Exploratory Data Analysis

Roger D. Peng

Exploratory Data Analysis with R

Roger D. Peng

ISBN 978-1-365-06006-9

Leanpub

This is a Leanpub book. Leanpub empowers authors and publishers with the Lean Publishing process. Lean Publishing is the act of publishing an in-progress ebook using lightweight tools and many iterations to get reader feedback, pivot until you have the right book and build traction once you do.

© 2015 - 2016 Roger D. Peng

Also By Roger D. Peng

R Programming for Data Science

The Art of Data Science

Report Writing for Data Science in R

Contents

1. **Stay in Touch!** 1
2. **Preface** 3
3. **Getting Started with R** 5
   - 3.1 Installation 5
   - 3.2 Getting started with the R interface 5
4. **Managing Data Frames with the `dplyr` package** 7
   - 4.1 Data Frames 7
   - 4.2 The `dplyr` Package 7
   - 4.3 `dplyr` Grammar 8
   - 4.4 Installing the `dplyr` package 8
   - 4.5 `select()` 9
   - 4.6 `filter()` 11
   - 4.7 `arrange()` 13
   - 4.8 `rename()` 14
   - 4.9 `mutate()` 14
   - 4.10 `group_by()` 15
   - 4.11 `%>%` 17
   - 4.12 Summary 19
5. **Exploratory Data Analysis Checklist** 21
   - 5.1 Formulate your question 21
   - 5.2 Read in your data 22
   - 5.3 Check the packaging 23
   - 5.4 Run `str()` 24
   - 5.5 Look at the top and the bottom of your data 24
   - 5.6 Check your "n"s 25
   - 5.7 Validate with at least one external data source 29
   - 5.8 Try the easy solution first 30
   - 5.9 Challenge your solution 33
   - 5.10 Follow up questions 35
6. **Principles of Analytic Graphics** 37

6.1	Show comparisons	37
6.2	Show causality, mechanism, explanation, systematic structure	39
6.3	Show multivariate data	41
6.4	Integrate evidence	45
6.5	Describe and document the evidence	45
6.6	Content, Content, Content	46
6.7	References	46

7. Exploratory Graphs ... 47

7.1	Characteristics of exploratory graphs	47
7.2	Air Pollution in the United States	47
7.3	Getting the Data	48
7.4	Simple Summaries: One Dimension	49
7.5	Five Number Summary	49
7.6	Boxplot	50
7.7	Histogram	52
7.8	Overlaying Features	55
7.9	Barplot	57
7.10	Simple Summaries: Two Dimensions and Beyond	58
7.11	Multiple Boxplots	59
7.12	Multiple Histograms	60
7.13	Scatterplots	61
7.14	Scatterplot - Using Color	62
7.15	Multiple Scatterplots	63
7.16	Summary	64

8. Plotting Systems ... 65

8.1	The Base Plotting System	65
8.2	The Lattice System	67
8.3	The ggplot2 System	68
8.4	References	70

9. Graphics Devices ... 71

9.1	The Process of Making a Plot	72
9.2	How Does a Plot Get Created?	72
9.3	Graphics File Devices	73
9.4	Multiple Open Graphics Devices	74
9.5	Copying Plots	74
9.6	Summary	75

10. The Base Plotting System ... 77

10.1	Base Graphics	77
10.2	Simple Base Graphics	78
10.3	Some Important Base Graphics Parameters	80

10.4	Base Plotting Functions	81
10.5	Base Plot with Regression Line	84
10.6	Multiple Base Plots	85
10.7	Summary	87

11. Plotting and Color in R **89**
11.1	Colors 1, 2, and 3	89
11.2	Connecting colors with data	91
11.3	Color Utilities in R	91
11.4	`colorRamp()`	92
11.5	`colorRampPalette()`	93
11.6	RColorBrewer Package	94
11.7	Using the RColorBrewer palettes	95
11.8	The `smoothScatter()` function	97
11.9	Adding transparency	97
11.10	Summary	99

12. Hierarchical Clustering **101**
12.1	Hierarchical clustering	102
12.2	How do we define close?	103
12.3	Example: Euclidean distance	103
12.4	Example: Manhattan distance	105
12.5	Example: Hierarchical clustering	105
12.6	Prettier dendrograms	112
12.7	Merging points: Complete	113
12.8	Merging points: Average	114
12.9	Using the `heatmap()` function	115
12.10	Notes and further resources	116

13. K-Means Clustering **119**
13.1	Illustrating the K-means algorithm	120
13.2	Stopping the algorithm	125
13.3	Using the `kmeans()` function	125
13.4	Building heatmaps from K-means solutions	127
13.5	Notes and further resources	128

14. Dimension Reduction **129**
14.1	Matrix data	129
14.2	Patterns in rows and columns	133
14.3	Related problem	134
14.4	SVD and PCA	135
14.5	Unpacking the SVD: u and v	135
14.6	SVD for data compression	136
14.7	Components of the SVD - Variance explained	137

CONTENTS

    14.8   Relationship to principal components 139
    14.9   What if we add a second pattern? 140
    14.10 Dealing with missing values 143
    14.11 Example: Face data 145
    14.12 Notes and further resources 148

15. The ggplot2 Plotting System: Part 1 . . . . **149**
    15.1   The Basics: `qplot()` 152
    15.2   Before You Start: Label Your Data 152
    15.3   ggplot2 "Hello, world!" 153
    15.4   Modifying aesthetics 154
    15.5   Adding a geom 155
    15.6   Histograms 156
    15.7   Facets 158
    15.8   Case Study: MAACS Cohort 161
    15.9   Summary of qplot() 170

16. The ggplot2 Plotting System: Part 2 . . . . **171**
    16.1   Basic Components of a ggplot2 Plot 171
    16.2   Example: BMI, PM2.5, Asthma 172
    16.3   Building Up in Layers 172
    16.4   First Plot with Point Layer 174
    16.5   Adding More Layers: Smooth 175
    16.6   Adding More Layers: Facets 177
    16.7   Modifying Geom Properties 178
    16.8   Modifying Labels 180
    16.9   Customizing the Smooth 181
    16.10 Changing the Theme 182
    16.11 More Complex Example 183
    16.12 A Quick Aside about Axis Limits 185
    16.13 Resources 188

17. Data Analysis Case Study: Changes in Fine Particle Air Pollution in the U.S. 189
    17.1   Synopsis 189
    17.2   Loading and Processing the Raw Data 189
    17.3   Results 192

18. About the Author **199**

1. Stay in Touch!

Thanks for purchasing this book. If you are interested in hearing more from me about things that I'm working on (books, data science courses, podcast, etc.), you can do two things:

- First, I encourage you to join my mailing list of Leanpub Readers[1]. On this list I send out updates of my own activities as well as occasional comments on data science current events. I'll also let you know what my co-conspirators Jeff Leek and Brian Caffo are up to because sometimes they do really cool stuff.
- Second, I have a regular podcast called Not So Standard Deviations[2] that I co-host with Dr. Hilary Parker, a Data Scientist at Stitch Fix. On this podcast, Hilary and I talk about the craft of data science and discuss common issues and problems in analyzing data. We'll also compare how data science is approached in both academia and industry contexts and discuss the latest industry trends. You can listen to recent episodes on our SoundCloud page or you can subscribe to it in iTunes[3] or your favorite podcasting app.

For those of you who purchased a **printed copy** of this book, I encourage you to go to the Leanpub web site and obtain the e-book version[4], which is available for free. The reason is that I will occasionally update the book with new material and readers who purchase the e-book version are entitled to free updates (this is unfortunately not yet possible with printed books).

Thanks again for purchasing this book and please do stay in touch!

[1] http://eepurl.com/bAJ3zj
[2] https://soundcloud.com/nssd-podcast
[3] https://itunes.apple.com/us/podcast/not-so-standard-deviations/id1040614570
[4] https://leanpub.com/exdata

2. Preface

Exploratory data analysis is a bit difficult to describe in concrete definitive terms, but I think most data analysts and statisticians know it when they see it. I like to think of it in terms of an analogy.

Filmmakers will shoot a lot of footage when making a movie or some film production, not all of which will be used. In addition, the footage will typically not be shot in the order that the storyline takes place, because of actors' schedules or other complicating factors. In addition, in some cases, it may be difficult to figure out exactly how the story should be told while shooting the footage. Rather, it's sometimes easier to see how the story flows when putting the various clips together in the editing room.

In the editing room, the director and the editor can play around a bit with different versions of different scenes to see which dialogue sounds better, which jokes are funnier, or which scenes are more dramatic. Scenes that just "don't work" might get dropped, and scenes that are particularly powerful might get extended or re-shot. This "rough cut" of the film is put together quickly so that important decisions can be made about what to pursue further and where to back off. Finer details like color correction or motion graphics might not be implemented at this point. Ultimately, this rough cut will help the director and editor create the "final cut", which is what the audience will ultimately view.

Exploratory data analysis is what occurs in the "editing room" of a research project or any data-based investigation. EDA is the process of making the "rough cut" for a data analysis, the purpose of which is very similar to that in the film editing room. The goals are many, but they include identifying relationships between variables that are particularly interesting or unexpected, checking to see if there is any evidence for or against a stated hypothesis, checking for problems with the collected data, such as missing data or measurement error), or identifying certain areas where more data need to be collected. At this point, finer details of presentation of the data and evidence, important for the final product, are not necessarily the focus.

Ultimately, EDA is important because it allows the investigator to make critical decisions about what is interesting to follow up on and what probably isn't worth pursuing because the data just don't provide the evidence (and might never provide the evidence, even with follow up). These kinds of decisions are important to make if a project is to move forward and remain within its budget.

This book covers some of the basics of visualizing data in R and summarizing high-dimensional data with statistical multivariate analysis techniques. There is less of an emphasis on formal statistical inference methods, as inference is typically not the focus of EDA. Rather, the goal is to show the data, summarize the evidence and identify interesting patterns while eliminating ideas that likely won't pan out.

Throughout the book, we will focus on the R statistical programming language. We will cover the various plotting systems in R and how to use them effectively. We will also discuss how to implement dimension reduction techniques like clustering and the singular value decomposition. All of these techniques will help you to visualize your data and to help you make key decisions in any data analysis.

3. Getting Started with R

3.1 Installation

The first thing you need to do to get started with R is to install it on your computer. R works on pretty much every platform available, including the widely available Windows, Mac OS X, and Linux systems. If you want to watch a step-by-step tutorial on how to install R for Mac or Windows, you can watch these videos:

- Installing R on Windows[1]
- Installing R on the Mac[2]

There is also an integrated development environment available for R that is built by RStudio. I really like this IDE—it has a nice editor with syntax highlighting, there is an R object viewer, and there are a number of other nice features that are integrated. You can see how to install RStudio here

- Installing RStudio[3]

The RStudio IDE is available from RStudio's web site[4].

3.2 Getting started with the R interface

After you install R you will need to launch it and start writing R code. Before we get to exactly how to write R code, it's useful to get a sense of how the system is organized. In these two videos I talk about where to write code and how set your working directory, which let's R know where to find all of your files.

- Writing code and setting your working directory on the Mac[5]
- Writing code and setting your working directory on Windows[6]

---

[1] http://youtu.be/Ohnk9hcxf9M
[2] https://youtu.be/uxuuWXU-7UQ
[3] https://youtu.be/bM7Sfz-LADM
[4] http://rstudio.com
[5] https://youtu.be/8xT3hmJQskU
[6] https://youtu.be/XBcvH1BpIBo

4. Managing Data Frames with the `dplyr` package

Watch a video of this chapter[1]

4.1 Data Frames

The *data frame* is a key data structure in statistics and in R. The basic structure of a data frame is that there is one observation per row and each column represents a variable, a measure, feature, or characteristic of that observation. R has an internal implementation of data frames that is likely the one you will use most often. However, there are packages on CRAN that implement data frames via things like relational databases that allow you to operate on very very large data frames (but we won't discuss them here).

Given the importance of managing data frames, it's important that we have good tools for dealing with them. R obviously has some built-in tools like the `subset()` function and the use of [and $ operators to extract subsets of data frames. However, other operations, like filtering, re-ordering, and collapsing, can often be tedious operations in R whose syntax is not very intuitive. The `dplyr` package is designed to mitigate a lot of these problems and to provide a highly optimized set of routines specifically for dealing with data frames.

4.2 The `dplyr` Package

The `dplyr` package was developed by Hadley Wickham of RStudio and is an optimized and distilled version of his `plyr` package. The `dplyr` package does not provide any "new" functionality to R per se, in the sense that everything `dplyr` does could already be done with base R, but it *greatly* simplifies existing functionality in R.

One important contribution of the `dplyr` package is that it provides a "grammar" (in particular, verbs) for data manipulation and for operating on data frames. With this grammar, you can sensibly communicate what it is that you are doing to a data frame that other people can understand (assuming they also know the grammar). This is useful because it provides an abstraction for data manipulation that previously did not exist. Another useful contribution is that the `dplyr` functions are **very** fast, as many key operations are coded in C++.

---

[1] https://youtu.be/aywFompr1F4

4.3 dplyr Grammar

Some of the key "verbs" provided by the dplyr package are

- select: return a subset of the columns of a data frame, using a flexible notation
- filter: extract a subset of rows from a data frame based on logical conditions
- arrange: reorder rows of a data frame
- rename: rename variables in a data frame
- mutate: add new variables/columns or transform existing variables
- summarise / summarize: generate summary statistics of different variables in the data frame, possibly within strata
- %>%: the "pipe" operator is used to connect multiple verb actions together into a pipeline

The dplyr package as a number of its own data types that it takes advantage of. For example, there is a handy print method that prevents you from printing a lot of data to the console. Most of the time, these additional data types are transparent to the user and do not need to be worried about.

Common dplyr Function Properties

All of the functions that we will discuss in this Chapter will have a few common characteristics. In particular,

1. The first argument is a data frame.
2. The subsequent arguments describe what to do with the data frame specified in the first argument, and you can refer to columns in the data frame directly without using the $ operator (just use the column names).
3. The return result of a function is a new data frame
4. Data frames must be properly formatted and annotated for this to all be useful. In particular, the data must be tidy[2]. In short, there should be one observation per row, and each column should represent a feature or characteristic of that observation.

4.4 Installing the dplyr package

The dplyr package can be installed from CRAN or from GitHub using the devtools package and the install_github() function. The GitHub repository will usually contain the latest updates to the package and the development version.

To install from CRAN, just run

---

[2] http://www.jstatsoft.org/v59/i10/paper

```
> install.packages("dplyr")
```

To install from GitHub you can run

```
> install_github("hadley/dplyr")
```

After installing the package it is important that you load it into your R session with the `library()` function.

```
> library(dplyr)

Attaching package: 'dplyr'

The following object is masked from 'package:stats':

    filter

The following objects are masked from 'package:base':

    intersect, setdiff, setequal, union
```

You may get some warnings when the package is loaded because there are functions in the dplyr package that have the same name as functions in other packages. For now you can ignore the warnings.

NOTE: If you ever run into a problem where R is getting confused over which function you mean to call, you can specify the *full name* of a function using the :: operator. The full name is simply the package name from which the function is defined followed by :: and then the function name. For example, the filter function from the dplyr package has the full name dplyr::filter. Calling functions with their full name will resolve any confusion over which function was meant to be called.

4.5 select()

For the examples in this chapter we will be using a dataset containing air pollution and temperature data for the city of Chicago[3] in the U.S. The dataset is available from my web site.

After unzipping the archive, you can load the data into R using the readRDS() function.

---

[3] http://www.biostat.jhsph.edu/~rpeng/leanpub/rprog/chicago_data.zip

```
> chicago <- readRDS("chicago.rds")
```

You can see some basic characteristics of the dataset with the `dim()` and `str()` functions.

```
> dim(chicago)
[1] 6940    8
> str(chicago)
'data.frame':   6940 obs. of  8 variables:
 $ city      : chr  "chic" "chic" "chic" "chic" ...
 $ tmpd      : num  31.5 33 33 29 32 40 34.5 29 26.5 32.5 ...
 $ dptp      : num  31.5 29.9 27.4 28.6 28.9 ...
 $ date      : Date, format: "1987-01-01" "1987-01-02" ...
 $ pm25tmean2: num  NA NA NA NA NA NA NA NA NA NA ...
 $ pm10tmean2: num  34 NA 34.2 47 NA ...
 $ o3tmean2  : num  4.25 3.3 3.33 4.38 4.75 ...
 $ no2tmean2 : num  20 23.2 23.8 30.4 30.3 ...
```

The `select()` function can be used to select columns of a data frame that you want to focus on. Often you'll have a large data frame containing "all" of the data, but any *given* analysis might only use a subset of variables or observations. The `select()` function allows you to get the few columns you might need.

Suppose we wanted to take the first 3 columns only. There are a few ways to do this. We could for example use numerical indices. But we can also use the names directly.

```
> names(chicago)[1:3]
[1] "city" "tmpd" "dptp"
> subset <- select(chicago, city:dptp)
> head(subset)
  city tmpd   dptp
1 chic 31.5 31.500
2 chic 33.0 29.875
3 chic 33.0 27.375
4 chic 29.0 28.625
5 chic 32.0 28.875
6 chic 40.0 35.125
```

Note that the : normally cannot be used with names or strings, but inside the `select()` function you can use it to specify a range of variable names.

You can also *omit* variables using the `select()` function by using the negative sign. With `select()` you can do

```
> select(chicago, -(city:dptp))
```

which indicates that we should include every variable *except* the variables `city` through `dptp`. The equivalent code in base R would be

```
> i <- match("city", names(chicago))
> j <- match("dptp", names(chicago))
> head(chicago[, -(i:j)])
```

Not super intuitive, right?

The `select()` function also allows a special syntax that allows you to specify variable names based on patterns. So, for example, if you wanted to keep every variable that ends with a "2", we could do

```
> subset <- select(chicago, ends_with("2"))
> str(subset)
'data.frame':   6940 obs. of  4 variables:
 $ pm25tmean2: num  NA NA NA NA NA NA NA NA NA NA ...
 $ pm10tmean2: num  34 NA 34.2 47 NA ...
 $ o3tmean2  : num  4.25 3.3 3.33 4.38 4.75 ...
 $ no2tmean2 : num  20 23.2 23.8 30.4 30.3 ...
```

Or if we wanted to keep every variable that starts with a "d", we could do

```
> subset <- select(chicago, starts_with("d"))
> str(subset)
'data.frame':   6940 obs. of  2 variables:
 $ dptp: num  31.5 29.9 27.4 28.6 28.9 ...
 $ date: Date, format: "1987-01-01" "1987-01-02" ...
```

You can also use more general regular expressions if necessary. See the help page (`?select`) for more details.

4.6 `filter()`

The `filter()` function is used to extract subsets of rows from a data frame. This function is similar to the existing `subset()` function in R but is quite a bit faster in my experience.

Suppose we wanted to extract the rows of the `chicago` data frame where the levels of PM2.5 are greater than 30 (which is a reasonably high level), we could do

```
> chic.f <- filter(chicago, pm25tmean2 > 30)
> str(chic.f)
'data.frame':    194 obs. of  8 variables:
 $ city       : chr  "chic" "chic" "chic" "chic" ...
 $ tmpd       : num  23 28 55 59 57 57 75 61 73 78 ...
 $ dptp       : num  21.9 25.8 51.3 53.7 52 56 65.8 59 60.3 67.1 ...
 $ date       : Date, format: "1998-01-17" "1998-01-23" ...
 $ pm25tmean2 : num  38.1 34 39.4 35.4 33.3 ...
 $ pm10tmean2 : num  32.5 38.7 34 28.5 35 ...
 $ o3tmean2   : num  3.18 1.75 10.79 14.3 20.66 ...
 $ no2tmean2  : num  25.3 29.4 25.3 31.4 26.8 ...
```

You can see that there are now only 194 rows in the data frame and the distribution of the `pm25tmean2` values is.

```
> summary(chic.f$pm25tmean2)
   Min. 1st Qu.  Median    Mean 3rd Qu.    Max.
  30.05   32.12   35.04   36.63   39.53   61.50
```

We can place an arbitrarily complex logical sequence inside of `filter()`, so we could for example extract the rows where PM2.5 is greater than 30 *and* temperature is greater than 80 degrees Fahrenheit.

```
> chic.f <- filter(chicago, pm25tmean2 > 30 & tmpd > 80)
> select(chic.f, date, tmpd, pm25tmean2)
         date tmpd pm25tmean2
1  1998-08-23   81   39.60000
2  1998-09-06   81   31.50000
3  2001-07-20   82   32.30000
4  2001-08-01   84   43.70000
5  2001-08-08   85   38.83750
6  2001-08-09   84   38.20000
7  2002-06-20   82   33.00000
8  2002-06-23   82   42.50000
9  2002-07-08   81   33.10000
10 2002-07-18   82   38.85000
11 2003-06-25   82   33.90000
12 2003-07-04   84   32.90000
13 2005-06-24   86   31.85714
14 2005-06-27   82   51.53750
15 2005-06-28   85   31.20000
16 2005-07-17   84   32.70000
17 2005-08-03   84   37.90000
```

Now there are only 17 observations where both of those conditions are met.

4.7 arrange()

The `arrange()` function is used to reorder rows of a data frame according to one of the variables/columns. Reordering rows of a data frame (while preserving corresponding order of other columns) is normally a pain to do in R. The `arrange()` function simplifies the process quite a bit.

Here we can order the rows of the data frame by date, so that the first row is the earliest (oldest) observation and the last row is the latest (most recent) observation.

```
> chicago <- arrange(chicago, date)
```

We can now check the first few rows

```
> head(select(chicago, date, pm25tmean2), 3)
        date pm25tmean2
1 1987-01-01         NA
2 1987-01-02         NA
3 1987-01-03         NA
```

and the last few rows.

```
> tail(select(chicago, date, pm25tmean2), 3)
           date pm25tmean2
6938 2005-12-29    7.45000
6939 2005-12-30   15.05714
6940 2005-12-31   15.00000
```

Columns can be arranged in descending order too by useing the special `desc()` operator.

```
> chicago <- arrange(chicago, desc(date))
```

Looking at the first three and last three rows shows the dates in descending order.

```
> head(select(chicago, date, pm25tmean2), 3)
        date pm25tmean2
1 2005-12-31   15.00000
2 2005-12-30   15.05714
3 2005-12-29    7.45000
> tail(select(chicago, date, pm25tmean2), 3)
          date pm25tmean2
6938 1987-01-03         NA
6939 1987-01-02         NA
6940 1987-01-01         NA
```

4.8 rename()

Renaming a variable in a data frame in R is surprisingly hard to do! The `rename()` function is designed to make this process easier.

Here you can see the names of the first five variables in the `chicago` data frame.

```
> head(chicago[, 1:5], 3)
  city tmpd dptp       date pm25tmean2
1 chic   35 30.1 2005-12-31   15.00000
2 chic   36 31.0 2005-12-30   15.05714
3 chic   35 29.4 2005-12-29    7.45000
```

The `dptp` column is supposed to represent the dew point temperature and the `pm25tmean2` column provides the PM2.5 data. However, these names are pretty obscure or awkward and probably be renamed to something more sensible.

```
> chicago <- rename(chicago, dewpoint = dptp, pm25 = pm25tmean2)
> head(chicago[, 1:5], 3)
  city tmpd dewpoint       date     pm25
1 chic   35     30.1 2005-12-31 15.00000
2 chic   36     31.0 2005-12-30 15.05714
3 chic   35     29.4 2005-12-29  7.45000
```

The syntax inside the `rename()` function is to have the new name on the left-hand side of the = sign and the old name on the right-hand side.

I leave it as an exercise for the reader to figure how you do this in base R without `dplyr`.

4.9 mutate()

The `mutate()` function exists to compute transformations of variables in a data frame. Often, you want to create new variables that are derived from existing variables and `mutate()` provides a clean interface for doing that.

For example, with air pollution data, we often want to *detrend* the data by subtracting the mean from the data. That way we can look at whether a given day's air pollution level is higher than or less than average (as opposed to looking at its absolute level).

Here we create a `pm25detrend` variable that subtracts the mean from the `pm25` variable.

```
> chicago <- mutate(chicago, pm25detrend = pm25 - mean(pm25, na.rm = TRUE))
> head(chicago)
  city tmpd dewpoint       date     pm25 pm10tmean2 o3tmean2 no2tmean2
1 chic   35     30.1 2005-12-31 15.00000       23.5  2.531250  13.25000
2 chic   36     31.0 2005-12-30 15.05714       19.2  3.034420  22.80556
3 chic   35     29.4 2005-12-29  7.45000       23.5  6.794837  19.97222
4 chic   37     34.5 2005-12-28 17.75000       27.5  3.260417  19.28563
5 chic   40     33.6 2005-12-27 23.56000       27.0  4.468750  23.50000
6 chic   35     29.6 2005-12-26  8.40000        8.5 14.041667  16.81944
  pm25detrend
1   -1.230958
2   -1.173815
3   -8.780958
4    1.519042
5    7.329042
6   -7.830958
```

There is also the related `transmute()` function, which does the same thing as `mutate()` but then *drops all non-transformed variables*.

Here we detrend the PM10 and ozone (O3) variables.

```
> head(transmute(chicago,
+                pm10detrend = pm10tmean2 - mean(pm10tmean2, na.rm = TRUE),
+                o3detrend = o3tmean2 - mean(o3tmean2, na.rm = TRUE)))
  pm10detrend   o3detrend
1  -10.395206 -16.904263
2  -14.695206 -16.401093
3  -10.395206 -12.640676
4   -6.395206 -16.175096
5   -6.895206 -14.966763
6  -25.395206  -5.393846
```

Note that there are only two columns in the transmuted data frame.

4.10 `group_by()`

The `group_by()` function is used to generate summary statistics from the data frame within strata defined by a variable. For example, in this air pollution dataset, you might want to know what the average annual level of PM2.5 is. So the stratum is the year, and that is something we can derive from the `date` variable. In conjunction with the `group_by()` function we often use the `summarize()` function (or `summarise()` for some parts of the world).

The general operation here is a combination of splitting a data frame into separate pieces defined by a variable or group of variables (`group_by()`), and then applying a summary function across those subsets (`summarize()`).

First, we can create a `year` varible using `as.POSIXlt()`.

```
> chicago <- mutate(chicago, year = as.POSIXlt(date)$year + 1900)
```

Now we can create a separate data frame that splits the original data frame by year.

```
> years <- group_by(chicago, year)
```

Finally, we compute summary statistics for each year in the data frame with the `summarize()` function.

```
> summarize(years, pm25 = mean(pm25, na.rm = TRUE),
+           o3 = max(o3tmean2, na.rm = TRUE),
+           no2 = median(no2tmean2, na.rm = TRUE))
Source: local data frame [19 x 4]

   year     pm25       o3      no2
1  1987      NaN 62.96966 23.49369
2  1988      NaN 61.67708 24.52296
3  1989      NaN 59.72727 26.14062
4  1990      NaN 52.22917 22.59583
5  1991      NaN 63.10417 21.38194
6  1992      NaN 50.82870 24.78921
7  1993      NaN 44.30093 25.76993
8  1994      NaN 52.17844 28.47500
9  1995      NaN 66.58750 27.26042
10 1996      NaN 58.39583 26.38715
11 1997      NaN 56.54167 25.48143
12 1998 18.26467 50.66250 24.58649
13 1999 18.49646 57.48864 24.66667
14 2000 16.93806 55.76103 23.46082
15 2001 16.92632 51.81984 25.06522
16 2002 15.27335 54.88043 22.73750
17 2003 15.23183 56.16608 24.62500
18 2004 14.62864 44.48240 23.39130
19 2005 16.18556 58.84126 22.62387
```

`summarize()` returns a data frame with `year` as the first column, and then the annual averages of `pm25`, `o3`, and `no2`.

In a slightly more complicated example, we might want to know what are the average levels of ozone (o3) and nitrogen dioxide (no2) within quintiles of pm25. A slicker way to do this would be through a regression model, but we can actually do this quickly with group_by() and summarize().

First, we can create a categorical variable of pm25 divided into quintiles.

```
> qq <- quantile(chicago$pm25, seq(0, 1, 0.2), na.rm = TRUE)
> chicago <- mutate(chicago, pm25.quint = cut(pm25, qq))
```

Now we can group the data frame by the pm25.quint variable.

```
> quint <- group_by(chicago, pm25.quint)
```

Finally, we can compute the mean of o3 and no2 within quintiles of pm25.

```
> summarize(quint, o3 = mean(o3tmean2, na.rm = TRUE),
+           no2 = mean(no2tmean2, na.rm = TRUE))
Source: local data frame [6 x 3]

  pm25.quint       o3       no2
1  (1.7,8.7]  21.66401 17.99129
2  (8.7,12.4] 20.38248 22.13004
3 (12.4,16.7] 20.66160 24.35708
4 (16.7,22.6] 19.88122 27.27132
5 (22.6,61.5] 20.31775 29.64427
6          NA 18.79044 25.77585
```

From the table, it seems there isn't a strong relationship between pm25 and o3, but there appears to be a positive correlation between pm25 and no2. More sophisticated statistical modeling can help to provide precise answers to these questions, but a simple application of dplyr functions can often get you most of the way there.

4.11 %>%

The pipeline operater %>% is very handy for stringing together multiple dplyr functions in a sequence of operations. Notice above that every time we wanted to apply more than one function, the sequence gets buried in a sequence of nested function calls that is difficult to read, i.e.

```
> third(second(first(x)))
```

This nesting is not a natural way to think about a sequence of operations. The %>% operator allows you to string operations in a left-to-right fashion, i.e.

```
> first(x) %>% second %>% third
```

Take the example that we just did in the last section where we computed the mean of o3 and no2 within quintiles of pm25. There we had to

1. create a new variable pm25.quint
2. split the data frame by that new variable
3. compute the mean of o3 and no2 in the sub-groups defined by pm25.quint

That can be done with the following sequence in a single R expression.

```
> mutate(chicago, pm25.quint = cut(pm25, qq)) %>%
+         group_by(pm25.quint) %>%
+         summarize(o3 = mean(o3tmean2, na.rm = TRUE),
+                   no2 = mean(no2tmean2, na.rm = TRUE))
Source: local data frame [6 x 3]

  pm25.quint       o3       no2
1  (1.7,8.7] 21.66401 17.99129
2  (8.7,12.4] 20.38248 22.13004
3 (12.4,16.7] 20.66160 24.35708
4 (16.7,22.6] 19.88122 27.27132
5 (22.6,61.5] 20.31775 29.64427
6         NA 18.79044 25.77585
```

This way we don't have to create a set of temporary variables along the way or create a massive nested sequence of function calls.

Notice in the above code that I pass the chicago data frame to the first call to mutate(), but then afterwards I do not have to pass the first argument to group_by() or summarize(). Once you travel down the pipeline with %>%, the first argument is taken to be the output of the previous element in the pipeline.

Another example might be computing the average pollutant level by month. This could be useful to see if there are any seasonal trends in the data.

```
> mutate(chicago, month = as.POSIXlt(date)$mon + 1) %>%
+         group_by(month) %>%
+         summarize(pm25 = mean(pm25, na.rm = TRUE),
+                   o3 = max(o3tmean2, na.rm = TRUE),
+                   no2 = median(no2tmean2, na.rm = TRUE))
Source: local data frame [12 x 4]

   month      pm25       o3      no2
1      1  17.76996 28.22222 25.35417
2      2  20.37513 37.37500 26.78034
3      3  17.40818 39.05000 26.76984
4      4  13.85879 47.94907 25.03125
5      5  14.07420 52.75000 24.22222
6      6  15.86461 66.58750 25.01140
7      7  16.57087 59.54167 22.38442
8      8  16.93380 53.96701 22.98333
9      9  15.91279 57.48864 24.47917
10    10  14.23557 47.09275 24.15217
11    11  15.15794 29.45833 23.56537
12    12  17.52221 27.70833 24.45773
```

Here we can see that o3 tends to be low in the winter months and high in the summer while no2 is higher in the winter and lower in the summer.

4.12 Summary

The dplyr package provides a concise set of operations for managing data frames. With these functions we can do a number of complex operations in just a few lines of code. In particular, we can often conduct the beginnings of an exploratory analysis with the powerful combination of group_by() and summarize().

Once you learn the dplyr grammar there are a few additional benefits

- dplyr can work with other data frame "backends" such as SQL databases. There is an SQL interface for relational databases via the DBI package
- dplyr can be integrated with the data.table package for large fast tables

The dplyr package is handy way to both simplify and speed up your data frame management code. It's rare that you get such a combination at the same time!

5. Exploratory Data Analysis Checklist

In this chapter we will run through an informal "checklist" of things to do when embarking on an exploratory data analysis. As a running example I will use a dataset on hourly ozone levels in the United States for the year 2014. The elements of the checklist are

1. Formulate your question
2. Read in your data
3. Check the packaging
4. Run `str()`
5. Look at the top and the bottom of your data
6. Check your "n"s
7. Validate with at least one external data source
8. Try the easy solution first
9. Challenge your solution
10. Follow up

5.1 Formulate your question

Formulating a question can be a useful way to guide the exploratory data analysis process and to limit the exponential number of paths that can be taken with any sizeable dataset. In particular, a *sharp* question or hypothesis can serve as a dimension reduction tool that can eliminate variables that are not immediately relevant to the question.

For example, in this chapter we will be looking at an air pollution dataset from the U.S. Environmental Protection Agency (EPA). A general question one could as is

> Are air pollution levels higher on the east coast than on the west coast?

But a more specific question might be

> Are hourly ozone levels on average higher in New York City than they are in Los Angeles?

Note that both questions may be of interest, and neither is right or wrong. But the first question requires looking at all pollutants across the entire east and west coasts, while the second question only requires looking at single pollutant in two cities.

It's usually a good idea to spend a few minutes to figure out what is the question you're *really* interested in, and narrow it down to be as specific as possible (without becoming uninteresting).

For this chapter, we will focus on the following question:

> Which counties in the United States have the highest levels of ambient ozone pollution?

As a side note, one of the most important questions you can answer with an exploratory data analysis is "Do I have the right data to answer this question?" Often this question is difficult ot answer at first, but can become more clear as we sort through and look at the data.

5.2 Read in your data

The next task in any exploratory data analysis is to read in some data. Sometimes the data will come in a very messy format and you'll need to do some cleaning. Other times, someone else will have cleaned up that data for you so you'll be spared the pain of having to do the cleaning.

We won't go through the pain of cleaning up a dataset here, not because it's not important, but rather because there's often not much generalizable knowledge to obtain from going through it. Every dataset has its unique quirks and so for now it's probably best to not get bogged down in the details.

Here we have a relatively clean dataset from the U.S. EPA on hourly ozone measurements in the entire U.S. for the year 2014. The data are available from the EPA's Air Quality System web page[1]. I've simply downloaded the zip file from the web site, unzipped the archive, and put the resulting file in a directory called "data". If you want to run this code you'll have to use the same directory structure.

The dataset is a comma-separated value (CSV) file, where each row of the file contains one hourly measurement of ozone at some location in the country.

NOTE: Running the code below may take a few minutes. There are 7,147,884 rows in the CSV file. If it takes too long, you can read in a subset by specifying a value for the n_max argument to read_csv() that is greater than 0.

---

[1] http://aqsdr1.epa.gov/aqsweb/aqstmp/airdata/download_files.html

```
> library(readr)
> ozone <- read_csv("data/hourly_44201_2014.csv",
+                   col_types = "ccccinnccccccncnncccccc")
```

The `readr` package by Hadley Wickham is a nice package for reading in flat files *very* fast, or at least much faster than R's built-in functions. It makes some tradeoffs to obtain that speed, so these functions are not always appropriate, but they serve our purposes here.

The character string provided to the `col_types` argument specifies the class of each column in the dataset. Each letter represents the class of a column: "c" for character, "n" for numeric", and "i" for integer. No, I didn't magically know the classes of each column—I just looked quickly at the file to see what the column classes were. If there are too many columns, you can not specify `col_types` and `read_csv()` will try to figure it out for you.

Just as a convenience for later, we can rewrite the names of the columns to remove any spaces.

```
> names(ozone) <- make.names(names(ozone))
```

5.3 Check the packaging

Have you ever gotten a present *before* the time when you were allowed to open it? Sure, we all have. The problem is that the present is wrapped, but you desperately want to know what's inside. What's a person to do in those circumstances? Well, you can shake the box a bit, maybe knock it with your knuckle to see if it makes a hollow sound, or even weigh it to see how heavy it is. This is how you should think about your dataset before you start analyzing it for real.

Assuming you don't get any warnings or errors when reading in the dataset, you should now have an object in your workspace named `ozone`. It's usually a good idea to poke at that object a little bit before we break open the wrapping paper.

For example, you can check the number of rows and columns.

```
> nrow(ozone)
[1] 7147884
> ncol(ozone)
[1] 23
```

Remember when I said there were 7,147,884 rows in the file? How does that match up with what we've read in? This dataset also has relatively few columns, so you might be able to check the original text file to see if the number of columns printed out (23) here matches the number of columns you see in the original file.

5.4 Run `str()`

Another thing you can do is run `str()` on the dataset. This is usually a safe operation in the sense that even with a very large dataset, running `str()` shouldn't take too long.

```
> str(ozone)
Classes 'tbl_df', 'tbl' and 'data.frame':       7147884 obs. of  23 variables:
 $ State.Code         : chr  "01" "01" "01" "01" ...
 $ County.Code        : chr  "003" "003" "003" "003" ...
 $ Site.Num           : chr  "0010" "0010" "0010" "0010" ...
 $ Parameter.Code     : chr  "44201" "44201" "44201" "44201" ...
 $ POC                : int  1 1 1 1 1 1 1 1 1 1 ...
 $ Latitude           : num  30.5 30.5 30.5 30.5 30.5 ...
 $ Longitude          : num  -87.9 -87.9 -87.9 -87.9 -87.9 ...
 $ Datum              : chr  "NAD83" "NAD83" "NAD83" "NAD83" ...
 $ Parameter.Name     : chr  "Ozone" "Ozone" "Ozone" "Ozone" ...
 $ Date.Local         : chr  "2014-03-01" "2014-03-01" "2014-03-01" "2014-03-01" ...
 $ Time.Local         : chr  "01:00" "02:00" "03:00" "04:00" ...
 $ Date.GMT           : chr  "2014-03-01" "2014-03-01" "2014-03-01" "2014-03-01" ...
 $ Time.GMT           : chr  "07:00" "08:00" "09:00" "10:00" ...
 $ Sample.Measurement : num  0.047 0.047 0.043 0.038 0.035 0.035 0.034 0.037 0.044 0.046 ...
 $ Units.of.Measure   : chr  "Parts per million" "Parts per million" "Parts per million" "Parts per \
million" ...
 $ MDL                : num  0.005 0.005 0.005 0.005 0.005 0.005 0.005 0.005 0.005 0.005 ...
 $ Uncertainty        : num  NA NA NA NA NA NA NA NA NA NA ...
 $ Qualifier          : chr  "" "" "" "" ...
 $ Method.Type        : chr  "FEM" "FEM" "FEM" "FEM" ...
 $ Method.Name        : chr  "INSTRUMENTAL - ULTRA VIOLET" "INSTRUMENTAL - ULTRA VIOLET" "INSTRUMENT\
AL - ULTRA VIOLET" "INSTRUMENTAL - ULTRA VIOLET" ...
 $ State.Name         : chr  "Alabama" "Alabama" "Alabama" "Alabama" ...
 $ County.Name        : chr  "Baldwin" "Baldwin" "Baldwin" "Baldwin" ...
 $ Date.of.Last.Change: chr  "2014-06-30" "2014-06-30" "2014-06-30" "2014-06-30" ...
```

The output for `str()` duplicates some information that we already have, like the number of rows and columns. More importantly, you can examine the *classes* of each of the columns to make sure they are correctly specified (i.e. numbers are `numeric` and strings are `character`, etc.). Because I pre-specified all of the column classes in `read_csv()`, they all should match up with what I specified.

Often, with just these simple maneuvers, you can identify potential problems with the data before plunging in head first into a complicated data analysis.

5.5 Look at the top and the bottom of your data

I find it useful to look at the "beginning" and "end" of a dataset right after I check the packaging. This lets me know if the data were read in properly, things are properly formatted, and that everthing is there. If your data are time series data, then make sure the dates at the beginning and end of the dataset match what you expect the beginning and ending time period to be.

You can peek at the top and bottom of the data with the `head()` and `tail()` functions. Here's the top.

```
> head(ozone[, c(6:7, 10)])
  Latitude Longitude Date.Local
1   30.498 -87.88141 2014-03-01
2   30.498 -87.88141 2014-03-01
3   30.498 -87.88141 2014-03-01
4   30.498 -87.88141 2014-03-01
5   30.498 -87.88141 2014-03-01
6   30.498 -87.88141 2014-03-01
```

For brevity I've only taken a few columns. And here's the bottom.

```
> tail(ozone[, c(6:7, 10)])
        Latitude Longitude Date.Local
7147879 18.17794 -65.91548 2014-09-30
7147880 18.17794 -65.91548 2014-09-30
7147881 18.17794 -65.91548 2014-09-30
7147882 18.17794 -65.91548 2014-09-30
7147883 18.17794 -65.91548 2014-09-30
7147884 18.17794 -65.91548 2014-09-30
```

I find `tail()` to be particularly useful because often there will be some problem reading the end of a dataset and if you don't check that you'd never know. Sometimes there's weird formatting at the end or some extra comment lines that someone decided to stick at the end.

Make sure to check all the columns and verify that all of the data in each column looks the way it's supposed to look. This isn't a foolproof approach, because we're only looking at a few rows, but it's a decent start.

5.6 Check your "n"s

In general, counting things is usually a good way to figure out if anything is wrong or not. In the simplest case, if you're expecting there to be 1,000 observations and it turns out there's only 20, you know something must have gone wrong somewhere. But there are other areas that you can check depending on your application. To do this properly, you need to identify some *landmarks* that can be used to check against your data. For example, if you are collecting data on people, such as in a survey or clinical trial, then you should know how many people there are in your study. That's something you should check in your dataset, to make sure that you have data on all the people you thought you would have data on.

In this example, we will use the fact that the dataset purportedly contains *hourly* data for the *entire country*. These will be our two landmarks for comparison.

Here, we have hourly ozone data that comes from monitors across the country. The monitors should be monitoring continuously during the day, so all hours should be represented. We can take a look at the Time.Local variable to see what time measurements are recorded as being taken.

```
> table(ozone$Time.Local)

 00:00   00:01   01:00   01:02   02:00   02:03   03:00
288698       2  290871       2  283709       2  282951
 03:04   04:00   04:05   05:00   05:06   06:00   06:07
     2  288963       2  302696       2  302356       2
 07:00   07:08   08:00   08:09   09:00   09:10   10:00
300950       2  298566       2  297154       2  297132
 10:11   11:00   11:12   12:00   12:13   13:00   13:14
     2  298125       2  298297       2  299997       2
 14:00   14:15   15:00   15:16   16:00   16:17   17:00
301410       2  302636       2  303387       2  303806
 17:18   18:00   18:19   19:00   19:20   20:00   20:21
     2  303795       2  304268       2  304268       2
 21:00   21:22   22:00   22:23   23:00   23:24
303551       2  295701       2  294549       2
```

One thing we notice here is that while almost all measurements in the dataset are recorded as being taken on the hour, some are taken at slightly different times. Such a small number of readings are taken at these off times that we might not want to care. But it does seem a bit odd, so it might be worth a quick check.

We can take a look at which observations were measured at time "00:01".

```
> library(dplyr)
> filter(ozone, Time.Local == "13:14") %>%
+         select(State.Name, County.Name, Date.Local,
+                Time.Local, Sample.Measurement)
Source: local data frame [2 x 5]

  State.Name County.Name Date.Local Time.Local
1   New York    Franklin 2014-09-30      13:14
2   New York    Franklin 2014-09-30      13:14
Variables not shown: Sample.Measurement (dbl)
```

We can see that it's a monitor in Franklin County, New York and that the measurements were taken on September 30, 2014. What if we just pulled all of the measurements taken at this monitor on this date?

```
> filter(ozone, State.Code == "36"
+        & County.Code == "033"
+        & Date.Local == "2014-09-30") %>%
+     select(Date.Local, Time.Local,
+            Sample.Measurement) %>%
+     as.data.frame
   Date.Local Time.Local Sample.Measurement
1  2014-09-30      00:01              0.011
2  2014-09-30      01:02              0.012
3  2014-09-30      02:03              0.012
4  2014-09-30      03:04              0.011
5  2014-09-30      04:05              0.011
6  2014-09-30      05:06              0.011
7  2014-09-30      06:07              0.010
8  2014-09-30      07:08              0.010
9  2014-09-30      08:09              0.010
10 2014-09-30      09:10              0.010
11 2014-09-30      10:11              0.010
12 2014-09-30      11:12              0.012
13 2014-09-30      12:13              0.011
14 2014-09-30      13:14              0.013
15 2014-09-30      14:15              0.016
16 2014-09-30      15:16              0.017
17 2014-09-30      16:17              0.017
18 2014-09-30      17:18              0.015
19 2014-09-30      18:19              0.017
20 2014-09-30      19:20              0.014
21 2014-09-30      20:21              0.014
22 2014-09-30      21:22              0.011
23 2014-09-30      22:23              0.010
24 2014-09-30      23:24              0.010
25 2014-09-30      00:01              0.010
26 2014-09-30      01:02              0.011
27 2014-09-30      02:03              0.011
28 2014-09-30      03:04              0.010
29 2014-09-30      04:05              0.010
30 2014-09-30      05:06              0.010
31 2014-09-30      06:07              0.009
32 2014-09-30      07:08              0.008
33 2014-09-30      08:09              0.009
34 2014-09-30      09:10              0.009
35 2014-09-30      10:11              0.009
36 2014-09-30      11:12              0.011
37 2014-09-30      12:13              0.010
38 2014-09-30      13:14              0.012
39 2014-09-30      14:15              0.015
40 2014-09-30      15:16              0.016
41 2014-09-30      16:17              0.016
42 2014-09-30      17:18              0.014
43 2014-09-30      18:19              0.016
44 2014-09-30      19:20              0.013
```

```
45 2014-09-30      20:21              0.013
46 2014-09-30      21:22              0.010
47 2014-09-30      22:23              0.009
48 2014-09-30      23:24              0.009
```

Now we can see that this monitor just records its values at odd times, rather than on the hour. It seems, from looking at the previous output, that this is the only monitor in the country that does this, so it's probably not something we should worry about.

Since EPA monitors pollution across the country, there should be a good representation of states. Perhaps we should see exactly how many states are represented in this dataset.

```
> select(ozone, State.Name) %>% unique %>% nrow
[1] 52
```

So it seems the representation is a bit too good—there are 52 states in the dataset, but only 50 states in the U.S.!

We can take a look at the unique elements of the State.Name variable to see what's going on.

```
> unique(ozone$State.Name)
 [1] "Alabama"                "Alaska"
 [3] "Arizona"                "Arkansas"
 [5] "California"             "Colorado"
 [7] "Connecticut"            "Delaware"
 [9] "District Of Columbia"   "Florida"
[11] "Georgia"                "Hawaii"
[13] "Idaho"                  "Illinois"
[15] "Indiana"                "Iowa"
[17] "Kansas"                 "Kentucky"
[19] "Louisiana"              "Maine"
[21] "Maryland"               "Massachusetts"
[23] "Michigan"               "Minnesota"
[25] "Mississippi"            "Missouri"
[27] "Montana"                "Nebraska"
[29] "Nevada"                 "New Hampshire"
[31] "New Jersey"             "New Mexico"
[33] "New York"               "North Carolina"
[35] "North Dakota"           "Ohio"
[37] "Oklahoma"               "Oregon"
[39] "Pennsylvania"           "Rhode Island"
[41] "South Carolina"         "South Dakota"
[43] "Tennessee"              "Texas"
[45] "Utah"                   "Vermont"
[47] "Virginia"               "Washington"
[49] "West Virginia"          "Wisconsin"
[51] "Wyoming"                "Puerto Rico"
```

Now we can see that Washington, D.C. (District of Columbia) and Puerto Rico are the "extra" states included in the dataset. Since they are clearly part of the U.S. (but not official states of the union) that all seems okay.

This last bit of analysis made use of something we will discuss in the next section: external data. We knew that there are only 50 states in the U.S., so seeing 52 state names was an immediate trigger that something might be off. In this case, all was well, but validating your data with an external data source can be very useful.

5.7 Validate with at least one external data source

Making sure your data matches something outside of the dataset is very important. It allows you to ensure that the measurements are roughly in line with what they should be and it serves as a check on what *other* things might be wrong in your dataset. External validation can often be as simple as checking your data against a single number, as we will do here.

In the U.S. we have national ambient air quality standards, and for ozone, the current standard[2] set in 2008 is that the "annual fourth-highest daily maximum 8-hr concentration, averaged over 3 years" should not exceed 0.075 parts per million (ppm). The exact details of how to calculate this are not important for this analysis, but roughly speaking, the 8-hour average concentration should not be too much higher than 0.075 ppm (it can be higher because of the way the standard is worded).

Let's take a look at the hourly measurements of ozone.

```
> summary(ozone$Sample.Measurement)
   Min. 1st Qu.  Median    Mean 3rd Qu.    Max.
0.00000 0.02000 0.03200 0.03123 0.04200 0.34900
```

From the summary we can see that the maximum hourly concentration is quite high (0.349 ppm) but that in general, the bulk of the distribution is far below 0.075.

We can get a bit more detail on the distribution by looking at deciles of the data.

```
> quantile(ozone$Sample.Measurement, seq(0, 1, 0.1))
    0%    10%    20%    30%    40%    50%    60%    70%
 0.000  0.010  0.018  0.023  0.028  0.032  0.036  0.040
   80%    90%   100%
 0.044  0.051  0.349
```

Knowing that the national standard for ozone is something like 0.075, we can see from the data that

---
[2]http://www.epa.gov/ttn/naaqs/standards/ozone/s_o3_history.html

- The data are at least of the right order of magnitude (i.e. the units are correct)
- The range of the distribution is roughly what we'd expect, given the regulation around ambient pollution levels
- Some hourly levels (less than 10%) are above 0.075 but this may be reasonable given the wording of the standard and the averaging involved.

5.8 Try the easy solution first

Recall that our original question was

> Which counties in the United States have the highest levels of ambient ozone pollution?

What's the simplest answer we could provide to this question? For the moment, don't worry about whether the answer is correct, but the point is how could you provide *prima facie* evidence for your hypothesis or question. You may refute that evidence later with deeper analysis, but this is the first pass.

Because we want to know which counties have the *highest* levels, it seems we need a list of counties that are ordered from highest to lowest with respect to their levels of ozone. What do we mean by "levels of ozone"? For now, let's just blindly take the average across the entire year for each county and then rank counties according to this metric.

To identify each county we will use a combination of the State.Name and the County.Name variables.

```
> ranking <- group_by(ozone, State.Name, County.Name) %>%
+         summarize(ozone = mean(Sample.Measurement)) %>%
+         as.data.frame %>%
+         arrange(desc(ozone))
```

Now we can look at the top 10 counties in this ranking.

```
> head(ranking, 10)
   State.Name County.Name      ozone
1  California    Mariposa 0.04992485
2  California      Nevada 0.04866836
3     Wyoming      Albany 0.04834274
4     Arizona     Yavapai 0.04746346
5     Arizona        Gila 0.04722276
6  California        Inyo 0.04659648
7        Utah    San Juan 0.04654895
8     Arizona    Coconino 0.04605669
9  California   El Dorado 0.04595514
10     Nevada  White Pine 0.04465562
```

It seems interesting that all of these counties are in the western U.S., with 4 of them in California alone.

For comparison we can look at the 10 lowest counties too.

```
> tail(ranking, 10)
    State.Name         County.Name        ozone
781     Alaska    Matanuska Susitna  0.020911008
782 Washington              Whatcom  0.020114267
783     Hawaii             Honolulu  0.019813165
784  Tennessee                 Knox  0.018579452
785 California               Merced  0.017200647
786     Alaska  Fairbanks North Star 0.014993138
787   Oklahoma                Caddo  0.014677374
788 Puerto Rico              Juncos  0.013738328
789 Puerto Rico             Bayamon  0.010693529
790 Puerto Rico              Catano  0.004685369
```

Let's take a look at one of the higest level counties, Mariposa County, California. First let's see how many observations there are for this county in the dataset.

```
> filter(ozone, State.Name == "California" & County.Name == "Mariposa") %>% nrow
[1] 9328
```

Always be checking. Does that number of observations sound right? Well, there's 24 hours in a day and 365 days per, which gives us 8760, which is close to that number of observations. Sometimes the counties use alternate methods of measurement during the year so there may be "extra" measurements.

We can take a look at how ozone varies through the year in this county by looking at monthly averages. First we'll need to convert the date variable into a `Date` class.

```
> ozone <- mutate(ozone, Date.Local = as.Date(Date.Local))
```

Then we will split the data by month to look at the average hourly levels.

```
> filter(ozone, State.Name == "California" & County.Name == "Mariposa") %>%
+         mutate(month = factor(months(Date.Local), levels = month.name)) %>%
+         group_by(month) %>%
+         summarize(ozone = mean(Sample.Measurement))
Source: local data frame [10 x 2]

       month       ozone
1    January  0.04081929
2   February  0.03884305
3      March  0.04548374
4      April  0.04976124
5        May  0.05047637
6       June  0.05639331
7       July  0.05224286
8     August  0.05541681
9  September  0.05117737
10   October  0.04693361
```

A few things stand out here. First, ozone appears to be higher in the summer months and lower in the winter months. Second, there are two months missing (November and December) from the data. It's not immediately clear why that is, but it's probably worth investigating a bit later on.

Now let's take a look at one of the lowest level counties, Caddo County, Oklahoma.

```
> filter(ozone, State.Name == "Oklahoma" & County.Name == "Caddo") %>% nrow
[1] 5666
```

Here we see that there are perhaps fewer observations than we would expect for a monitor that was measuring 24 hours a day all year. We can check the data to see if anything funny is going on.

```
> filter(ozone, State.Name == "Oklahoma" & County.Name == "Caddo") %>%
+         mutate(month = factor(months(Date.Local), levels = month.name)) %>%
+         group_by(month) %>%
+         summarize(ozone = mean(Sample.Measurement))
Source: local data frame [9 x 2]

       month        ozone
1    January  0.018732719
2   February  0.002060543
3      March  0.002000000
4      April  0.023208955
5        May  0.024182927
6       June  0.020195936
7       July  0.019112745
8     August  0.020869376
9  September  0.002000000
```

Here we can see that the levels of ozone are much lower in this county and that also three months are missing (October, November, and December). Given the seasonal nature of ozone, it's possible that the levels of ozone are so low in those months that it's not even worth measuring. In fact some of the monthly averages are below the typical method detection limit of the measurement technology, meaning that those values are highly uncertain and likely not distinguishable from zero.

5.9 Challenge your solution

The easy solution is nice because it is, well, easy, but you should never allow those results to hold the day. You should always be thinking of ways to challenge the results, especially if those results comport with your prior expectation.

Now, the easy answer seemed to work okay in that it gave us a listing of counties that had the highest average levels of ozone for 2014. However, the analysis raised some issues. For example, some counties do not have measurements every month. Is this a problem? Would it affect our ranking of counties if we had those measurements?

Also, how stable are the rankings from year to year? We only have one year's worth of data for the moment, but we could perhaps get a sense of the stability of the rankings by shuffling the data around a bit to see if anything changes. We can imagine that from year to year, the ozone data are somewhat different randomly, but generally follow similar patterns across the country. So the shuffling process could approximate the data changing from one year to the next. It's not an ideal solution, but it could give us a sense of how stable the rankings are.

First we set our random number generator and resample the indices of the rows of the data frame with replacement. The statistical jargon for this approach is a bootstrap sample. We use the resampled indices to create a new dataset, ozone2, that shares many of the same qualities as the original but is randomly perturbed.

```
> set.seed(10234)
> N <- nrow(ozone)
> idx <- sample(N, N, replace = TRUE)
> ozone2 <- ozone[idx, ]
```

Now we can reconstruct our rankings of the counties based on this resampled data.

```
> ranking2 <- group_by(ozone2, State.Name, County.Name) %>%
+         summarize(ozone = mean(Sample.Measurement)) %>%
+         as.data.frame %>%
+         arrange(desc(ozone))
```

We can then compare the top 10 counties from our original ranking and the top 10 counties from our ranking based on the resampled data.

```
> cbind(head(ranking, 10),
+       head(ranking2, 10))
   State.Name County.Name      ozone State.Name
1  California    Mariposa 0.04992485 California
2  California      Nevada 0.04866836 California
3     Wyoming      Albany 0.04834274    Wyoming
4     Arizona     Yavapai 0.04746346    Arizona
5     Arizona        Gila 0.04722276    Arizona
6  California        Inyo 0.04659648 California
7        Utah    San Juan 0.04654895       Utah
8     Arizona    Coconino 0.04605669 California
9  California   El Dorado 0.04595514    Arizona
10     Nevada  White Pine 0.04465562     Nevada
   County.Name      ozone
1     Mariposa 0.04975053
2       Nevada 0.04875887
3       Albany 0.04818458
4      Yavapai 0.04734300
5         Gila 0.04713265
6         Inyo 0.04666913
7     San Juan 0.04658873
8    El Dorado 0.04618268
9     Coconino 0.04601939
10  White Pine 0.04469161
```

We can see that the rankings based on the resampled data (columns 4–6 on the right) are very close to the original, with the first 7 being identical. Numbers 8 and 9 get flipped in the resampled rankings but that's about it. This might suggest that the original rankings are somewhat stable.

We can also look at the bottom of the list to see if there were any major changes.

```
> cbind(tail(ranking, 10),
+       tail(ranking2, 10))
    State.Name          County.Name       ozone
781     Alaska    Matanuska Susitna 0.020911008
782 Washington              Whatcom 0.020114267
783     Hawaii             Honolulu 0.019813165
784  Tennessee                 Knox 0.018579452
785 California               Merced 0.017200647
786     Alaska  Fairbanks North Star 0.014993138
787   Oklahoma                Caddo 0.014677374
788 Puerto Rico               Juncos 0.013738328
789 Puerto Rico              Bayamon 0.010693529
790 Puerto Rico               Catano 0.004685369
    State.Name          County.Name       ozone
781  Louisiana    West Baton Rouge 0.020718069
782     Hawaii            Honolulu 0.019891068
783 Washington             Whatcom 0.019728567
784  Tennessee                Knox 0.019200000
```

```
785    California              Merced 0.016519393
786        Alaska Fairbanks North Star 0.014925359
787      Oklahoma               Caddo 0.014764086
788   Puerto Rico              Juncos 0.013535870
789   Puerto Rico             Bayamon 0.010889964
790   Puerto Rico              Catano 0.004602808
```

Here we can see that the bottom 7 counties are identical in both rankings, but after that things shuffle a bit. We're less concerned with the counties at the bottom of the list, but this suggests there is also reasonable stability.

5.10 Follow up questions

In this chapter I've presented some simple steps to take when starting off on an exploratory analysis. The example analysis conducted in this chapter was far from perfect, but it got us thinking about the data and the question of interest. It also gave us a number of things to follow up on in case we continue to be interested in this question.

At this point it's useful to consider a few followup questions.

1. **Do you have the right data?** Sometimes at the conclusion of an exploratory data analysis, the conclusion is that the dataset is not really appropriate for this question. In this case, the dataset seemed perfectly fine for answering the question of which counties had the highest levels of ozone.
2. **Do you need other data?** One sub-question we tried to address was whether the county rankings were stable across years. We addressed this by resampling the data once to see if the rankings changed, but the better way to do this would be to simply get the data for previous years and re-do the rankings.
3. **Do you have the right question?** In this case, it's not clear that the question we tried to answer has immediate relevance, and the data didn't really indicate anything to increase the question's relevance. For example, it might have been more interesting to assess which counties were in violation of the national ambient air quality standard, because determining this could have regulatory implications. However, this is a much more complicated calculation to do, requiring data from at least 3 previous years.

The goal of exploratory data analysis is to get you thinking about your data and reasoning about your question. At this point, we can refine our question or collect new data, all in an iterative process to get at the truth.

6. Principles of Analytic Graphics

Watch a video of this chapter[1].

The material for this chapter is inspired by Edward Tufte's wonderful book *Beautiful Evidence*, which I strongly encourage you to buy if you are able. He discusses how to make informative and useful data graphics and lays out six principles that are important to achieving that goal. Some of these principles are perhaps more relevant to making "final" graphics as opposed to more "exploratory" graphics, but I believe they are all important principles to keep in mind.

6.1 Show comparisons

Showing comparisons is really the basis of all good scientific investigation. Evidence for a hypothesis is always *relative* to another competing hypothesis. When you say "the evidence favors hypothesis A", what you mean to say is that "the evidence favors hypothesis A versus hypothesis B". A good scientist is always asking "Compared to What?" when confronted with a scientific claim or statement. Data graphics should generally follow this same principle. You should always be comparing at least two things.

For example, take a look at the plot below. This plot shows the change in symptom-free days in a group of children enrolled in a clinical trial[2] testing whether an air cleaner installed in a child's home improves their asthma-related symptoms. This study was conducted at the Johns Hopkins University School of Medicine and was conducted in homes where a smoker was living for at least 4 days a week. Each child was assessed at baseline and then 6-months later at a second visit. The aim was to improve a child's symptom-free days over the 6-month period. In this case, a higher number is better, indicating that they had *more* symptom-free days.

---

[1] https://youtu.be/6lOvA_y7p7w
[2] http://www.ncbi.nlm.nih.gov/pubmed/21810636

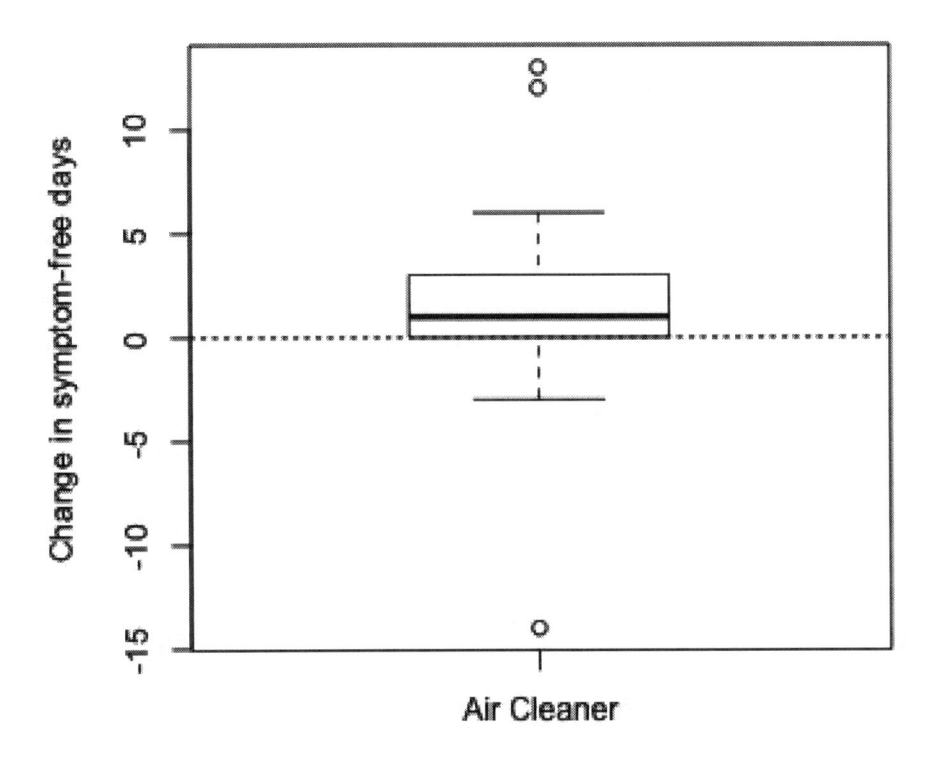

Change in symptom-free days with air cleaner

There were 47 children who received the air cleaner, and you can see from the boxplot that on average the number of symptom-free days increased by about 1 day (the solid line in the middle of the box is the median of the data).

But the question of "compared to what?" is not answered in this plot. In particular, we don't know from the plot what would have happened if the children had *not* received the air cleaner. But of course, we do have that data and we can show both the group that received the air cleaner and the control group that did not.

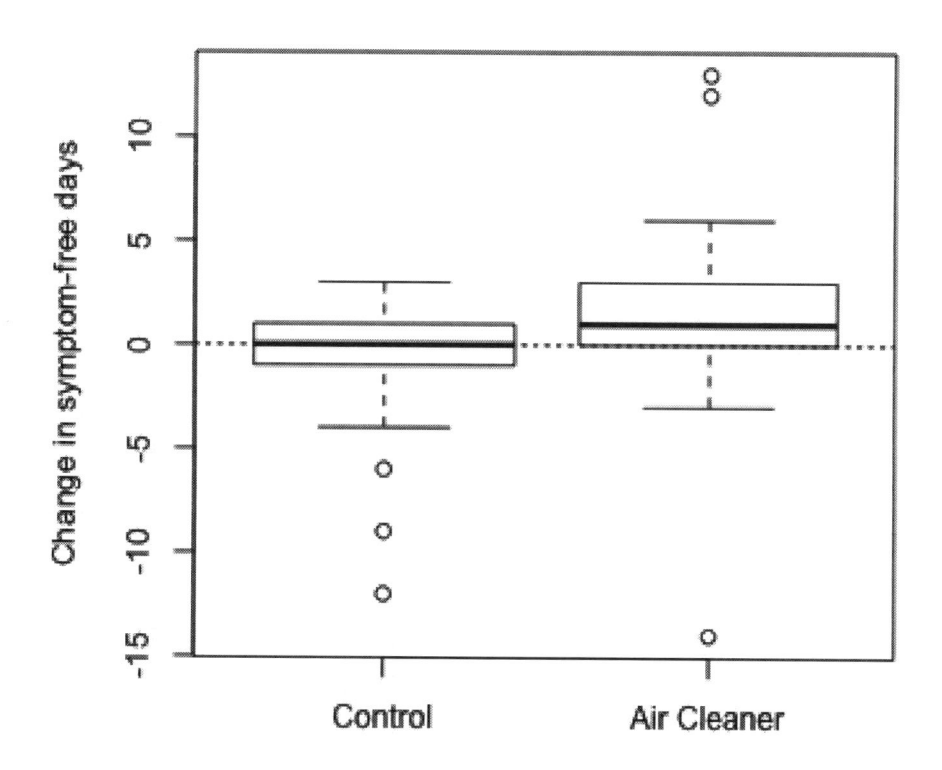

Change in symptom-free days by treatment group

Here we can see that on average, the control group children changed very little in terms of their symptom free days. Therefore, *compared to children who did not receive an air cleaner*, children receiving an air cleaner experienced improved asthma morbidity.

6.2 Show causality, mechanism, explanation, systematic structure

If possible, it's always useful to show your causal framework for thinking about a question. Generally, it's difficult to prove that one thing causes another thing even with the most carefully collected data. But it's still often useful for your data graphics to indicate what you are thinking about in terms of cause. Such a display may suggest hypotheses or refute them, but most importantly, they will raise new questions that can be followed up with new data or analyses.

In the plot below, which is reproduced from the previous section, I show the change in symptom-free days for a group of children who received an air cleaner and a group of children who received no intervention.

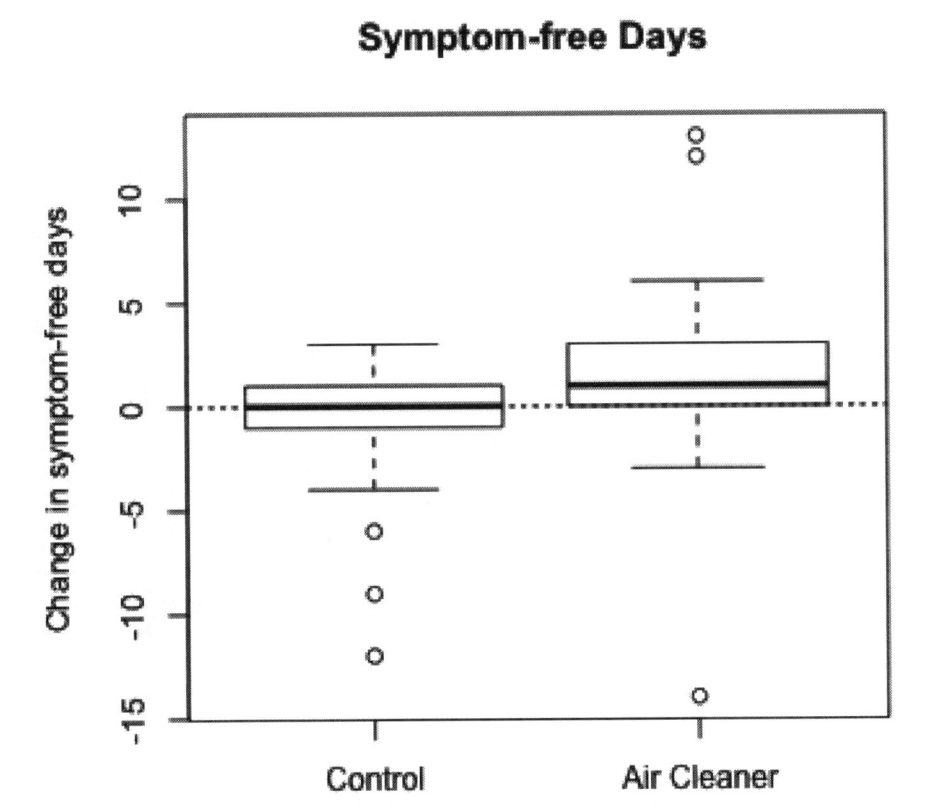

Symptom-free Days

Change in symptom-free days by treatment group

From the plot, it seems clear that on average, the group that received an air cleaner experienced improved asthma morbidity (more symptom-free days, a good thing).

An interesting question might be "Why do the children with the air cleaner improve?" This may not be the *most* important question—you might just care that the air cleaners help things—but answering the question of "why?" might lead to improvements or new developments.

The hypothesis behind air cleaners improving asthma morbidity in children is that the air cleaners remove airborne particles from the air. Given that the homes in this study all had smokers living in them, it is likely that there is a high level of particles in the air, primarily from second-hand smoke.

It's fairly well-understood that inhaling fine particles can exacerbate asthma symptoms, so it stands to reason that reducing the presence in the air should improve asthma symptoms. Therefore, we'd expect that *the group receiving the air cleaners* should on average see a decrease in airborne particles. In this case we are tracking *fine particulate matter*, also called PM2.5 which stands for particulate matter less than or equal to 2.5 microns in aerodynamic diameter.

In the plot below, you can see both the change in symptom-free days for both groups (left) and the change in PM2.5 in both groups (right).

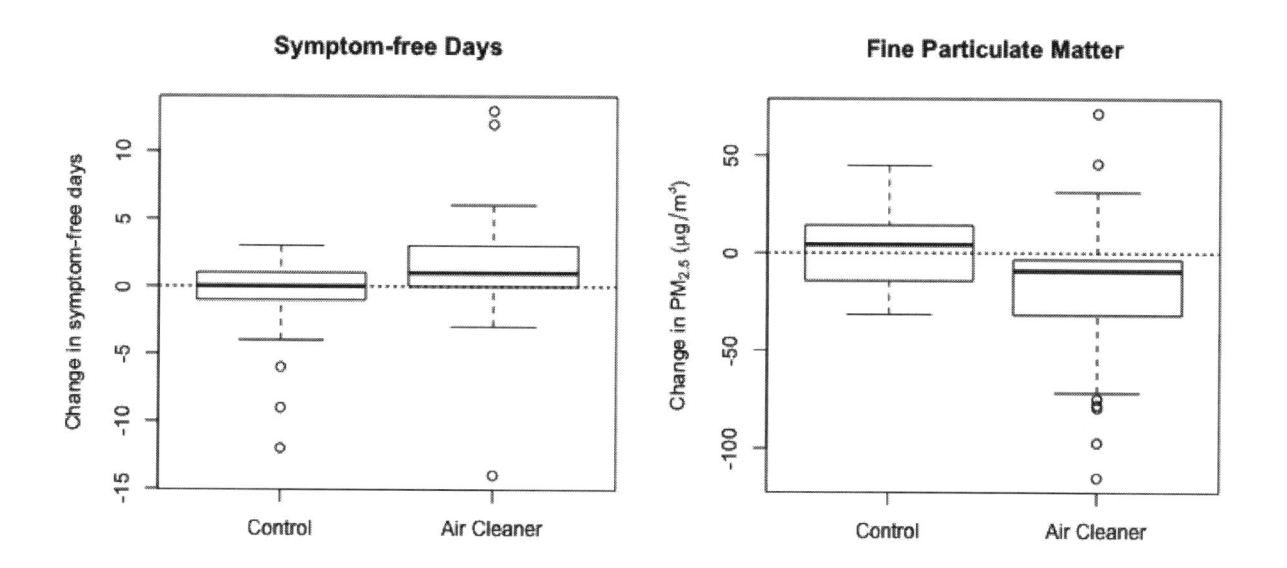

Change in symptom-free days and change in PM2.5 levels in-home

Now we can see from the right-hand plot that on average in the control group, the level of PM2.5 actually increased a little bit while in the air cleaner group the levels decreased on average. This pattern shown in the plot above is consistent with the idea that air cleaners improve health by reducing airborne particles. However, it is not conclusive proof of this idea because there may be other unmeasured confounding factors that can lower levels of PM2.5 and improve symptom-free days.

6.3 Show multivariate data

The real world is multivariate. For anything that you might study, there are usually many attributes that you can measure. The point is that data graphics should attempt to show this information as much as possible, rather than reduce things down to one or two features that we can plot on a page. There are a variety of ways that you can show multivariate data, and you don't need to wear 3-D classes to do it.

Here is just a quick example. Below is data on daily airborne particulate matter ("PM10") in New York City and mortality from 1987 to 2000. Each point on the plot represents the average PM10 level for that day (measured in micrograms per cubic meter) and the number of deaths on that day. The PM10 data come from the U.S. Environmental Protection Agency and the mortality data come from the U.S. National Center for Health Statistics.

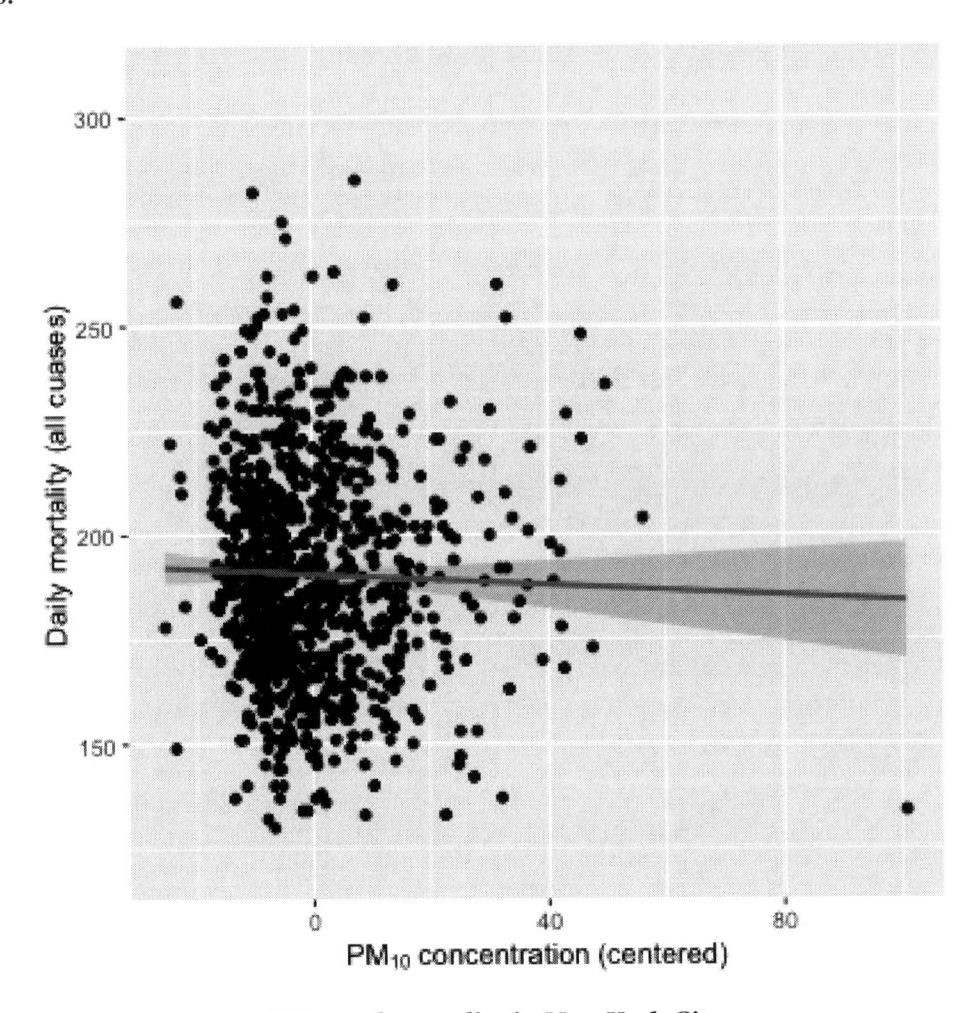

PM10 and mortality in New York City

This is a bivariate plot showing two variables in this dataset. From the plot it seems that there is a slight negative relationship between the two variables. That is, higher daily average levels of PM10 appear to be associated with lower levels of mortality (fewer deaths per day).

However, there are other factors that are associated with both mortality and PM10 levels. One example is the season. It's well known that mortality tends to be higher in the winter than in the summer. That can be easily shown in the following plot of mortality and date.

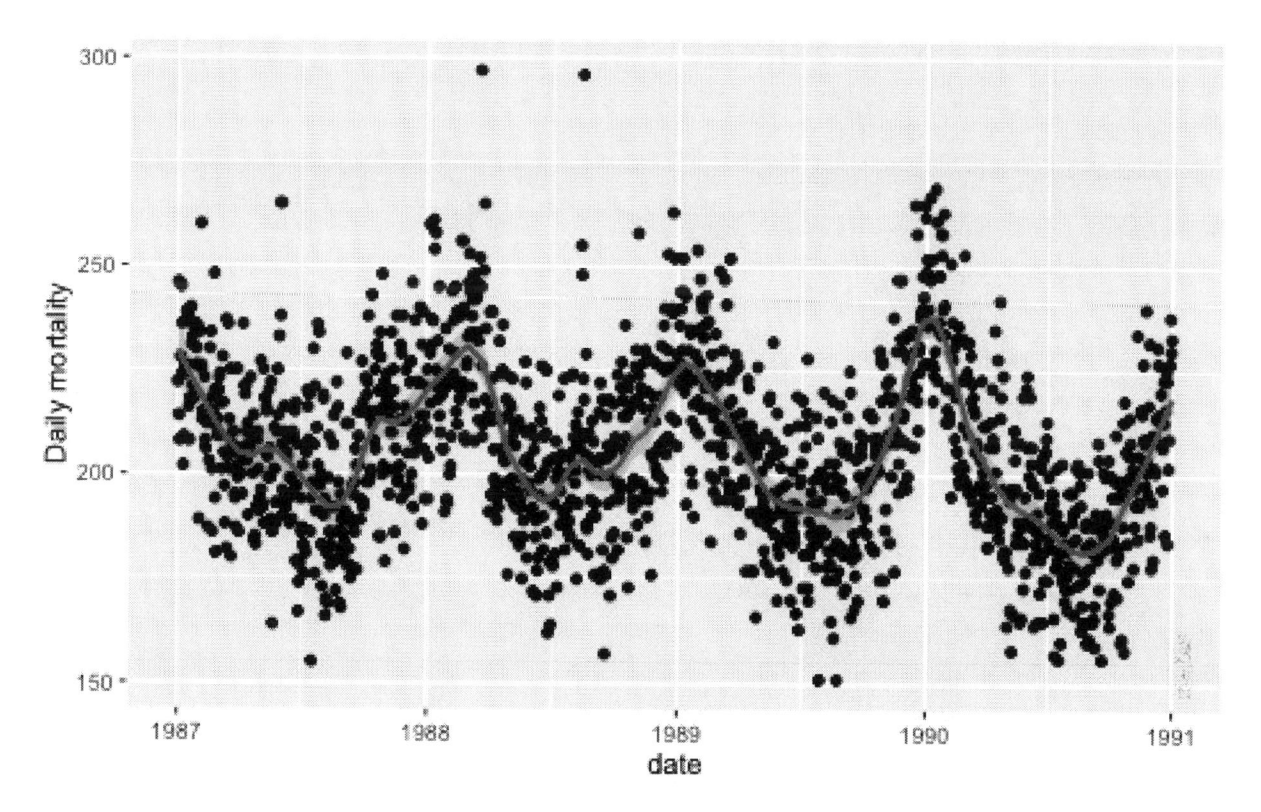

Daily mortality in New York City

Similarly, we can show that in New York City, PM10 levels tend to be high in the summer and low in the winter. Here's the plot for daily PM10 over the same time period. Note that the PM10 data have been centered (the overall mean has been subtracted from them) so that is why there are both positive and negative values.

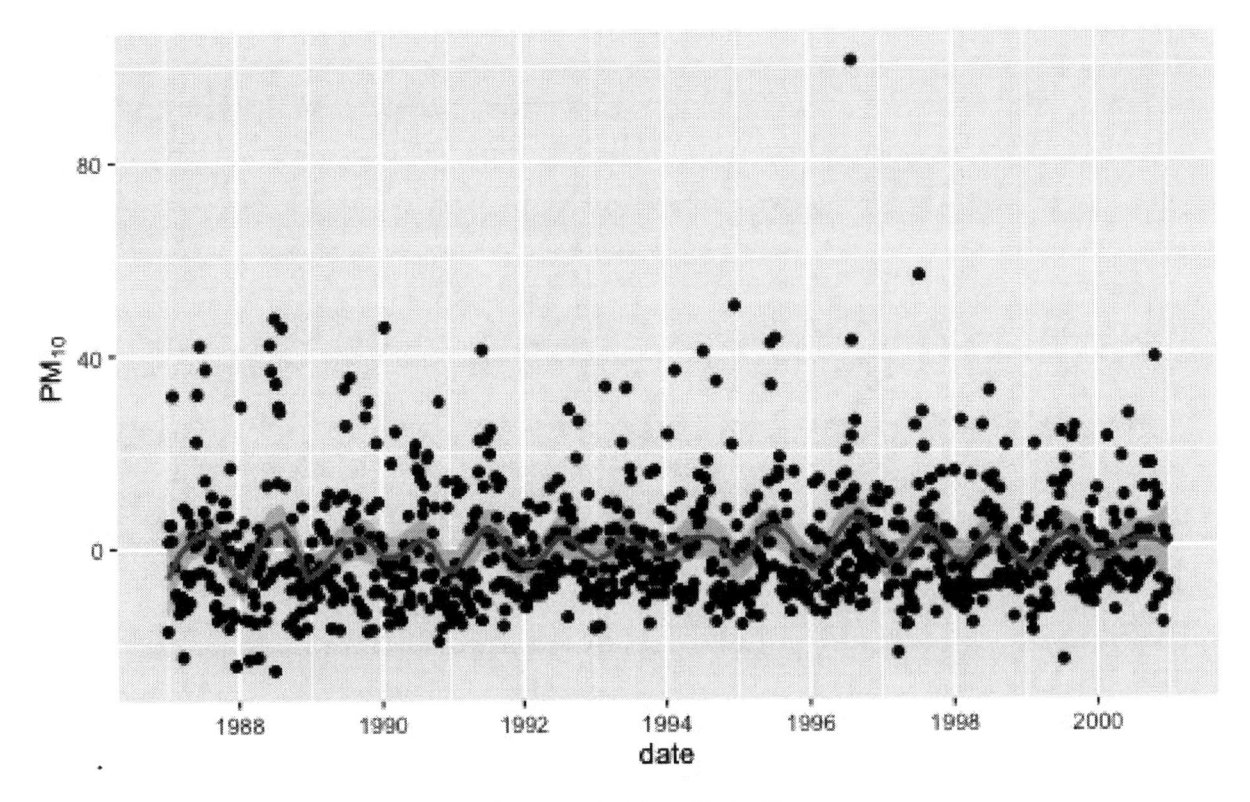

Daily PM10 in New York City

From the two plots we can see that PM10 and mortality have opposite seasonality with mortality being high in the winter and PM10 being high in the summer. What happens if we plot the relationship between mortality and PM10 *by season*? That plot is below.

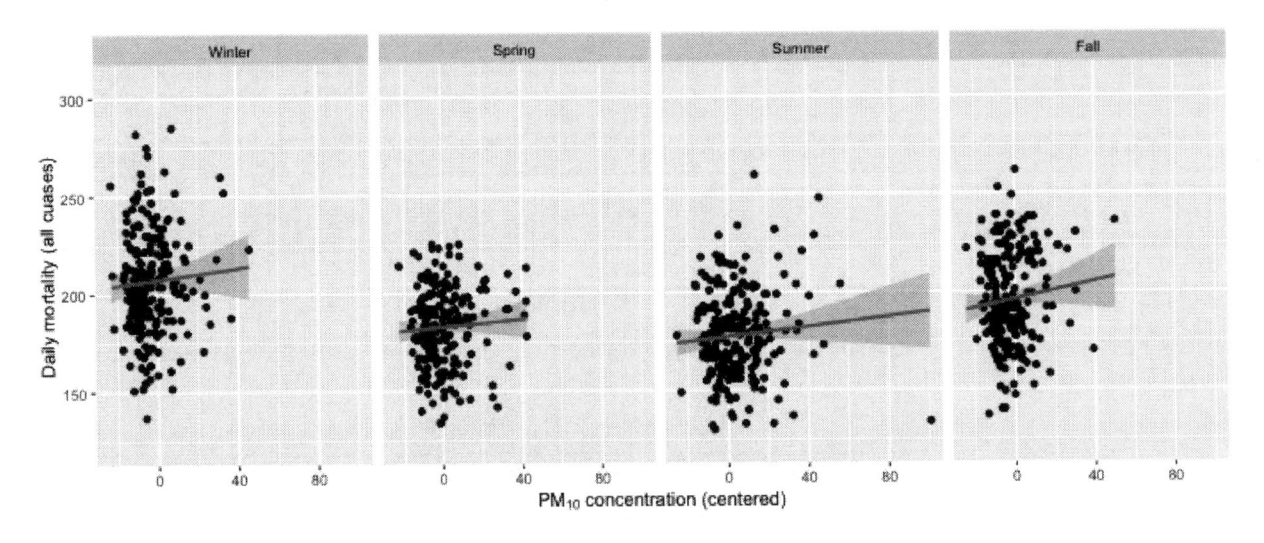

PM10 and mortality in New York City by season

Interestingly, before, when we plotted PM10 and mortality by itself, the relationship appeared to be slightly negative. However, in each of the plots above, the relationship is slightly positive. This set of plots illustrates the effect of confounding by season, because season is related to both PM10 levels and to mortality counts, but in different ways for each one.

This example illustrates just one of many reasons why it can be useful to plot multivariate data and to show as many features as intelligently possible. In some cases, you may uncover unexpected relationships depending on how they are plotted or visualized.

6.4 Integrate evidence

Just because you may be making data graphics, doesn't mean you have to rely solely on circles and lines to make your point. You can also include printed numbers, words, images, and diagrams to tell your story. In other words, data graphics should make use of many modes of data presentation simultaneously, not just the ones that are familiar to you or that the software can handle. One should never let the tools available drive the analysis; one should integrate as much evidence as possible on to a graphic as possible.

6.5 Describe and document the evidence

Data graphics should be appropriately documented with labels, scales, and sources. A general rule for me is that a data graphic should tell a complete story all by itself. You should not have to refer to extra text or descriptions when interpreting a plot, if possible. Ideally, a plot would have all of the necessary descriptions attached to it. You might think that this level of documentation should be reserved for "final" plots as opposed to exploratory ones, but it's good to get in the habit of documenting your evidence sooner rather than later.

Imagine if you were writing a paper or a report, and a data graphic was presented to make the primary point. Imagine the person you hand the paper/report to has very little time and will only focus on the graphic. Is there enough information on that graphic for the person to get the story? While it is certainly possible to be too detailed, I tend to err on the side of more information rather than less.

In the simple example below, I plot the same data twice (this is the PM10 data from the previous section of this chapter).

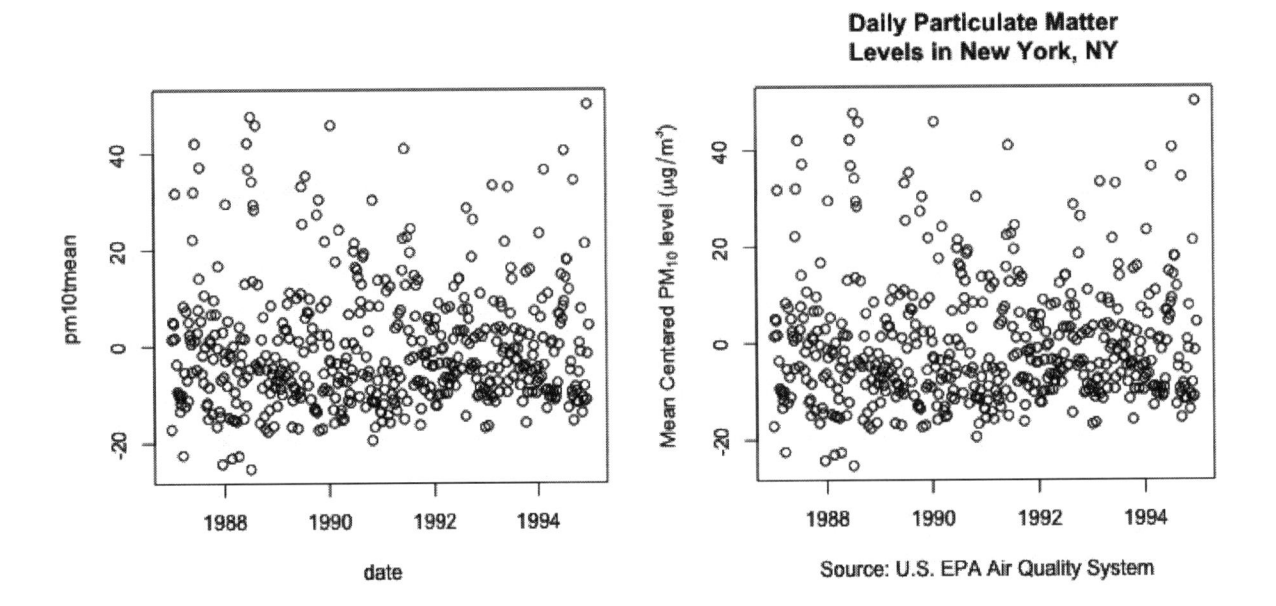

Labelling and annotation of data graphics

The plot on the left is a default plot generated by the `plot` function in R. The plot on the right uses the same `plot` function but adds annotations like a title, y-axis label, x-axis label. Key information included is where the data were collected (New York), the units of measurement, the time scale of measurements (daily), and the source of the data (EPA).

6.6 Content, Content, Content

Analytical presentations ultimately stand or fall depending on the quality, relevance, and integrity of their content. This includes the question being asked and the evidence presented in favor of certain hypotheses. No amount of visualization magic or bells and whistles can make poor data, or more importantly, a poorly formed question, shine with clarity. Starting with a good question, developing a sound approach, and only presenting information that is necessary for answering that question, is essential to every data graphic.

6.7 References

This chapter is inspired by the work of Edward Tufte. I encourage you to take a look at his books, in particular the following book:

Edward Tufte (2006). *Beautiful Evidence*, Graphics Press LLC. www.edwardtufte.com[3]

---

[3] http://www.edwardtufte.com

7. Exploratory Graphs

Watch a video of this chapter: Part 1[1] Part 2[2]

There are many reasons to use graphics or plots in exploratory data analysis. If you just have a few data points, you might just print them out on the screen or on a sheet of paper and scan them over quickly before doing any real analysis (technique I commonly use for small datasets or subsets). If you have a dataset with more than just a few data points, then you'll typically need some assistance to visualize the data.

Visualizing the data via graphics can be important at the beginning stages of data analysis to understand basic properties of the data, to find simple patterns in data, and to suggest possible modeling strategies. In later stages of an analysis, graphics can be used to "debug" an analysis, if an unexpected (but not necessarily wrong) result occurs, or ultimately, to communicate your findings to others.

7.1 Characteristics of exploratory graphs

For the purposes of this chapter (and the rest of this book), we will make a distinction between *exploratory* graphs and *final* graphs. This distinction is not a very formal one, but it serves to highlight the fact that graphs are used for many different purposes. Exploratory graphs are usually made very quickly and a lot of them are made in the process of checking out the data.

The goal of making exploratory graphs is usually developing a personal understanding of the data and to prioritize tasks for follow up. Details like axis orientation or legends, while present, are generally cleaned up and prettified if the graph is going to be used for communication later. Often color and plot symbol size are used to convey various dimensions of information.

7.2 Air Pollution in the United States

For this chapter, we will use a simple case study to demonstrate the kinds of simple graphs that can be useful in exploratory analyses. The data we will be using come from the U.S. Environmental Protection Agency (EPA), which is the U.S. government agency that sets national air quality standards for outdoor air pollution[3]. One of the national

---

[1] https://youtu.be/ma6-0PSNLHo
[2] https://youtu.be/UyopqXQ8TTM
[3] http://www.epa.gov/air/criteria.html

ambient air quality standards in the U.S. concerns the long-term average level of fine particle pollution, also referred to as PM2.5. Here, the standard says that the "annual mean, averaged over 3 years" cannot exceed 12 micrograms per cubic meter. Data on daily PM2.5 are available from the U.S. EPA web site, or specifically, the EPA Air Quality System[4] web site.

One key question we are interested is: **Are there any counties in the U.S. that exceed the national standard for fine particle pollution?** This question has important consequences because counties that are found to be in violation of the national standards can face serious legal consequences. In particular, states that have counties in violation of the standards are required to create a State Implementation Plan (SIP) that shows how those counties will come within the national standards within a given period of time.

7.3 Getting the Data

First, we can read the data into R with read.csv(). This dataset contains the annual mean PM2.5 averaged over the period 2008 through 2010

```
> class <- c("numeric", "character", "factor", "numeric", "numeric")
> pollution <- read.csv("data/avgpm25.csv", colClasses = class)
```

Here are the first few rows of the data frame.

```
> head(pollution)
       pm25  fips region longitude latitude
1  9.771185 01003   east -87.74826 30.59278
2  9.993817 01027   east -85.84286 33.26581
3 10.688618 01033   east -87.72596 34.73148
4 11.337424 01049   east -85.79892 34.45913
5 12.119764 01055   east -86.03212 34.01860
6 10.827805 01069   east -85.35039 31.18973
```

Each row contains the 5-digit code indicating the county (fips), the region of the country in which the county resides, the longitude and latitude of the centroid for that county, and the average PM2.5 level.

Here's a bit more information on the dataset as given by str().

---

[4]http://www.epa.gov/ttn/airs/airsaqs/detaildata/downloadaqsdata.htm

```
> str(pollution)
'data.frame':       576 obs. of  5 variables:
 $ pm25     : num  9.77 9.99 10.69 11.34 12.12 ...
 $ fips     : chr  "01003" "01027" "01033" "01049" ...
 $ region   : Factor w/ 2 levels "east","west": 1 1 1 1 1 1 1 1 1 1 ...
 $ longitude: num  -87.7 -85.8 -87.7 -85.8 -86 ...
 $ latitude : num  30.6 33.3 34.7 34.5 34 ...
```

Back to the question, though. How can we see if any counties exceed the standard of 12 micrograms per cubic meter?

7.4 Simple Summaries: One Dimension

For one dimensional summarize, there are number of options in R.

- **Five-number summary**: This gives the minimum, 25th percentile, median, 75th percentile, maximum of the data and is quick check on the distribution of the data (see the `fivenum()`)
- **Boxplots**: Boxplots are a visual representation of the five-number summary plus a bit more information. In particular, boxplots commonly plot outliers that go beyond the bulk of the data. This is implemented via the `boxplot()` function
- **Barplot**: Barplots are useful for visualizing categorical data, with the number of entries for each category being proportional to the height of the bar. Think "pie chart" but actually useful. The barplot can be made with the `barplot()` function.
- **Histograms**: Histograms show the complete empirical distribution of the data, beyond the five data points shown by the boxplots. Here, you can easily check skewwness of the data, symmetry, multi-modality, and other features. The `hist()` function makes a histogram, and a handy function to go with it sometimes is the `rug()` function.
- **Density plot**: The `density()` function computes a non-parametric estimate of the distribution of a variables

7.5 Five Number Summary

A five-number summary can be computed with the `fivenum()` function, which takes a vector of numbers as input. Here, we compute a five-number summary of the PM2.5 data in the pollution dataset.

```
> fivenum(pollution$pm25)
[1]  3.382626  8.547590 10.046697 11.356829 18.440731
```

We can see that the median across all the counties in the dataset is about 10 micrograms per cubic meter.

For interactive work, it's often a bit nice to use the summary() function, which has a default method for numeric vectors.

```
> summary(pollution$pm25)
   Min. 1st Qu.  Median    Mean 3rd Qu.    Max.
  3.383   8.549  10.050   9.836  11.360  18.440
```

You'll notice that in addition to the five-number summary, the summary() function also adds the mean of the data, which can be compared to the median to identify any skewness in the data. Given that the mean is fairly close to the median, there doesn't appear to be a dramatic amount of skewness in the distribution of PM2.5 in this dataset.

7.6 Boxplot

Here's a quick boxplot of the PM2.5 data. Note that in a boxplot, the "whiskers" that stick out above and below the box have a length of 1.5 times the *inter-quartile range*, or IQR, which is simply the distance from the bottom of the box to the top of the box. Anything beyond the whiskers is marked as an "outlier" and is plotted separately as an individual point.

```
> boxplot(pollution$pm25, col = "blue")
```

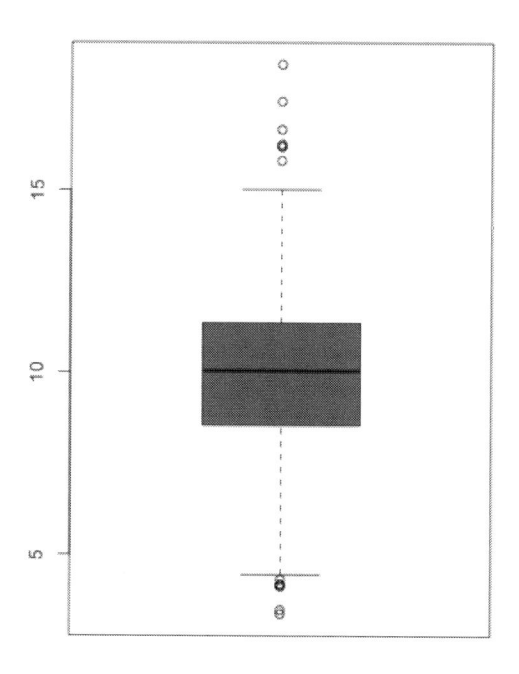

Boxplot of PM2.5 data

From the boxplot, we can see that there are a few points on both the high and the low end that appear to be outliers according to the `boxplot()` algorithm. These points migth be worth looking at individually.

From the plot, it appears that the high points are all above the level of 15, so we can take a look at those data points directly. Note that although the current national ambient air quality standard is 12 micrograms per cubic meter, it used to be 15.

```
> library(dplyr)
> filter(pollution, pm25 > 15)
      pm25  fips region longitude latitude
1 16.19452 06019   west -119.9035 36.63837
2 15.80378 06029   west -118.6833 35.29602
3 18.44073 06031   west -119.8113 36.15514
4 16.66180 06037   west -118.2342 34.08851
5 15.01573 06047   west -120.6741 37.24578
6 17.42905 06065   west -116.8036 33.78331
7 16.25190 06099   west -120.9588 37.61380
8 16.18358 06107   west -119.1661 36.23465
```

These counties are all in the western U.S. (`region == west`) and in fact are all in California because the first two digits of the `fips` code are `06`.

We can make a quick map of these counties to get a sense of where they are in California.

```
> library(maps)
> map("county", "california")
> with(filter(pollution, pm25 > 15), points(longitude, latitude))
```

Map of California counties

At this point, you might decide to follow up on these counties, or ignore them if you are interested in other features. Since these counties appear to have very high levels, relative to the distribution of levels in the other counties in the U.S., they may be worth following up on if you are interested in describing counties that are potentially in violation of the standards.

Note that the plot/map above is not very pretty, but it was made quickly and it gave us a sense of where these outlying counties were located and conveyed enough information to help decide if we an to follow up or not.

7.7 Histogram

A histogram is useful to look at when we want to see more detail on the full distribution of the data. The boxplot is quick and handy, but fundamentally only gives us a bit of information.

Here is a histogram of the PM2.5 annual average data.

```
> hist(pollution$pm25, col = "green")
```

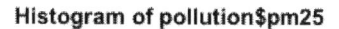

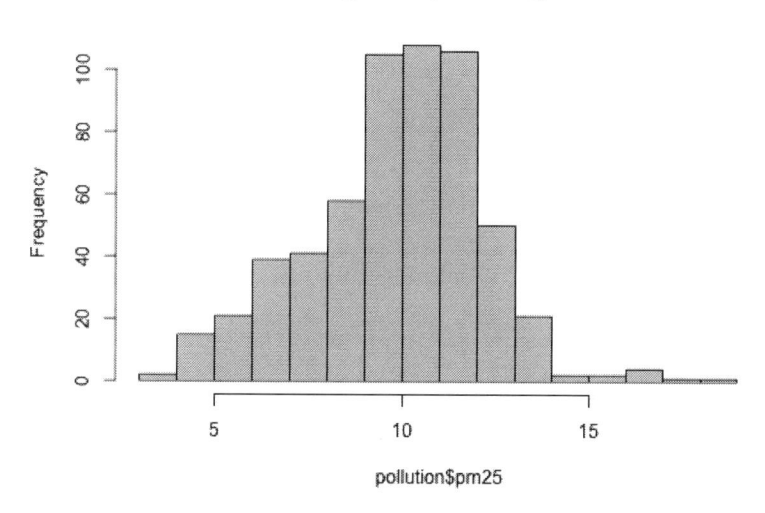

Histogram of PM2.5 data

This distribution is interesting because there appears to be a high concentration of counties in the neighborhood of 9 to 12 micrograms per cubic meter. We can get a little more detail of we use the `rug()` function to show us the actual data points.

```
> hist(pollution$pm25, col = "green")
> rug(pollution$pm25)
```

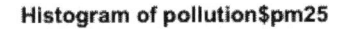

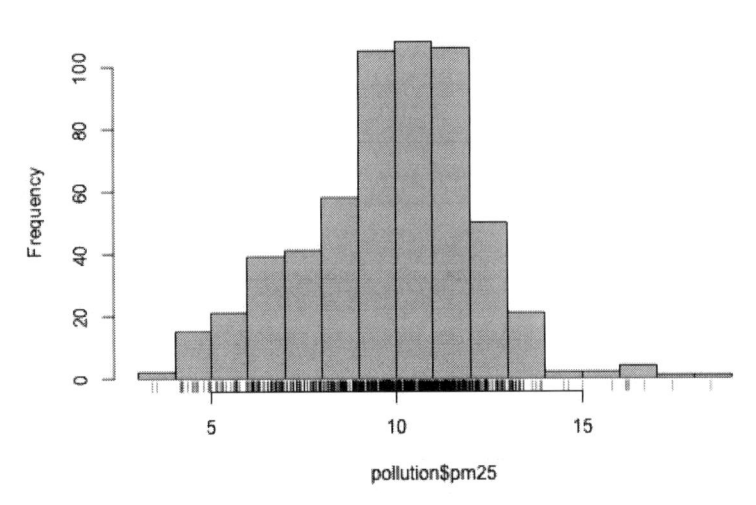

Histogram of PM2.5 data with rug

The large cluster of data points in the 9 to 12 range is perhaps not surprising in this context. It's not uncommon to observe this behavior in situations where you have a strict limit imposed at a certain level. Note that there are still quite a few counties above the level of 12, which may be worth investigating.

The `hist()` function has a default algorithm for determining the number of bars to use in the histogram based on the density of the data (see `?nclass.Sturges`). However, you can override the default option by setting the `breaks` argument to something else. Here, we use more bars to try to get more detail.

```
> hist(pollution$pm25, col = "green", breaks = 100)
> rug(pollution$pm25)
```

Histogram of pollution$pm25

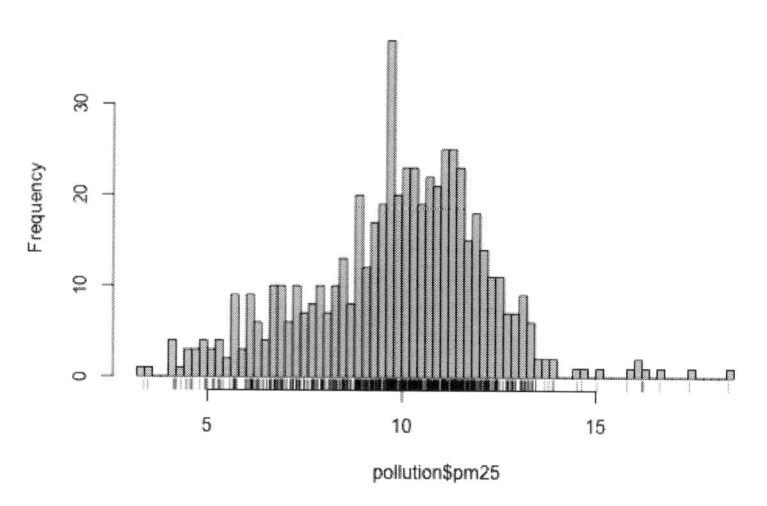

Histogram of PM2.5 data with more breaks

Now we see that there's a rather large spike 9 micrograms per cubic meter. It's not immediately clear why, but again, it might be worth following up on.

7.8 Overlaying Features

Once we start seeing interesting features in our data, it's often useful to lay down annotations on our plots as reference points are markers. For example in our boxplot above, we might want to draw a horizontal line at 12 where the national standard is.

```
> boxplot(pollution$pm25, col = "blue")
> abline(h = 12)
```

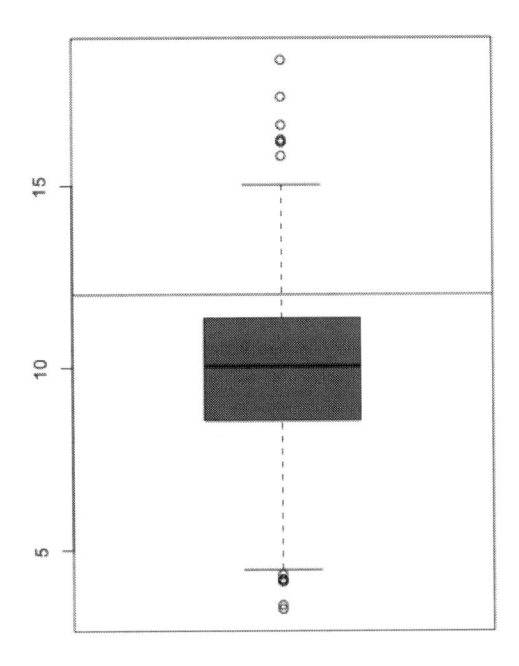

Boxplot of PM2.5 data with added line

We can see that a reasonable portion of the distribution as displayed by the boxplot is above the line (i.e. potentially in violation of the standard).

While the boxplot gives a sense, the histogram might be better suited to visualizing the data here. In the plot below, we see the histogram and draw two lines, one at the median of the data and one at 12, the level of the standard.

```
> hist(pollution$pm25, col = "green")
> abline(v = 12, lwd = 2)
> abline(v = median(pollution$pm25), col = "magenta", lwd = 4)
```

Histogram of pollution$pm25

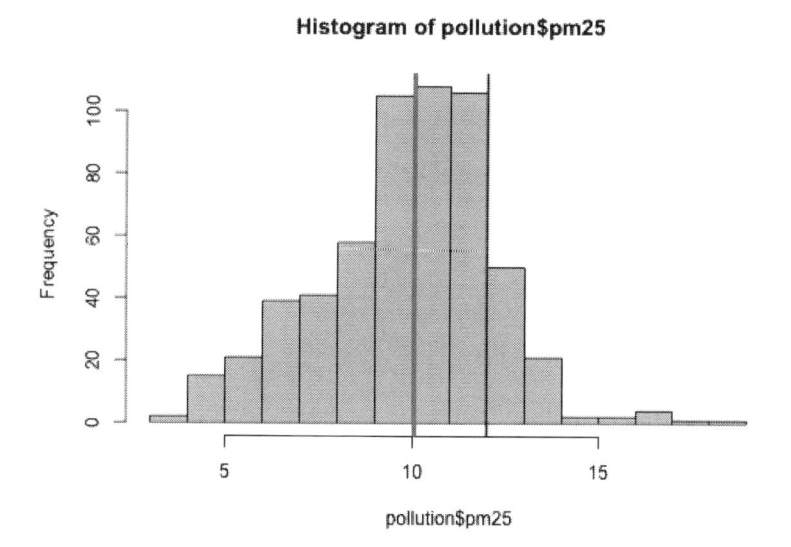

Histogram of PM2.5 data with annotation

Note that for the vertical lines, we can use both color (col) and the line width (lwd) to indicate different components of information.

7.9 Barplot

The barplot is useful for summarizing categorical data. Here we have one categorical variable, the region in which a county resides (east or west). We can see how many western and eastern counties there are with barplot(). We use the table() function to do the actual tabulation of how many counties there are in each region.

```
> library(dplyr)
> table(pollution$region) %>% barplot(col = "wheat")
```

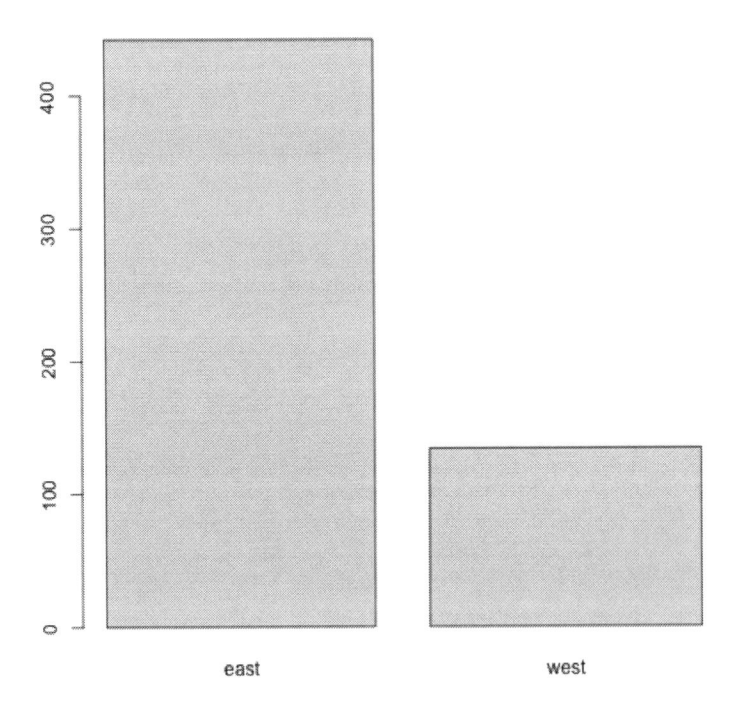

plot of chunk unnamed-chunk-14

We can see quite clearly that there are many more counties in the eastern U.S. in this dataset than in the western U.S.

7.10 Simple Summaries: Two Dimensions and Beyond

So far we've covered some of the main tools used to summarize one dimensional data. For investigating data in two dimensions and beyond, there is an array of additional tools. Some of the key approaches are

- **Multiple or overlayed 1-D plots** (Lattice/ggplot2): Using multiple boxplots or multiple histograms can be useful for seeing the relationship between two variables, especially when on is naturally categorical.
- **Scatterplots**: Scatterplots are the natural tool for visualizing two continuous variables. Transformations of the variables (e.g. log or square-root transformation) may be necessary for effective visualization.
- **Smooth scatterplots**: Similar in concept to scatterplots but rather plots a 2-D histogram of the data. Can be useful for scatterplots that may contain many many data points.

For visualizing data in more than 2 dimensions, without resorting to 3-D animations (or glasses!), we can often combine the tools that we've already learned:

- **Overlayed or multiple 2-D plots; conditioning plots (coplots)**: A conditioning plot, or coplot, shows the relationship between two variables as a third (or more) variable changes. For example, you might want to see how the relationship between air pollution levels and mortality changes with the season of the year. Here, air pollution and mortality are the two primary variables and season is the third variable varying in the background.
- **Use color, size, shape to add dimensions**: Plotting points with different colors or shapes is useful for indicating a third dimension, where different colors can indicate different categories or ranges of something. Plotting symbols with different sizes can also achieve the same effect when the third dimension is continuous.
- **Spinning/interactive plots**: Spinning plots can be used to simulate 3-D plots by allowing the user to essentially quickly cycle through many different 2-D projections so that the plot feels 3-D. These are sometimes helpful to capture unusual structure in the data, but I rarely use them.
- **Actual 3-D plots (not that useful)**: Actual 3-D plots (for example, requiring 3-D glasses) are relatively few and far between and are generally impractical for communicating to a large audience. Of course, this may change in the future with improvements in technology....

7.11 Multiple Boxplots

One of the simplest ways to show the relationship between two variables (in this case, one categorical and one continuous) is to show side-by-side boxplots. Using the pollution data described above, we can show the difference in PM2.5 levels between the eastern and western parts of the U.S. with the boxplot() function.

```
> boxplot(pm25 ~ region, data = pollution, col = "red")
```

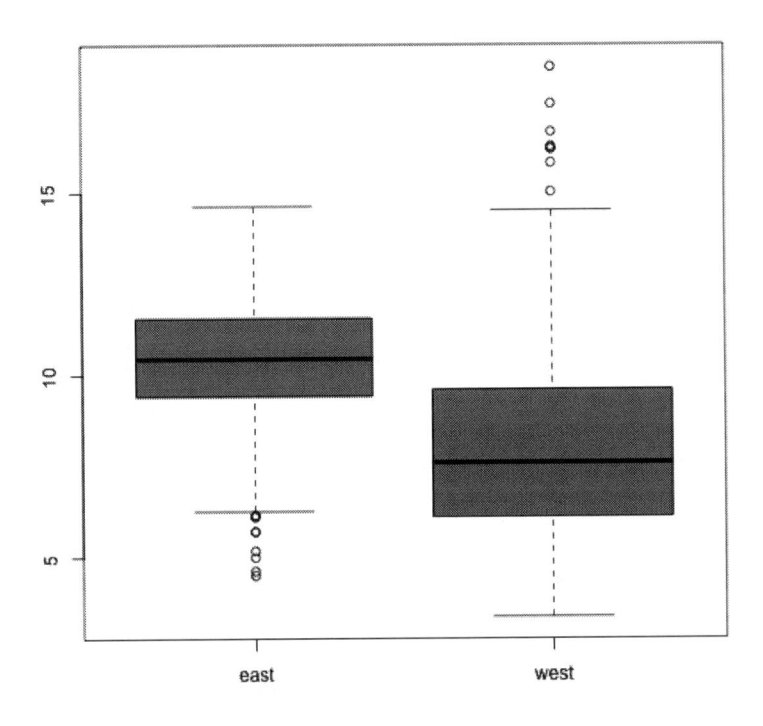

Boxplot of PM2.5 by region

The `boxplot()` function can take a *formula*, with the left hand side indicating the variable for which we want to create the boxplot (continuous) and the right hand side indicating the variable that stratifies the left hand side into categories. Since the `region` variable only has two categories, we end up with two boxplots. Side-by-side boxplots are useful because you can often fit many on a page to get a rich sense of any trends or changes in a variable. Their compact format allow you to visualize a lot of data in a small space.

From the plot above, we can see rather clearly that the levels in eastern counties are on average higher than the levels in western counties.

7.12 Multiple Histograms

It can sometimes be useful to plot multiple histograms, much like with side-by-side boxplots, to see changes in the shape of the distribution of a variable across different categories. However, the number of histograms that you can effectively put on a page is limited.

Here is the distribution of PM2.5 in the eastern and western regions of the U.S.

```
> par(mfrow = c(2, 1), mar = c(4, 4, 2, 1))
> hist(subset(pollution, region == "east")$pm25, col = "green")
> hist(subset(pollution, region == "west")$pm25, col = "green")
```

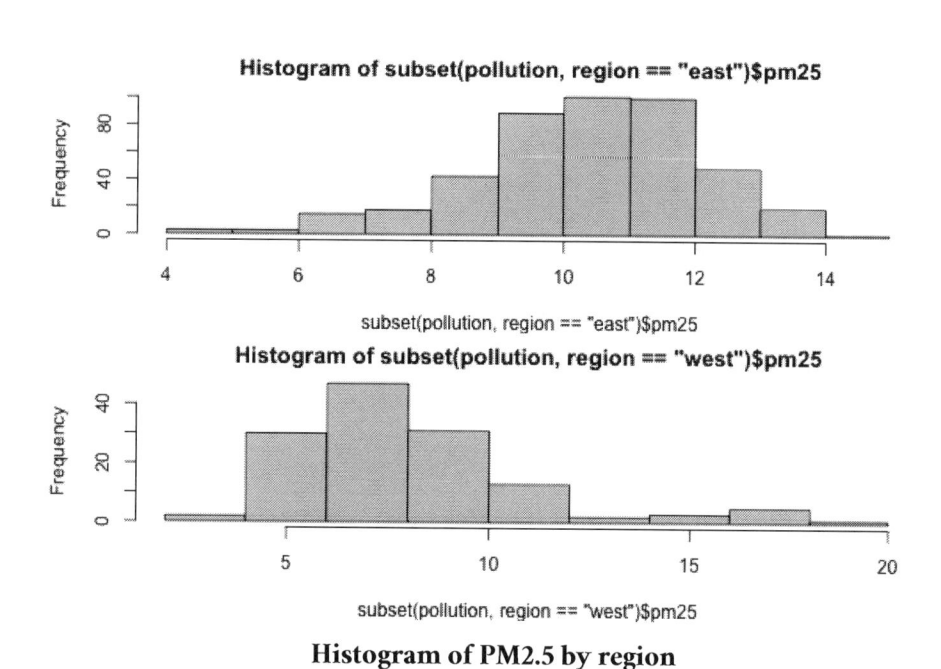

Histogram of PM2.5 by region

You can see here that the PM2.5 in the western U.S. tends to be right-skewed with some outlying counties with very high levels. The PM2.5 in the east tends to be left skewed some counties having very low levels.

7.13 Scatterplots

For continuous variables, the most common visualization technique is the scatterplot, which simply maps each variable to an x- or y-axis coordinate. Here is a scatterplot of latitude and PM2.5, which can be made with the `plot()` function.

```
> with(pollution, plot(latitude, pm25))
> abline(h = 12, lwd = 2, lty = 2)
```

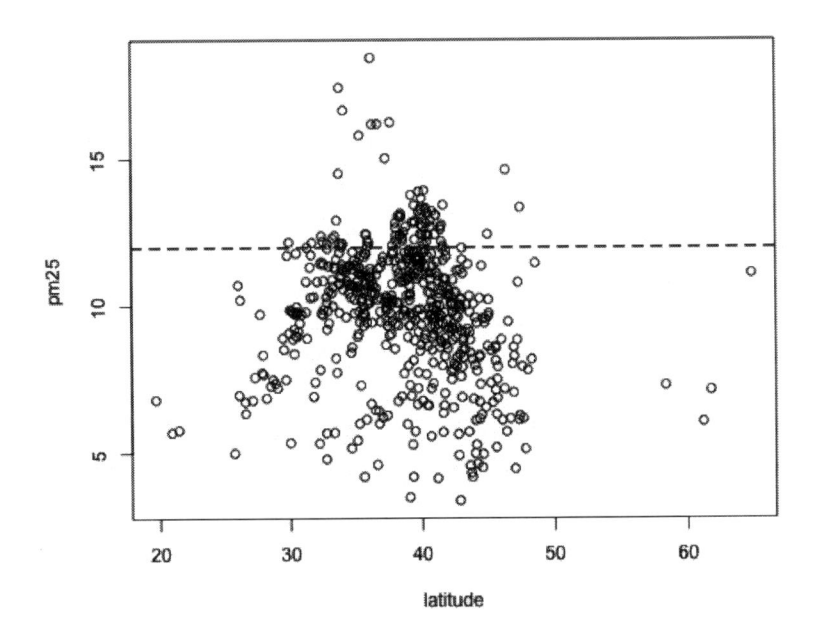

Scatterplot of PM2.5 and latitude

As you go from south to north in the U.S., we can see that the highest levels of PM2.5 tend to be in the middle region of the country.

7.14 Scatterplot - Using Color

If we wanted to add a third dimension to the scatterplot above, say the region variable indicating east and west, we could use color to highlight that dimension. Here we color the circles in the plot to indicate east (black) or west (red).

```
> with(pollution, plot(latitude, pm25, col = region))
> abline(h = 12, lwd = 2, lty = 2)
```

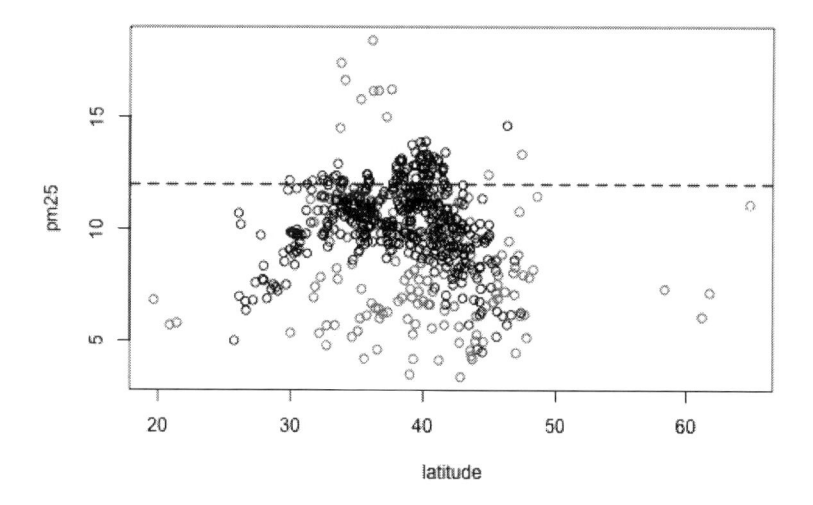

Scatterplot of PM2.5 and latitude by region

It may be confusing at first to figure out which color gets mapped to which region. We can find out by looking directly at the levels of the region variable.

```
> levels(pollution$region)
[1] "east" "west"
```

Here we see that the first level is "east" and the second level is "west". So the color for "east" will get mapped to 1 and the color for "west" will get mapped to 2. For plotting functions, col = 1 is black (the default color) and col = 2 is red.

7.15 Multiple Scatterplots

Using multiple scatterplots can be necessary when overlaying points with different colors or shapes is confusing (sometimes because of the volume of data). Separating the plots out can sometimes make visualization easier.

```
> par(mfrow = c(1, 2), mar = c(5, 4, 2, 1))
> with(subset(pollution, region == "west"), plot(latitude, pm25, main = "West"))
> with(subset(pollution, region == "east"), plot(latitude, pm25, main = "East"))
```

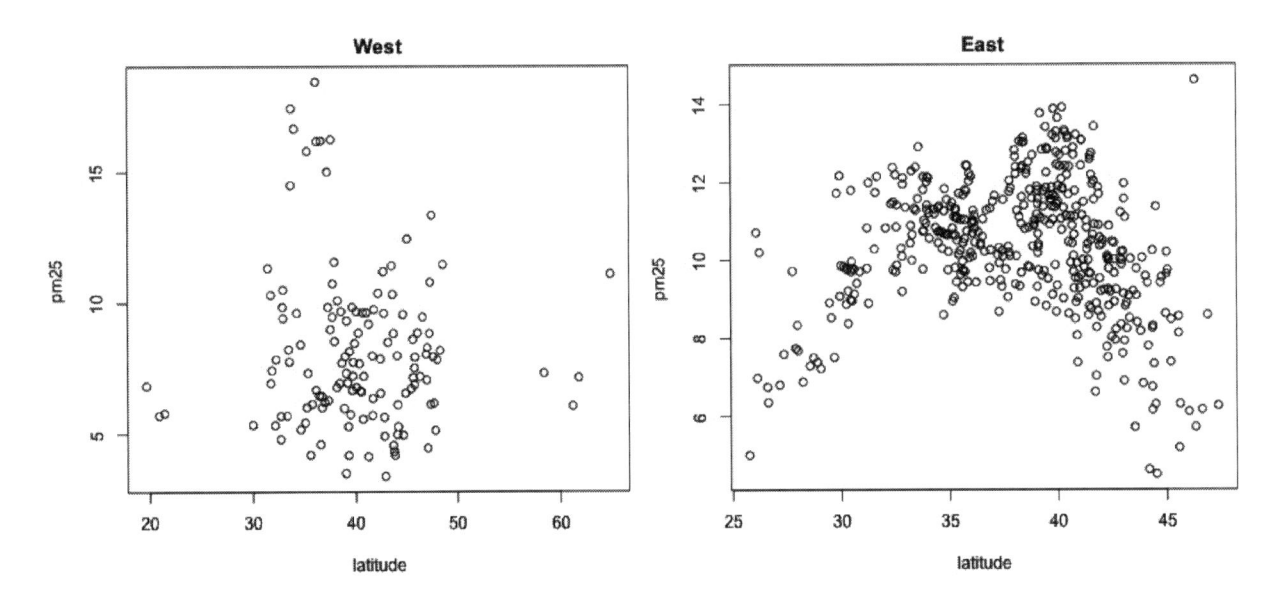

Multiple Scatterplots of PM2.5 and latitude by region

These kinds of plots, sometimes called panel plots, are generally easier to make with either the lattice or ggplot2 system, which we will learn about in greater detail in later chapters..

```
> ## Lattice
> library(lattice)
> xyplot(pm25 ~ latitude | region, data = pollution)
>
> ## ggplot2
> library(ggplot2)
> qplot(latitude, pm25, data = pollution, facets = . ~ region)
```

7.16 Summary

Exploratory plots are "quick and dirty" and their purpose is to let you summarize the data and highlight any broad features. They are also useful for exploring basic questions about the data and for judging the evidence for or against certain hypotheses. Ultimately, they may be useful for suggesting modeling strategies that can be employed in the "next step" of the data analysis process.

8. Plotting Systems

Watch a video of this chapter[1].

There are three different plotting systems in R and they each have different characteristics and modes of operation. They three systems are the base plotting system, the lattice system, and the ggplot2 system. This chapter (and this book) will focus primarily on the base plotting system.

8.1 The Base Plotting System

The base plotting system is the original plotting system for R. The basic model is sometimes referred to as the "artist's palette" model. The idea is you start with blank canvas and build up from there.

In more R-specific terms, you typically start with `plot` function (or similar plot creating function) to *initiate* a plot and then *annotate* the plot with various annotation functions (`text, lines, points, axis`)

The base plotting system is often the most convenient plotting system to use because it mirrors how we sometimes think of building plots and analyzing data. If we don't have a completely well-formed idea of how we want to look at some data, often we'll start by "throwing some data on the page" and then slowly add more information to it as our thought process evolves.

For example, we might look at a simple scatterplot and then decide to add a linear regression line or a smoother to it to highlight the trends.

```
> data(airquality)
> with(airquality, {
+         plot(Temp, Ozone)
+         lines(loess.smooth(Temp, Ozone))
+ })
```

[1]https://youtu.be/a4mvbyNGdBA

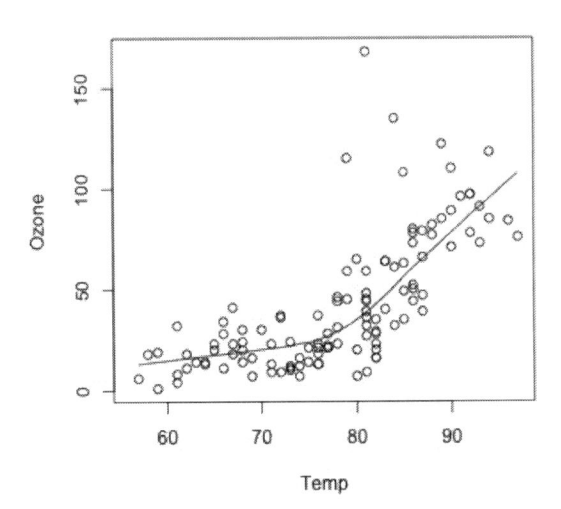

Scatterplot with loess curve

In the code above, the `plot` function creates the initial plot and draws the points (circles) on the canvas. The `lines` function is used to annotate or add to the plot; in this case it adds a loess smoother to the scatterplot.

Here we use the `plot` function to draw the points on the scatterplot and then use the `title` function to add a main title to the plot.

One downside with constructing base plots is that you canâ€™t go backwards once the plot has started. So it's possible that you could start down the road of constructing a plot and realize later (when it's too late) that you don't have enough room to add a y-axis label or something like that.

If you have specific plot in mind, there is then a need to plan in advance to make sure, for example, that you've set your margins to be the right size to fit all of the annotations that you may want to include. While the base plotting system is nice in that it gives you the flexibility to specify these kinds of details to painstaking accuracy, sometimes it would be nice if the system could just figure it out for you.

Another downside of the base plotting system is that it's difficult to describe or translate a plot to others because there's no clear graphical language or grammar that can be used to communicate what you've done. The only real way to describe what you've done in a base plot is to just list the series of commands/functions that you've executed, which is not a particularly compact way of communicating things. This is one problem that the `ggplot2` package attempts to address.

Another typical base plot is constructed with the following code.

```
> data(cars)
> 
> ## Create the plot / draw canvas
> with(cars, plot(speed, dist))
> 
> ## Add annotation
> title("Speed vs. Stopping distance")
```

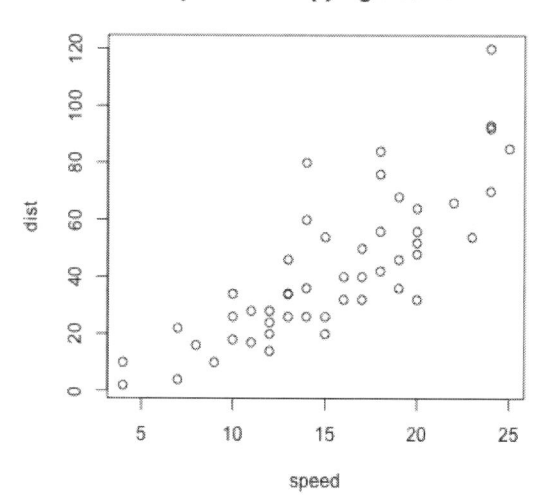

Base plot with title

We will go into more detail on what these functions do in later chapters.

8.2 The Lattice System

The lattice plotting system is implemented in the `lattice` package which comes with every installation of R (although it is not loaded by default). To use the lattice plotting functions you must first load the `lattice` package with the `library` function.

```
> library(lattice)
```

With the lattice system, plots are created with a single function call, such as `xyplot` or `bwplot`. There is no real distinction between functions that create or initiate plots and functions that annotate plots because it all happens at once.

Lattice plots tend to be most useful for conditioning types of plots, i.e. looking at how y changes with x across levels of z. These types of plots are useful for looking at multi-dimensional data and often allow you to squeeze a lot of information into a single window or page.

Another aspect of lattice that makes it different from base plotting is that things like margins and spacing are set automatically. This is possible because entire plot is specified at once via a single function call, so all of the available information needed to figure out the spacing and margins is already there.

Here is an example of a lattice plot that looks at the relationship between life expectancy and income and how that relationship varies by region in the United States.

```
> state <- data.frame(state.x77, region = state.region)
> xyplot(Life.Exp ~ Income | region, data = state, layout = c(4, 1))
```

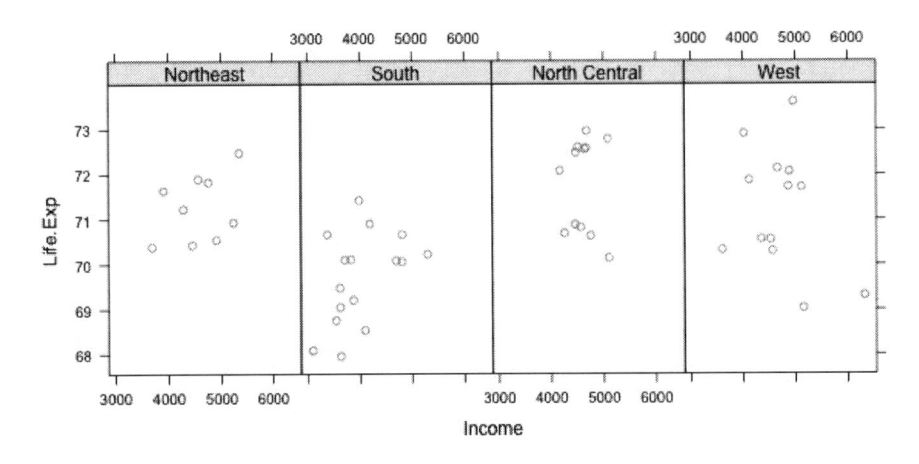

Lattice plot

You can see that the entire plot was generated by the call to xyplot and all of the data for the plot were stored in the state data frame. The plot itself contains four panels—one for each region—and within each panel is a scatterplot of life expectancy and income. The notion of *panels* comes up a lot with lattice plots because you typically have many panels in a lattice plot (each panel typically represents a *condition*, like "region").

One downside with the lattice system is that it can sometimes be very awkward to specify an entire plot in a single function call (you end up with functions with many many arguments). Also, annotation in panels in plots is not especially intuitive and can be difficult to explain. In particular, the use of custom panel functions and subscripts can be difficult to wield and requires intense preparation. Finally, once a plot is created, you cannot "add" to the plot (but of course you can just make it again with modifications).

8.3 The ggplot2 System

The ggplot2 plottings system attempts to split the difference between base and lattice in a number of ways. Taking cues from lattice, the ggplot2 system automatically deals with spacings, text, titles but also allows you to annotate by "adding" to a plot.

The ggplot2 system is implemented in the `ggplot2` package, which is available from CRAN (it does not come with R). You can install it from CRAN via

```
> install.packages("ggplot2")
```

and then load it into R via the `library` function.

```
> library(ggplot2)
Loading required package: methods
```

Superficially, the ggplot2 functions are similar to lattice, but the system is generally easier and more intuitive to use. The defaults used in ggplot2 make many choices for you, but you can still customize plots to your heart's desire.

A typical plot with the `ggplot` package looks as follows.

```
> data(mpg)
> qplot(displ, hwy, data = mpg)
```

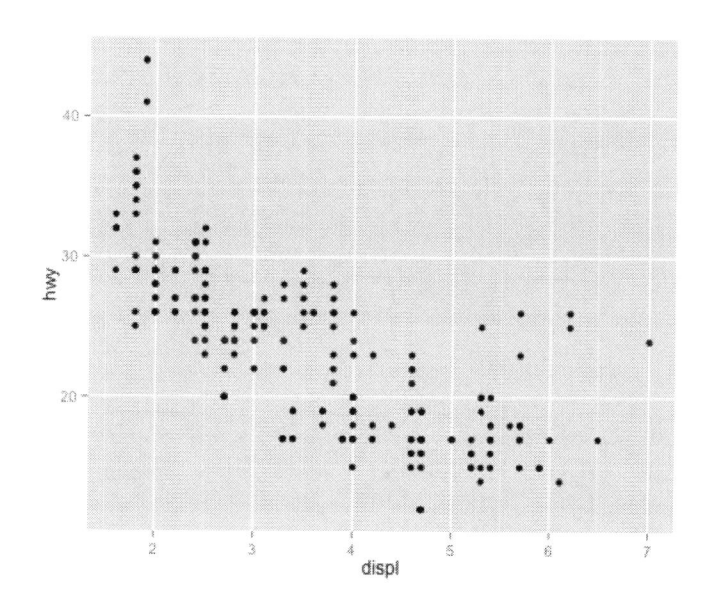

ggplot2 plot

The `qplot` function in `ggplot2` is what you use to "quickly get some data on the screen". There are additional functions in `ggplot2` that allow you to make arbitrarily sophisticated plots.

8.4 References

Paul Murrell (2011). *R Graphics*, CRC Press.

Hadley Wickham (2009). *ggplot2*, Springer.

Deepayan Sarkar (2008). *Lattice: Multivariate Data Visualization with R*, Springer.

9. Graphics Devices

Watch a video of this chapter: Part 1[1] Part 2[2]

A graphics device is something where you can make a plot appear. Examples include

- A window on your computer (screen device)
- A PDF file (file device)
- A PNG or JPEG file (file device)
- A scalable vector graphics (SVG) file (file device)

When you make a plot in R, it has to be "sent" to a specific graphics device. The most common place for a plot to be "sent" is the *screen device*. On a Mac the screen device is launched with the `quartz()` function, on Windows the screen device is launched with `windows()` function, and on Unix/Linux the screen device is launched with `x11()` function.

When making a plot, you need to consider how the plot will be used to determine what device the plot should be sent to. The list of devices supported by your installation of R is found in `?Devices`. There are also graphics devices that have been created by users and these are aviailable through packages on CRAN.

For quick visualizations and exploratory analysis, usually you want to use the screen device. Functions like `plot` in base, `xyplot` in lattice, or `qplot` in ggplot2 will default to sending a plot to the screen device. On a given platform, such as Mac, Windows, or Unix/Linux, there is only one screen device.

For plots that may be printed out or be incorporated into a document, such as papers, reports, or slide presentations, usually a *file device* is more appropriate, there are many different file devices to choose from and exactly which one to use in a given situation is something we discuss later.

Note that typically, not all graphics devices are available on all platforms. For example, you cannot launch the `windows()` device on a Mac or the `quartz()` device on Windows. The code for mst of the key graphics devices is implemented in the `grDevices` package, which comes with a standard R installation and is typically loaded by default.

---

[1] https://youtu.be/ftc6_hqRYuY
[2] https://youtu.be/ci6ogllxVxg

9.1 The Process of Making a Plot

When making a plot one must first make a few considerations (not necessarily in this order):

- Where will the plot be made? On the screen? In a file?
- How will the plot be used?
    - Is the plot for viewing temporarily on the screen?
    - Will it be presented in a web browser?
    - Will it eventually end up in a paper that might be printed?
    - Are you using it in a presentation?
- Is there a large amount of data going into the plot? Or is it just a few points?
- Do you need to be able to dynamically resize the graphic?
- What graphics system will you use: base, lattice, or ggplot2? These generally cannot be mixed.

Base graphics are usually constructed piecemeal, with each aspect of the plot handled separately through a series of function calls; this is sometimes conceptually simpler and allows plotting to mirror the thought process. Lattice graphics are usually created in a single function call, so all of the graphics parameters have to specified at once; specifying everything at once allows R to automatically calculate the necessary spacings and font sizes. The ggplot2 system combines concepts from both base and lattice graphics but uses an independent implementation.

9.2 How Does a Plot Get Created?

There are two basic approaches to plotting. The first is most common. This involves

1. Call a *plotting* function like plot, xyplot, or qplot
2. The plot appears on the screen device
3. Annotate the plot if necessary
4. Enjoy

Here's an example of this process in making a plot with the plot() function.

```
> ## Make plot appear on screen device
> with(faithful, plot(eruptions, waiting))
> 
> ## Annotate with a title
> title(main = "Old Faithful Geyser data")
```

The second basic approach to plotting is most commonly used for file devices:

1. Explicitly launch a graphics device
2. Call a plotting function to make a plot (Note: if you are using a file device, no plot will appear on the screen)
3. Annotate the plot if necessary
4. Explicitly close graphics device with `dev.off()` (this is very important!)

Here's an example of how to make a plot using this second approach. In this case we make a plot that gets saved in a PDF file.

```
> ## Open PDF device; create 'myplot.pdf' in my working directory
> pdf(file = "myplot.pdf")
> 
> ## Create plot and send to a file (no plot appears on screen)
> with(faithful, plot(eruptions, waiting))
> 
> ## Annotate plot; still nothing on screen
> title(main = "Old Faithful Geyser data")
> 
> ## Close the PDF file device
> dev.off()
> 
> ## Now you can view the file 'myplot.pdf' on your computer
```

9.3 Graphics File Devices

There are two basic types of file devices to consider: *vector* and *bitmap* devices. Some of the key vector formats are

- `pdf`: useful for line-type graphics, resizes well, usually portable, not efficient if a plot has many objects/points
- `svg`: XML-based scalable vector graphics; supports animation and interactivity, potentially useful for web-based plots
- `win.metafile`: Windows metafile format (only on Windows)
- `postscript`: older format, also resizes well, usually portable, can be used to create encapsulated postscript files; Windows systems often donâ€™t have a postscript viewer

Some examples of bitmap formats are

- `png`: bitmapped format, good for line drawings or images with solid colors, uses lossless compression (like the old GIF format), most web browsers can read this format natively, good for plotting many many many points, does not resize well
- `jpeg`: good for photographs or natural scenes, uses lossy compression, good for plotting many many many points, does not resize well, can be read by almost any computer and any web browser, not great for line drawings
- `tiff`: Creates bitmap files in the TIFF format; supports lossless compression
- `bmp`: a native Windows bitmapped format

9.4 Multiple Open Graphics Devices

It is possible to open multiple graphics devices (screen, file, or both), for example when viewing multiple plots at once. Plotting can only occur on one graphics device at a time, though.

The **currently active** graphics device can be found by calling `dev.cur()` Every open graphics device is assigned an integer starting with 2 (there is no graphics device 1). You can change the active graphics device with `dev.set(<integer>)` where `<integer>` is the number associated with the graphics device you want to switch to

9.5 Copying Plots

Copying a plot to another device can be useful because some plots require a lot of code and it can be a pain to type all that in again for a different device. Of course, it is always good to save the code that creates your plots, especially for any plots that you might publish or give to other people.

The `dev.copy()` can be used to copy a plot from one device to another. For example you might copy a plot from the screen device to a file device. The `dev.copy2pdf()` function is used specifically to copy a plot from the current device (usually the screen device) to a PDF file.

Note that copying a plot is not an exact operation, so the result may not be identical to the original. In particular, when copying from the screen device to a file, depending on the size of the file device, many annotations such as axis labels may not look right.

```
> library(datasets)
>
> ## Create plot on screen device
> with(faithful, plot(eruptions, waiting))
>
> ## Add a main title
> title(main = "Old Faithful Geyser data")
>
> ## Copy my plot to a PNG file
> dev.copy(png, file = "geyserplot.png")
>
> ## Don't forget to close the PNG device!
> dev.off()
```

9.6 Summary

Plots must be created on a graphics device. The default graphics device is almost always the screen device, which is most useful for exploratory analysis. File devices are useful for creating plots that can be included in other documents or sent to other people

For file devices, there are vector and bitmap formats

- Vector formats are good for line drawings and plots with solid colors using a modest number of points
- Bitmap formats are good for plots with a large number of points, natural scenes or web-based plots

10. The Base Plotting System

Watch a video of this chapter: Part 1[1] Part 2[2]

The core plotting and graphics engine in R is encapsulated in the following packages:

- graphics: contains plotting functions for the "base" graphing systems, including plot, hist, boxplot and many others.
- grDevices: contains all the code implementing the various graphics devices, including X11, PDF, PostScript, PNG, etc.

The grDevices package was discussed in the previous chapter and it contains the functionality for sending plots to various output devices. The graphics package contains the code for actually constructing and annotating plots.

In this chapter, we focus on using the **base plotting system** to create graphics on the **screen device**.

10.1 Base Graphics

Base graphics are used most commonly and are a very powerful system for creating data graphics. There are two *phases* to creating a base plot:

1. Initializing a new plot
2. Annotating (adding to) an existing plot

Calling plot(x, y) or hist(x) will launch a graphics device (if one is not already open) and draw a new plot on the device. If the arguments to plot are not of some special class, then the *default* method for plot is called; this function has *many* arguments, letting you set the title, x axis label, y axis label, etc.

The base graphics system has *many* global parameters that can set and tweaked. These parameters are documented in ?par and are used to control the global behavior of plots, such as the margins, axis orientation, and other details. It wouldnâ€™t hurt to try to memorize at least part of this help page!

---

[1]https://youtu.be/AAXh0egb5WM
[2]https://youtu.be/bhyb1gCeAVk

10.2 Simple Base Graphics

Histogram

Here is an example of a simple histogram made using the `hist()` function in the `graphics` package. If you run this code and your graphics window is not already open, it should open once you call the `hist()` function.

```
> library(datasets)
>
> ## Draw a new plot on the screen device
> hist(airquality$Ozone)
```

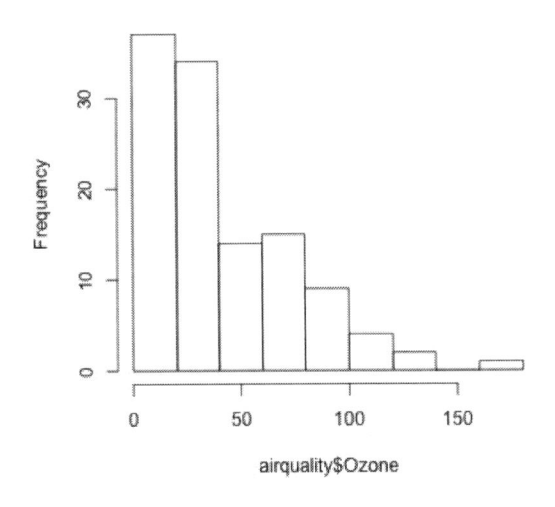

Ozone levels in New York City

Boxplot

Boxplots can be made in R using the `boxplot()` function, which takes as its first argument a *formula*. The formula has form of y-axis ~ x-axis. Anytime you see a ~ in R, it's a formula. Here, we are plotting ozone levels in New York *by month*, and the right hand side of the ~ indicate the month variable. However, we first have to transform the month variable in to a factor before we can pass it to `boxplot()`, or else `boxplot()` will treat the month variable as continuous.

```
> airquality <- transform(airquality, Month = factor(Month))
> boxplot(Ozone ~ Month, airquality, xlab = "Month", ylab = "Ozone (ppb)")
```

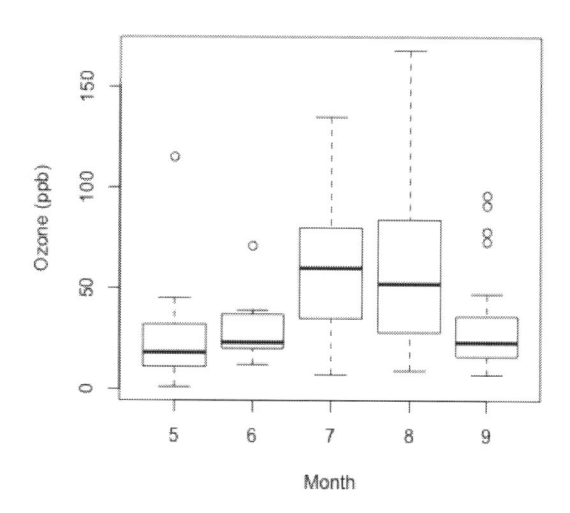

Ozone levels by month in New York City

Each boxplot shows the median, 25th and 75th percentiles of the data (the "box"), as well as +/- 1.5 times the interquartile range (IQR) of the data (the "whiskers"). Any data points beyond 1.5 times the IQR of the data are indicated separately with circles.

In this case the monthly boxplots show some interesting features. First, the levels of ozone tend to be highest in July and August. Second, the *variability* of ozone is also highest in July and August. This phenomenon is common with environmental data where the mean and the variance are often related to each other.

Scatterplot

Here is a simple scatterplot made with the `plot()` function.

```
> with(airquality, plot(Wind, Ozone))
```

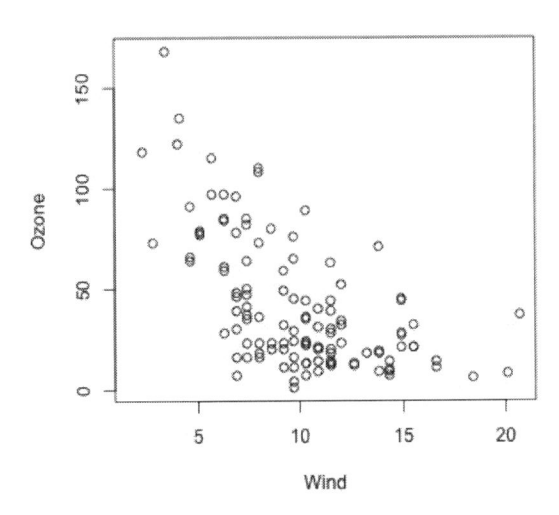

Scatterplot of wind and ozone in New York City

Generally, the `plot()` function takes two vectors of numbers: one for the x-axis coordinates and one for the y-axis coordinates. However, `plot()` is what's called a *generic function* in R, which means its behavior can change depending on what kinds of data are passed to the function. We won't go into detail about that behavior for now. The remainder of this chapter will focus on the *default* behavior of the `plot()` function.

One thing to note here is that although we did not provide labels for the x- and the y-axis, labels were automatically created from the *names* of the variables (i.e. "Wind" and "Ozone"). This can be useful when you are making plots quickly, but it demands that you have useful descriptive names for the your variables and R objects.

10.3 Some Important Base Graphics Parameters

Many base plotting functions share a set of global parameters. Here are a few key ones:

- `pch`: the plotting symbol (default is open circle)
- `lty`: the line type (default is solid line), can be dashed, dotted, etc.
- `lwd`: the line width, specified as an integer multiple
- `col`: the plotting color, specified as a number, string, or hex code; the `colors()` function gives you a vector of colors by name
- `xlab`: character string for the x-axis label
- `ylab`: character string for the y-axis label

The `par()` function is used to specify the *global* graphics parameters that affect all plots in an R session. These parameters can be overridden when they are specified as arguments to specific plotting functions.

- `las`: the orientation of the axis labels on the plot
- `bg`: the background color
- `mar`: the margin size
- `oma`: the outer margin size (default is 0 for all sides)
- `mfrow`: number of plots per row, column (plots are filled row-wise)
- `mfcol`: number of plots per row, column (plots are filled column-wise)

You can see the default values for global graphics parameters by calling the `par()` function and passing the name of the parameter in quotes.

```
> par("lty")
[1] "solid"
> par("col")
[1] "black"
> par("pch")
[1] 1
```

Here are some more default values for global graphics parameters.

```
> par("bg")
[1] "white"
> par("mar")
[1] 5.1 4.1 4.1 2.1
> par("mfrow")
[1] 1 1
```

For the most part, you usually don't have to modify these when making quick plots. However, you might need to tweak them for finalizing finished plots.

10.4 Base Plotting Functions

The most basic base plotting function is `plot()`. The `plot()` function makes a scatterplot, or other type of plot depending on the class of the object being plotted. Calling `plot()` will draw a plot on the screen device (and open the screen device if not already open). After that, annotation functions can be called to add to the already-made plot.

Some key annotation functions are

- `lines`: add lines to a plot, given a vector of x values and a corresponding vector of y values (or a 2-column matrix); this function just connects the dots
- `points`: add points to a plot
- `text`: add text labels to a plot using specified x, y coordinates

- `title`: add annotations to x, y axis labels, title, subtitle, outer margin
- `mtext`: add arbitrary text to the margins (inner or outer) of the plot
- `axis`: adding axis ticks/labels

Here's an example of creating a base plot and the adding some annotation. First we make the plot with the `plot()` function and then add a title to the top of the plot with the `title()` function.

```
> library(datasets)
>
> ## Make the initial plot
> with(airquality, plot(Wind, Ozone))
>
> ## Add a title
> title(main = "Ozone and Wind in New York City")
```

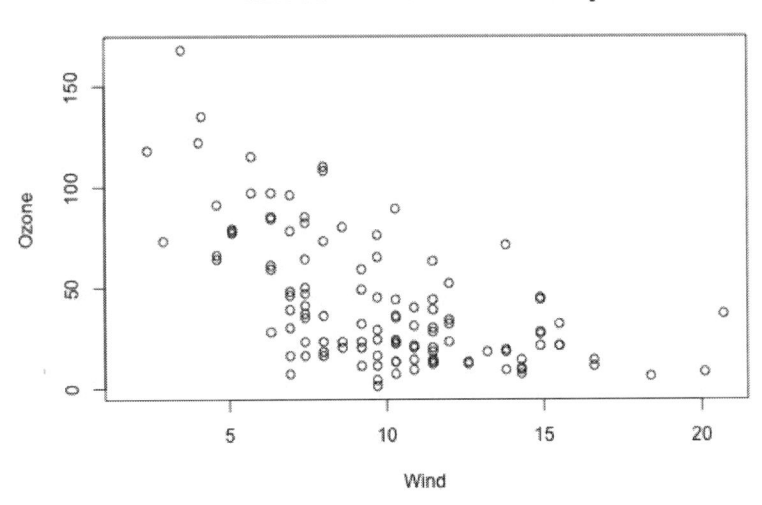

Base plot with annotation

Here, I start with the same plot as above (although I add the title right away using the `main` argument to `plot()`) and then annotate it by coloring blue the data points corresponding to the month of May.

```
> with(airquality, plot(Wind, Ozone, main = "Ozone and Wind in New York City"))
> with(subset(airquality, Month == 5), points(Wind, Ozone, col = "blue"))
```

Ozone and Wind in New York City

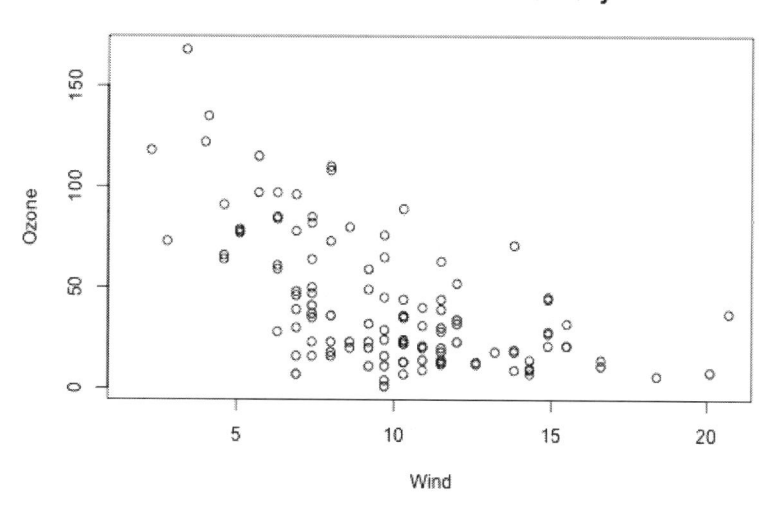

Base plot with annotation

The following plot colors the data points for the month of May blue and colors all of the other points red.

Notice that when constructing the initial plot, we use the option `type = "n"` in the call to `plot()`. This is a common paradigm as `plot()` will draw everything in the plot except for the data points inside the plot window. Then you can use annotation functions like `points()` to add data points. So here, we create the plot without drawing the data points, then add the blue points and then add the red points. Finally, we add a legend with the `legend()` function explaining the meaning of the different colors in the plot.

```
> with(airquality, plot(Wind, Ozone, main = "Ozone and Wind in New York City", type = "n"))
> with(subset(airquality, Month == 5), points(Wind, Ozone, col = "blue"))
> with(subset(airquality, Month != 5), points(Wind, Ozone, col = "red"))
> legend("topright", pch = 1, col = c("blue", "red"), legend = c("May", "Other Months"))
```

Ozone and Wind in New York City

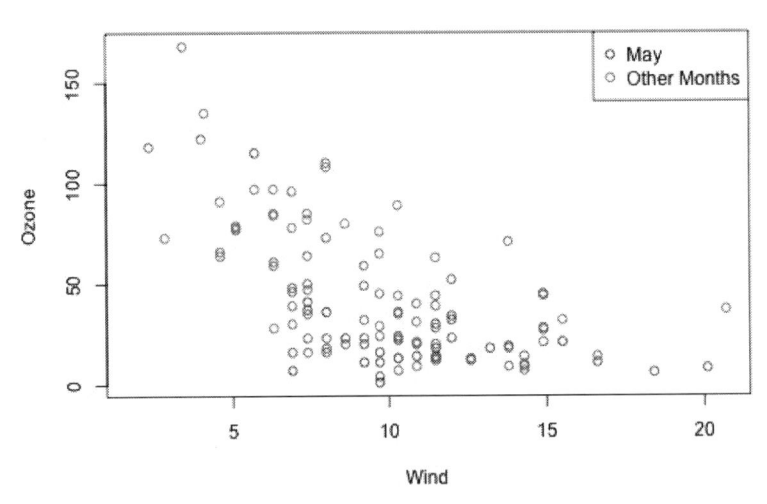

Base plot with multiple annotations

10.5 Base Plot with Regression Line

It's fairly common to make a scatterplot and then want to draw a simple linear regression line through the data. This can be done with the `abline()` function.

Below, we first make the plot (as above). Then we fit a simple linear regression model using the `lm()` function. Here, we try to model Ozone as a function of Wind. Then we take the output of `lm()` and pass it to the `abline()` function which automatically takes the information from the `model` object and calculates the corresponding regression line.

Note that in the call to `plot()` below, we set `pch = 20` to change the plotting symbol to a filled circle.

```
> with(airquality, plot(Wind, Ozone, main = "Ozone and Wind in New York City", pch = 20))
> 
> ## Fit a simple linear regression model
> model <- lm(Ozone ~ Wind, airquality)
> 
> ## Draw regression line on plot
> abline(model, lwd = 2)
```

Ozone and Wind in New York City

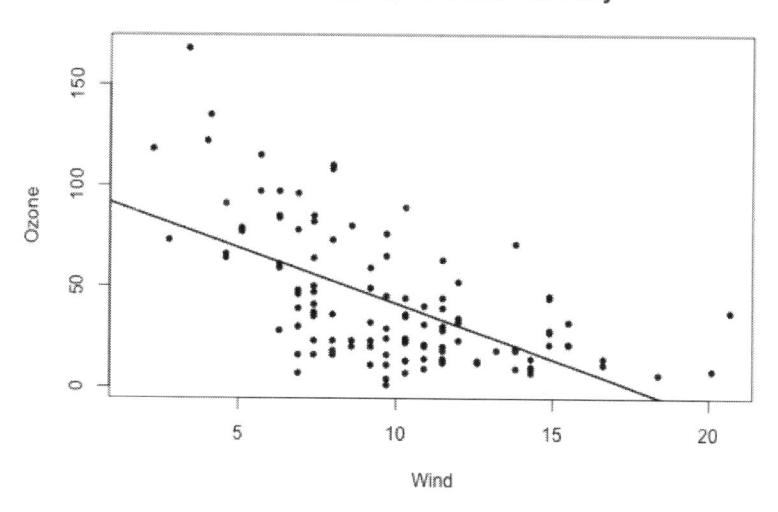

(scatterplot of Ozone vs Wind with linear regression line)

Scatterplot with linear regresion line

10.6 Multiple Base Plots

Making multiple plots side by side is a useful way to visualize many relationships between variables with static 2-D plots. Often the repetition of data across a single plot window can be a useful way to identify patterns in the data. In order to do this, the `mfrow` and `mfcol` parameters set by the `par()` function are critical.

Both the `mfrow` and `mfcol` parameters take two numbers: the number of rows of plots followed by the number of columns. The multiple plots will be arranged in a matrix-like pattern. The only difference between the two parameters is that if `mfrow` is set, then the plots will be drawn row-wise; if `mfcol` is set, the plots will be drawn column-wise.

In the example below, we make two plots: one of Ozone and Wind and another with Ozone and Solar.R. We set `par(mfrow = c(1, 2))`, which indicates that we one row of plots and two columns of plots.

```
> par(mfrow = c(1, 2))
> with(airquality, {
+       plot(Wind, Ozone, main = "Ozone and Wind")
+       plot(Solar.R, Ozone, main = "Ozone and Solar Radiation")
+ })
```

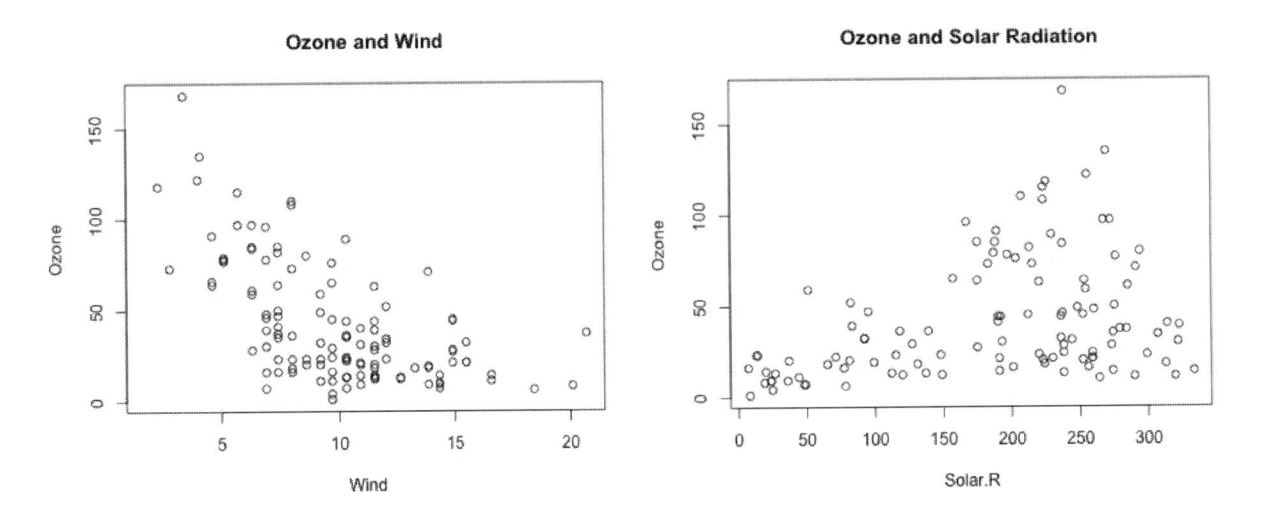

Panel plot with two plots

The example below creates three plots in a row by setting par(mfrow = c(1, 3)). Here we also change the plot margins with the mar parameter. The various margin parameters, like mar, are specified by setting a value for each *side* of the plot. Side 1 is the bottom of the plot, side 2 is the left hand side, side 3 is the top, and side 4 is the right hand side. In the example below we also modify the outer margin via the oma parameter to create a little more space for the plots and to place them closer together.

```
> par(mfrow = c(1, 3), mar = c(4, 4, 2, 1), oma = c(0, 0, 2, 0))
> with(airquality, {
+         plot(Wind, Ozone, main = "Ozone and Wind")
+         plot(Solar.R, Ozone, main = "Ozone and Solar Radiation")
+         plot(Temp, Ozone, main = "Ozone and Temperature")
+         mtext("Ozone and Weather in New York City", outer = TRUE)
+ })
```

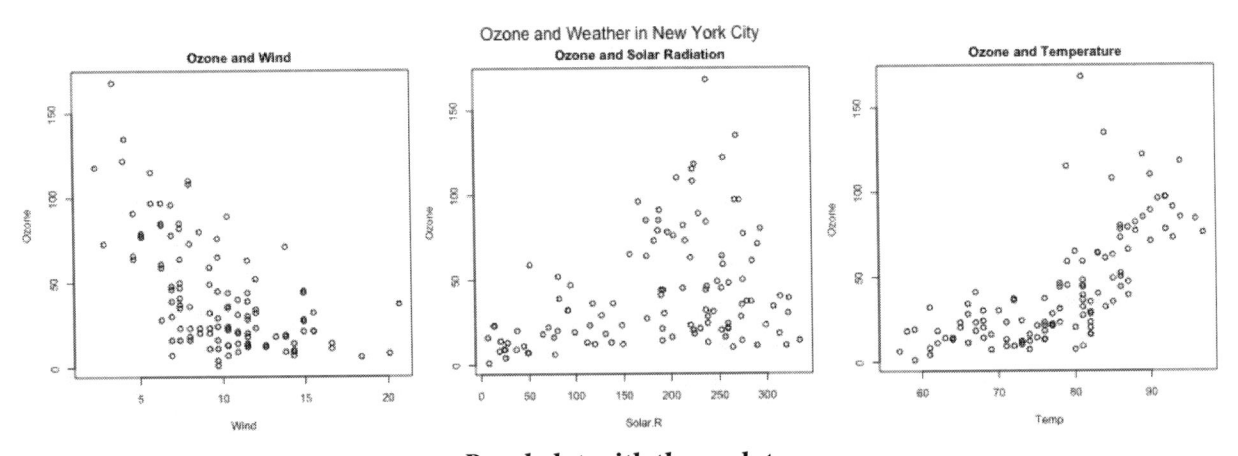

Panel plot with three plots

In the above example, the `mtext()` function was used to create an overall title for the panel of plots. Hence, each individual plot has a title, while the overall set of plots also has a summary title. The `mtext()` function is important for adding text annotations that aren't specific to a single plot.

10.7 Summary

- Plots in the base plotting system are created by calling successive R functions to "build up" a plot
- Plotting occurs in two stages:

  ```
  - Creation of a plot
  - Annotation of a plot (adding lines, points, text, legends)
  ```

- The base plotting system is very flexible and offers a high degree of control over plotting

11. Plotting and Color in R

Watch a video of this chapter: Part 1[1] Part 2[2] Part 3[3] Part 4[4]

The default color schemes for most plots in R are horrendous. I am as guilty as anyone of using these horrendous color schemes but I am actively trying to work at improving my habits. R has much better ways for handling the specification of colors in plots and graphs and you should make use of them when possible. But, in order to do that, it's important to know a little about how colors work in R.

11.1 Colors 1, 2, and 3

Quite often, with plots made in R, you'll see something like the following Christmas-themed plot.

```
> set.seed(19)
> x <- rnorm(30)
> y <- rnorm(30)
> plot(x, y, col = rep(1:3, each = 10), pch = 19)
> legend("bottomright", legend = paste("Group", 1:3), col = 1:3, pch = 19, bty = "n")
```

[1] https://youtu.be/7QaR91TCc3k
[2] https://youtu.be/3Q1ormd5oMA
[3] https://youtu.be/4JJfGpVHTq4
[4] https://youtu.be/9-cn0auNV58

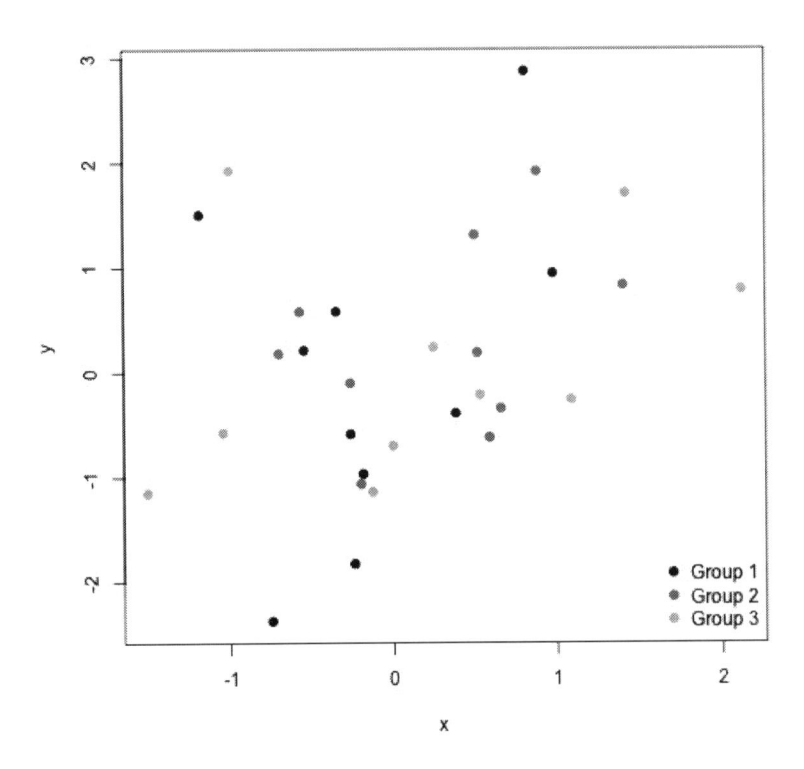

Default colors in R

The reason is simple. In R, the color black is denoted by col = 1 in most plotting functions, red is denoted by col = 2, and green is denoted by col = 3. So if you're plotting multiple groups of things, it's natural to plot them using colors 1, 2, and 3.

Here's another set of common color schemes used in R, this time via the image() function.

```
> par(mfrow = c(1, 2))
> image(volcano, col = heat.colors(10), main = "heat.colors()")
> image(volcano, col = topo.colors(10), main = "topo.colors()")
```

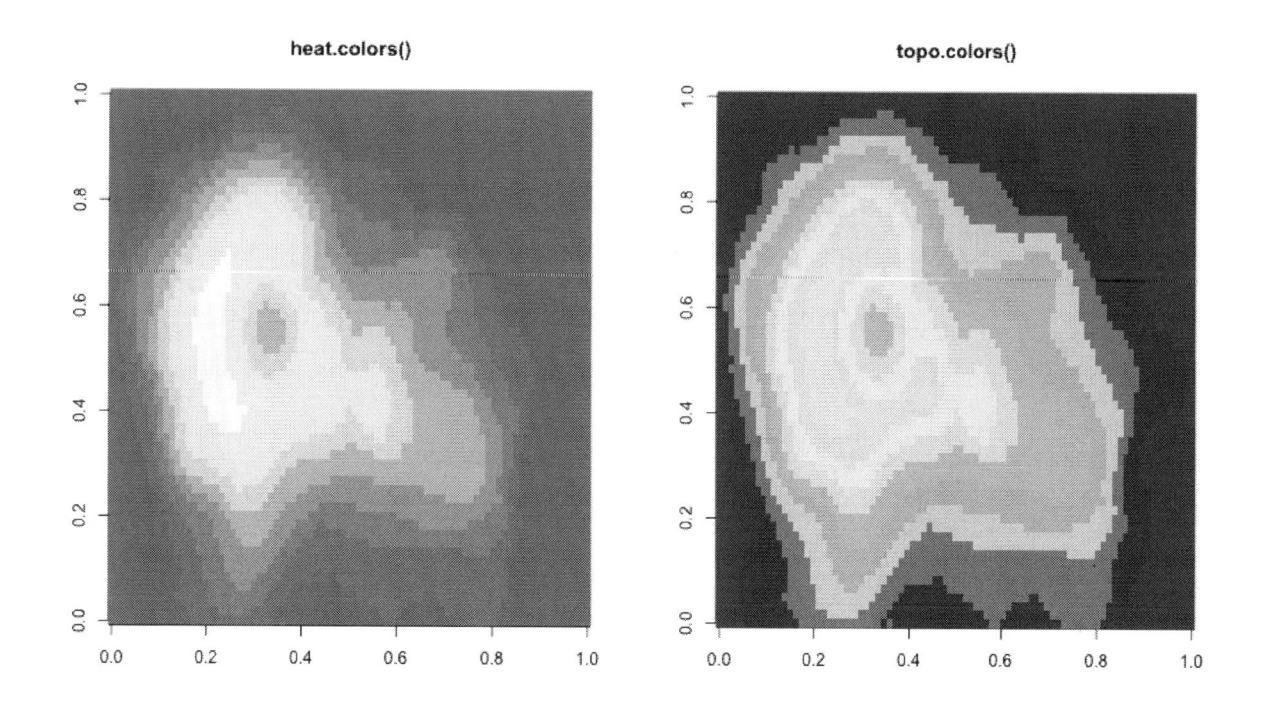

Image plots in R

11.2 Connecting colors with data

Typically we add color to a plot, not to improve its artistic value, but to add another dimension to the visualization (i.e. to "escape flatland"[5]). Therefore, it makes sense that *the range and palette of colors you use will depend on the kind of data you are plotting*. While it may be common to just choose colors at random, choosing the colors for your plot should require careful consideration. Because careful choices of plotting color can have an impact on how people interpret your data and draw conclusions from them.

11.3 Color Utilities in R

R has a number of utilities for dealing with colors and color palettes in your plots. For starters, the grDevices package has two functions

- colorRamp: Take a palette of colors and return a function that takes valeus between 0 and 1, indicating the extremes of the color palette (e.g. see the gray() function)

---

[5] http://www.edwardtufte.com/tufte/books_vdqi

- `colorRampPalette`: Take a palette of colors and return a function that takes integer arguments and returns a vector of colors interpolating the palette (like `heat.colors()` or `topo.colors()`)

Both of these functions take palettes of colors and help to interpolate between the colors on the palette. They differ only in the type of object that they return.

Finally, the function `colors()` lists the names of colors you can use in any plotting function. Typically, you would specify the color in a (base) plotting function via the `col` argument.

11.4 `colorRamp()`

For both `colorRamp()` and `colorRampPalette()`, imagine you're a painter and you have your palette in your hand. On your palette are a set of colors, say red and blue. Now, between red and blue you can a imagine an entire spectrum of colors that can be created by mixing together different amounts of read and blue. Both `colorRamp()` and `colorRampPalette()` handle that "mixing" process for you.

Let's start with a simple palette of "red" and "blue" colors and pass them to `colorRamp()`.

```
> pal <- colorRamp(c("red", "blue"))
> pal(0)
     [,1] [,2] [,3]
[1,]  255    0    0
```

Notice that `pal` is in fact a function that was returned by `colorRamp()`. When we call `pal(0)` we get a 1 by 3 matrix. The numbers in the matrix will range from 0 to 255 and indicate the quantities of red, green, and blue (RGB) in columns 1, 2, and 3 respectively. Simple math tells us there are over 16 million colors that can be expressed in this way. Calling `pal(0)` gives us the maximum value (255) on red and 0 on the other colors. So this is just the color red.

We can pass any value between 0 and 1 to the `pal()` function.

```
> ## blue
> pal(1)
     [,1] [,2] [,3]
[1,]    0    0  255
>
> ## purple-ish
> pal(0.5)
      [,1] [,2]  [,3]
[1,] 127.5    0 127.5
```

You can also pass a sequence of numbers to the `pal()` function.

```
> pal(seq(0, 1, len = 10))
             [,1] [,2]        [,3]
 [1,] 255.00000    0    0.00000
 [2,] 226.66667    0   28.33333
 [3,] 198.33333    0   56.66667
 [4,] 170.00000    0   85.00000
 [5,] 141.66667    0  113.33333
 [6,] 113.33333    0  141.66667
 [7,]  85.00000    0  170.00000
 [8,]  56.66667    0  198.33333
 [9,]  28.33333    0  226.66667
[10,]   0.00000    0  255.00000
```

The idea here is that `colorRamp()` gives you a function that allows you to interpolate between the two colors red and blue. You do not have to provide just two colors in your initial color palette; you can start with multiple colors and `colorRamp()` will interpolate between all of them.

11.5 `colorRampPalette()`

The `colorRampPalette()` function in manner similar to `colorRamp(()`, however the function that it returns gives you a fixed number of colors that interpolate the palette.

```
> pal <- colorRampPalette(c("red", "yellow"))
```

Again we have a function `pal()` that was returned by `colorRampPalette()`, this time interpolating a palette containing the colors red and yellow. But now, the `pal()` function takes an integer argument specifing the number of interpolated colors to return.

```
> ## Just return red and yellow
> pal(2)
[1] "#FF0000" "#FFFF00"
```

Note that the colors are represented as hexadecimal strings. After the # symbol, the first two characters indicate the red amount, the second two the green amount, and the last two the blue amount. Because each position can have 16 possible values (0-9 and A-F), the two positions together allow for 256 possibilities per color. In this example above, since we only asked for two colors, it gave us red and yellow, the two extremes of the palette.

We can ask for more colors though.

```
> ## Return 10 colors in between red and yellow
> pal(10)
 [1] "#FF0000" "#FF1C00" "#FF3800" "#FF5500" "#FF7100" "#FF8D00" "#FFAA00"
 [8] "#FFC600" "#FFE200" "#FFFF00"
```

You'll see that the first color is still red ("FF" in the red position) and the last color is still yellow ("FF" in both the red and green positions). But now there are 8 more colors in between. These values, in hexadecimal format, can also be specified to base plotting functions via the `col` argument.

Note that the `rgb()` function can be used to produce any color via red, green, blue proportions and return a hexadecimal representation.

```
> rgb(0, 0, 234, maxColorValue = 255)
[1] "#0000EA"
```

11.6 RColorBrewer Package

Part of the art of creating good color schemes in data graphics is to start with an appropriate color palette that you can then interpolate with a function like `colorRamp()` or `colorRampPalette()`. One package on CRAN that contains interesting and useful color palettes is the `RColorBrewer`[6] package.

The `RColorBrewer` packge offers three types of palettes

- Sequential: for numerical data that are ordered
- Diverging: for numerical data that can be positive or negative, often representing deviations from some norm or baseline
- Qualitative: for qualitative unordered data

---
[6]http://cran.r-project.org/package=RColorBrewer

All of these palettes can be used in conjunction with the `colorRamp()` and `colorRamp-Palette()`.

Here is a display of all the color palettes available from the `RColorBrewer` package.

```
> library(RColorBrewer)
> display.brewer.all()
```

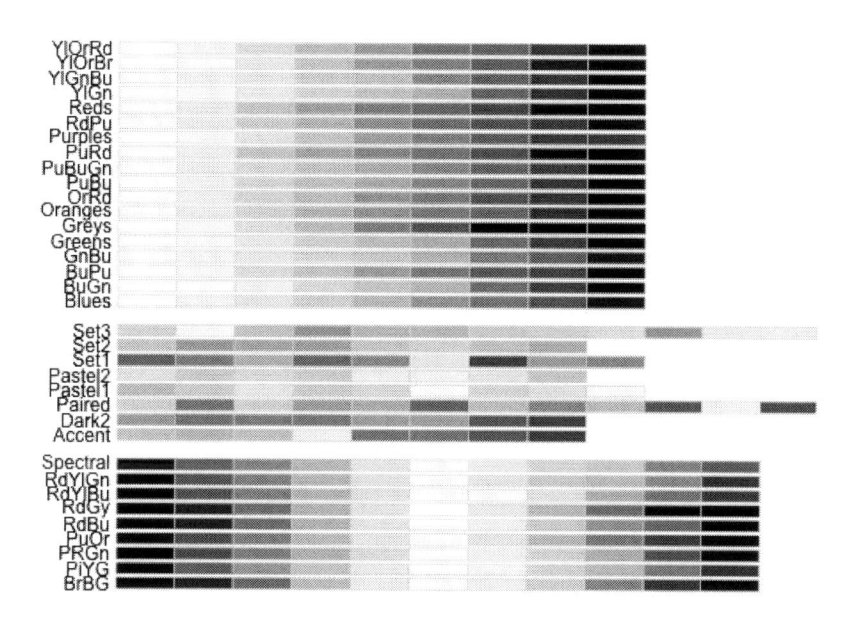

RColorBrewer palettes

11.7 Using the RColorBrewer palettes

The only real function in the `RColorBrewer` package is the `brewer.pal()` function which has two arguments

- `name`: the name of the color palette you want to use
- `n`: the number of colors you want from the palette (integer)

Below we choose to use 3 colors from the "BuGn" palette, which is a sequential palette.

```
> library(RColorBrewer)
> cols <- brewer.pal(3, "BuGn")
> cols
[1] "#E5F5F9" "#99D8C9" "#2CA25F"
```

Those three colors make up my initial palette. Then I can pass them to colorRamp-Palette() to create my interpolating function.

```
> pal <- colorRampPalette(cols)
```

Now I can plot the volcano data using this color ramp. Note that the volcano dataset contains elevations of a volcano, which is continuous, ordered, numerical data, for which a sequential palette is appropriate.

```
> image(volcano, col = pal(20))
```

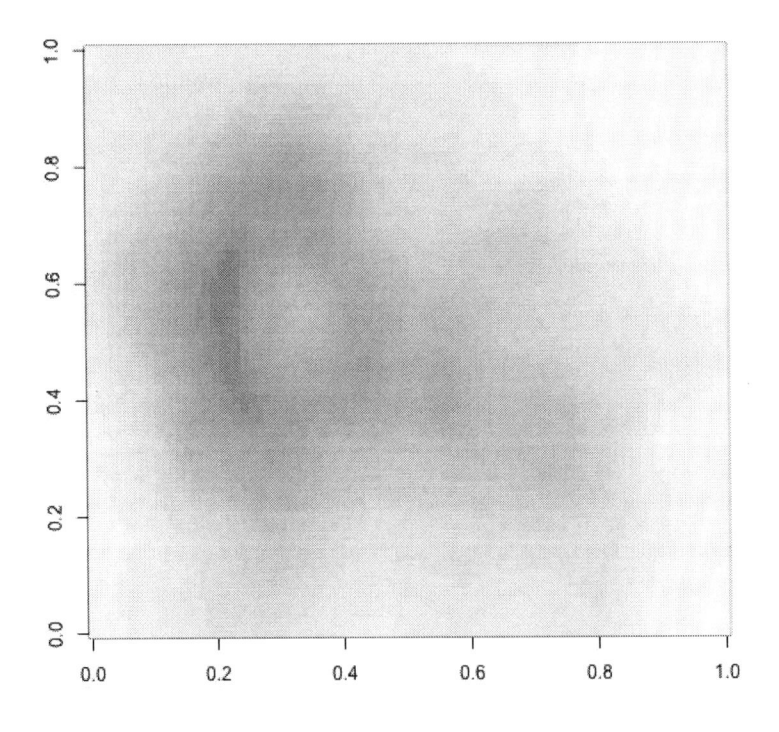

Volcano data with color ramp palette

11.8 The `smoothScatter()` function

A function that takes advantage of the color palettes in `RColorBrewer` is the `smoothScatter()` function, which is very useful for making scatterplots of very large datasets. The `smoothScatter()` function essentially gives you a 2-D histogram of the data using a sequential palette (here "Blues").

```
> set.seed(1)
> x <- rnorm(10000)
> y <- rnorm(10000)
> smoothScatter(x, y)
```

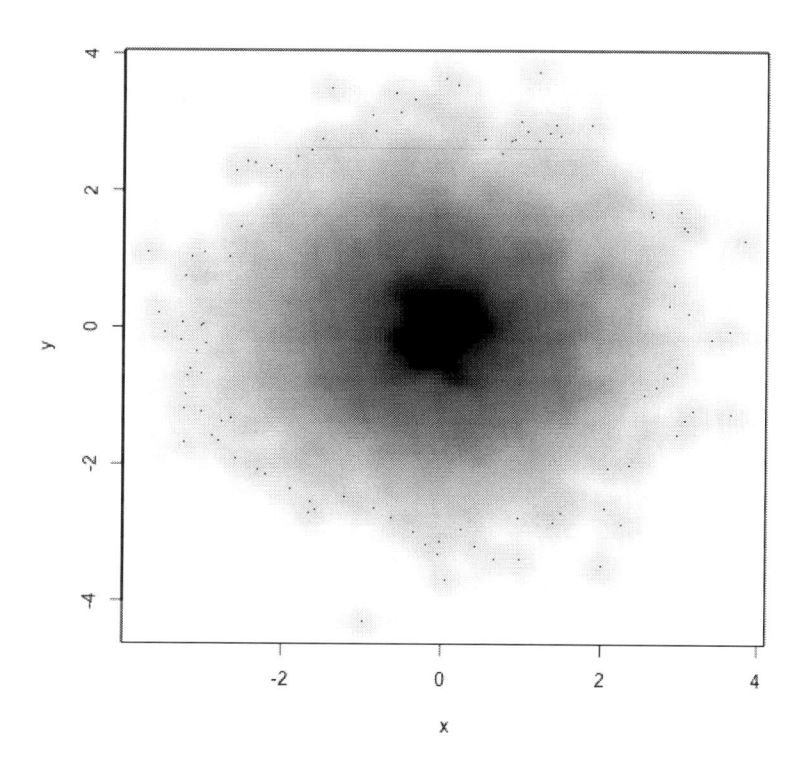

smoothScatter function

11.9 Adding transparency

Color transparency can be added via the `alpha` parameter to `rgb()` to produce color specifications with varying levels of transparency. When transparency is used you'll notice an extra two characters added to the right side of the hexadecimal representation (there will be 8 positions instead of 6).

For example, if I wanted the color red with a high level of transparency, I could specify

```
> rgb(1, 0, 0, 0.1)
[1] "#FF00001A"
```

Transparency can be useful when you have plots with a high density of points or lines. For example, teh scatterplot below has a lot of overplotted points and it's difficult to see what's happening in the middle of the plot region.

```
> set.seed(2)
> x <- rnorm(2000)
> y <- rnorm(2000)
> plot(x, y, pch = 19)
```

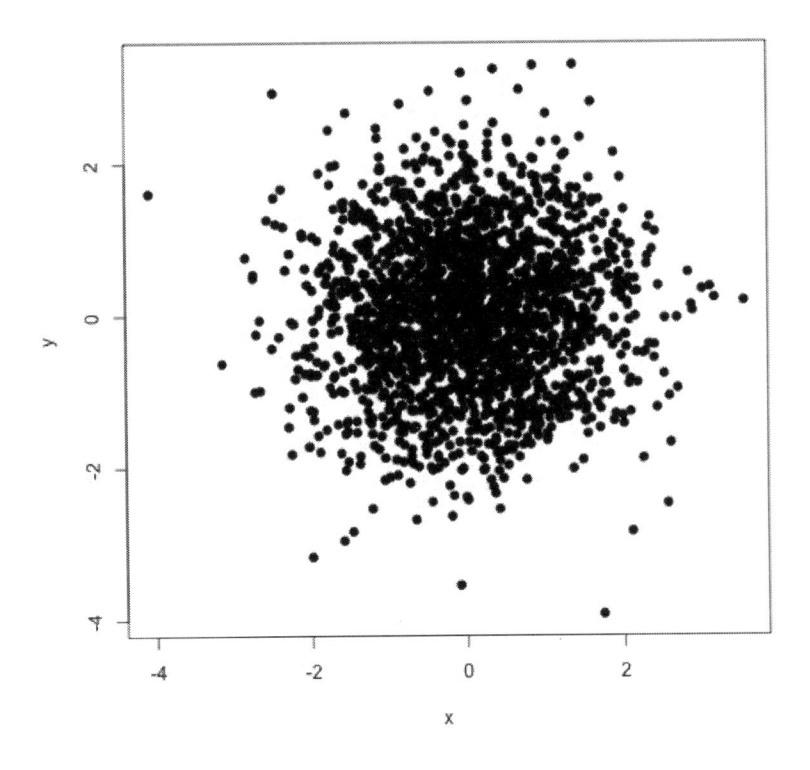

Scatterplot with no transparency

If we add some transparency to the black circles, we can get a better sense of the varying density of the points in the plot.

```
> plot(x, y, pch = 19, col = rgb(0, 0, 0, 0.15))
```

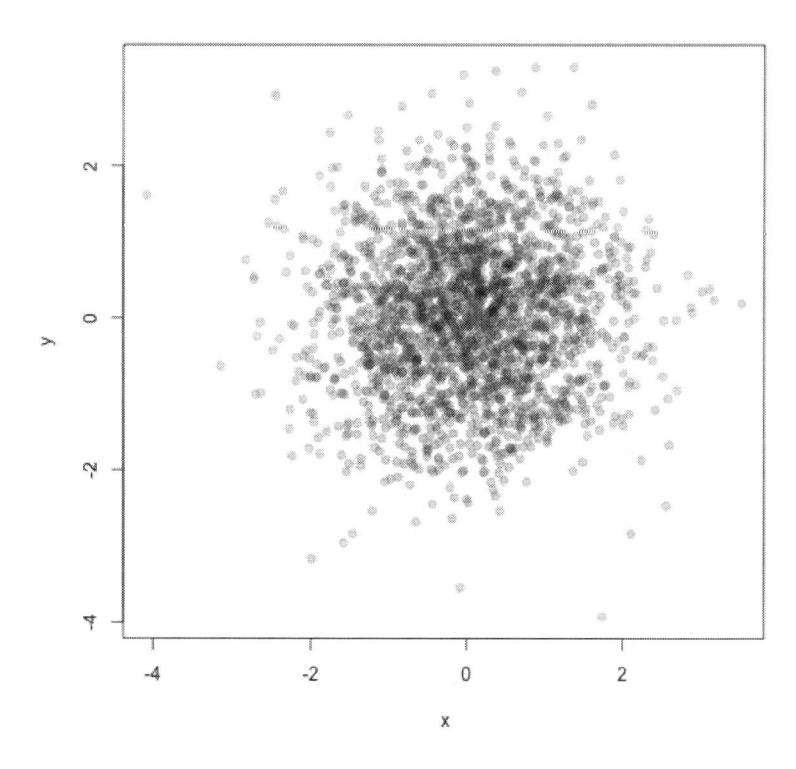

Scatterplot with transparency

Better, right?

11.10 Summary

- Careful use of colors in plots, images, maps, and other data graphics can make it easier for the reader to get what you're trying to say (why make it harder?).
- The RColorBrewer package is an R package that provides color palettes for sequential, categorical, and diverging data
- The colorRamp and colorRampPalette functions can be used in conjunction with color palettes to connect data to colors
- Transparency can sometimes be used to clarify plots with many points

12. Hierarchical Clustering

Watch a video of this chapter: Part 1[1] Part 2[2] Part 3[3]

Clustering or cluster analysis is a bread and butter technique for visualizing high dimensional or multidimensional data. It's very simple to use, the ideas are fairly intuitive, and it can serve as a really quick way to get a sense of what's going on in a very high dimensional data set.

Cluster analysis is a really important and widely used technique. If you just type "cluster analysis" into Google, there are many millions of results that come back.

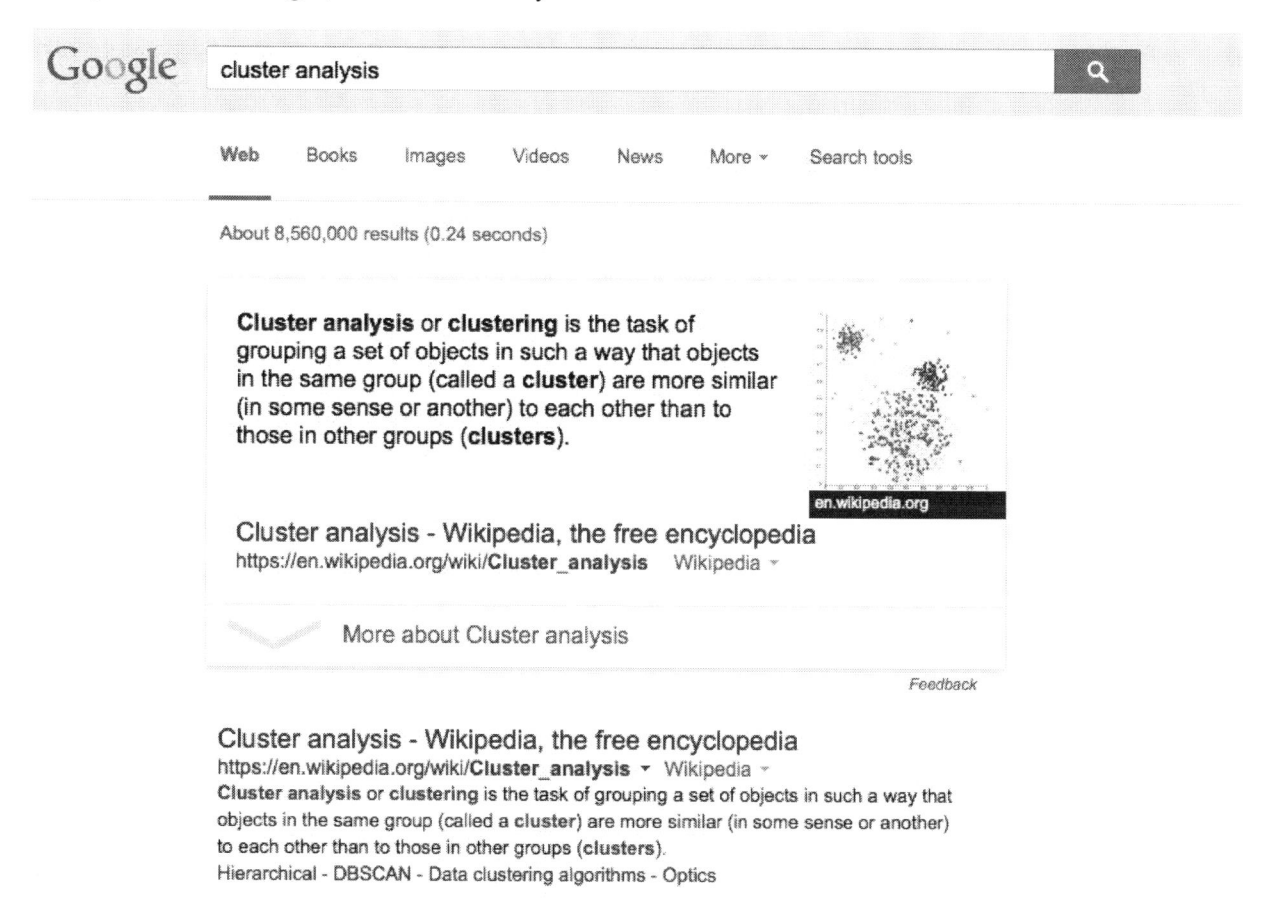

Google search results for "cluster analysis"

---

[1] https://youtu.be/BKoChxguelA
[2] https://youtu.be/ZQYLGS7ptWM
[3] https://youtu.be/lmSMEZAjE-4

And it's a widely applied method in many different areas of science, business, and other applications. So it's useful to know how these techniques work.

The point of clustering is to organize things or observations that are **close** together and separate them into groups. Of course, this simple definition raises some immediate questions:

- How do we define close?
- How do we group things?
- How do we visualize the grouping?
- How do we interpret the grouping?

All clustering techniques confront a basic issue, which is how do we define when things are close together and when things are far apart? Essentially, the wide variety of clustering techniques out there that you can apply to data differ in the ways that they answer these questions.

12.1 Hierarchical clustering

Hierarchical clustering, as is denoted by the name, involves organizing your data into a kind of hierarchy. The common approach is what's called an agglomerative approach. This is a kind of bottom up approach, where you start by thinking of the data as individual data points. Then you start lumping them together into clusters little by little until eventually your entire data set is just one big cluster.

Imagine there's all these little particles floating around (your data points), and you start kind of grouping them together into little balls. And then the balls get grouped up into bigger balls, and the bigger balls get grouped together into one big massive cluster. That's the agglomerative approach to clustering, and that's what we're going to talk about here.

The algorithm is recursive and goes as follows:

1. Find closest two things points in your dataset
2. Put them together and call them a "point"
3. Use your new "dataset" with this new point and repeat

This methodology requires that you have a way to measure the *distance* between two points and that you have an approach to *merging* two points to create a new "point". A benefit of this clustering methodology is that you can produce a tree showing how close things are to each other, which is simply a by product of running the algorithm.

12.2 How do we define close?

Defining closeness is a key aspect of defining a clustering method. Ultimately, the old rule of "garbage in, garbage out" applies. If you don't use a distance metric that makes sense for your data, then you won't get any useful information out of the clustering.

There are a number of commonly used metrics for characterizing distance or its inverse, similarity:

- Euclidean distance: A continuous metric which can be thought of in geometric terms as the "straight-line" distance between two points.
- Correlation similarity: Similar in nature to Euclidean distance
- "Manhattan" distance: on a grid or lattice, how many "city blocks" would you have to travel to get from point A to point B?

The important thing is to always pick a distance or similarity metric that makes sense for your problem.

12.3 Example: Euclidean distance

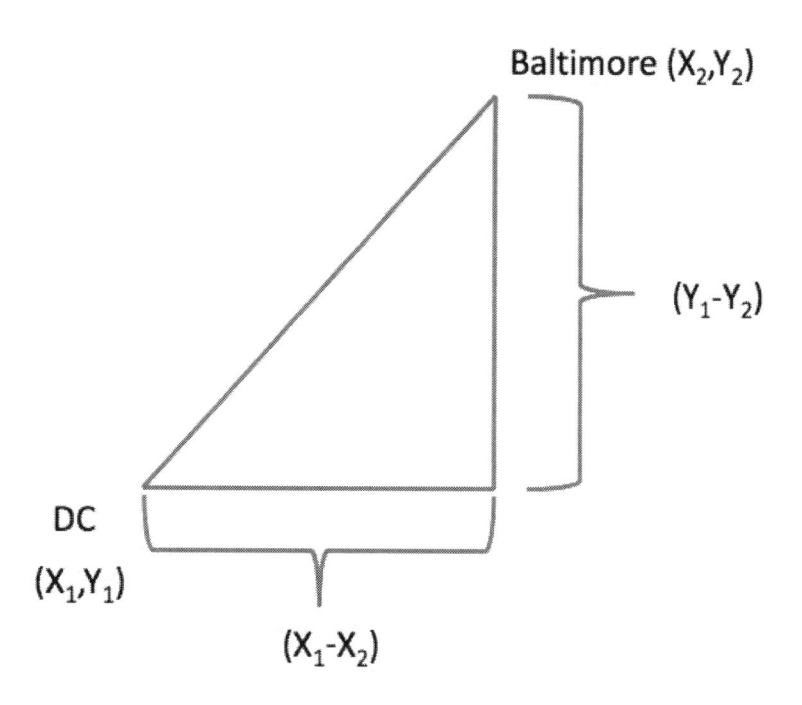

Baltimore (X_2, Y_2)

$(Y_1 - Y_2)$

DC (X_1, Y_1)

$(X_1 - X_2)$

Euclidean distance

source[4]

For example, take two cities, say, Baltimore and Washington D.C., and put them on a map. If you imagine that the center of each city has an X and a Y coordinate (say, longitude and latitude), and you want to map the distance between the centers of the two cities, then you can draw a straight diagonal line between the two cities. The distance can be calculated in the usual way, which is going to be a function of the difference in the x coordinates and the difference in the y coordinates. In the two-dimensional plane, you take the distance in the x coordinates, square it, take the difference in the y coordinates, square that, and then add the two squares together and take the square root of the whole thing. In other words,

$$Distance = [(X_1 - X_2)^2 + (Y_1 - Y_2)^2]^{1/2}$$

That's the classical definition of Euclidian distance. You can imagine if a bird were to fly from Washington, D.C. to Baltimore, it would just fly straight from one city to another. This is possible because a bird isn't impeded by things like roads or mountains, or whatever. Whether that makes sense for you depends on, among other things, whether you're a bird or not. And so you have to think about the properties of this distance metric in the context of your problem.

One nice feature of Euclidean distance is that it's easily generalizable to higher dimensions. If instead of two dimensions you have 100 dimensions, you can easily take the differences between each of the 100 dimensions, square them, sum them together and then take the square root. So the Euclidean distance metric extends very naturally to very high dimensions problems.

In general the formula for Euclidean distance between point

$$A = (A_1, A_2, \ldots, A_n)$$

and

$$B = (B_1, B_2, \ldots, B_n)$$

is

$$Distance = ((A_1 - B_1)^2 + (A_2 - B_2)^2 + \cdots + (A_n - B_n)^2)^{(1/2)}$$

---

[4] http://rafalab.jhsph.edu/688/lec/lecture5-clustering.pdf

12.4 Example: Manhattan distance

The Manhattan distance gets its name from the idea that you can look at points as being on a grid or lattice, not unlike the grid making up the streets of Manhattan in New York City.

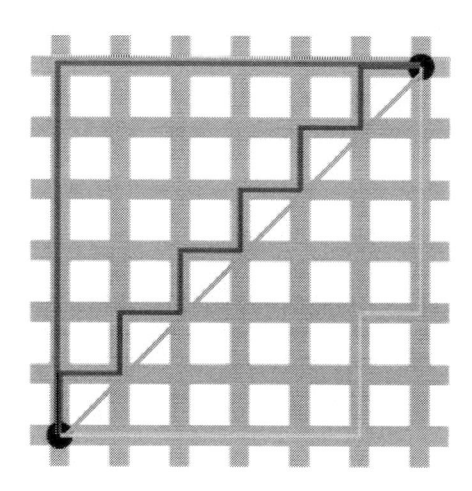

Manhattan distance

In a city, if you want to go from point A to point B, you usually cannot take the direct route there because there will be buildings in the way. So instead, you have to follow the streets, or the grid layout, of the city to navigate around. That's the idea behind Manhattan distance

In the figure above, the red, blue, and yellow lines show various way of getting between the two black circles using the grid layout, while the green line shows the Euclidean distance. The Manhattan distance between the points is simply the sum of the right-left moves plus the sum of all the up-down moves on the grid.

In general:

$$Distance = |A_1 - B_1| + |A_2 - B_2| + \cdots + |A_n - B_n|$$

Check out Wikipedia's page on taxicab geometry[5] for a fun diversion.

12.5 Example: Hierarchical clustering

Here is a simple example demonstrating how hierarchical clustering works. First we'll simulate some data in three separate clusters.

---
[5]http://en.wikipedia.org/wiki/Taxicab_geometry

```
> set.seed(1234)
> x <- rnorm(12, rep(1:3, each = 4), 0.2)
> y <- rnorm(12, rep(c(1, 2, 1), each = 4), 0.2)
> plot(x, y, col = "blue", pch = 19, cex = 2)
> text(x + 0.05, y + 0.05, labels = as.character(1:12))
```

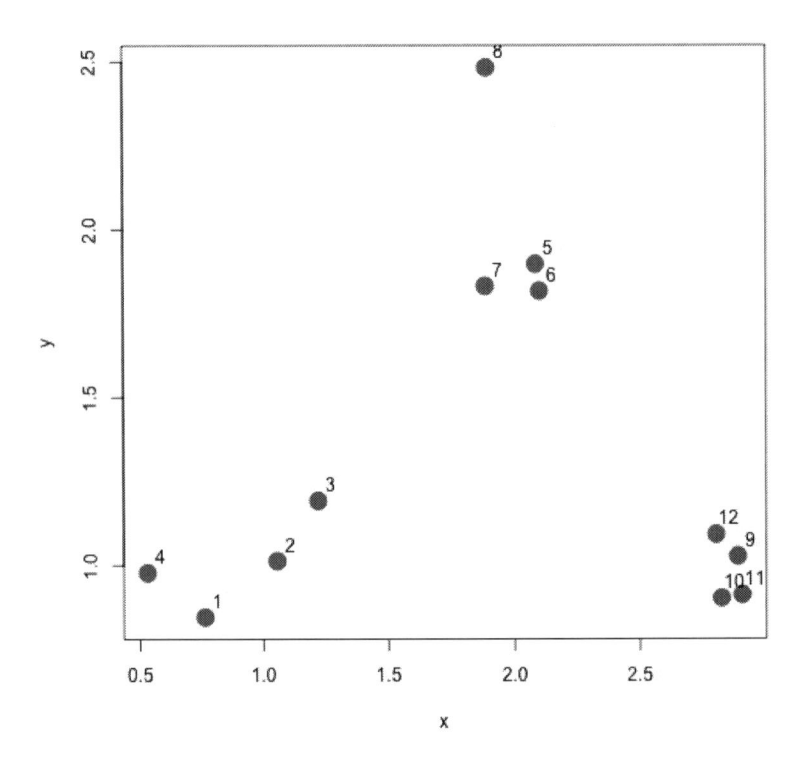

Simulated clustered data

The first step in the basic clustering approach is to calculate the distance between every point with every other point. The result is a *distance matrix,* which can be computed with the `dist()` function in R.

Here is just a piece of the distance matrix associated with the figure above.

```
> dataFrame <- data.frame(x=x, y=y)
> dist(dataFrame)
            1          2          3          4          5          6
2   0.34120511
3   0.57493739 0.24102750
4   0.26381786 0.52578819 0.71861759
5   1.69424700 1.35818182 1.11952883 1.80666768
6   1.65812902 1.31960442 1.08338841 1.78081321 0.08150268
7   1.49823399 1.16620981 0.92568723 1.60131659 0.21110433 0.21666557
8   1.99149025 1.69093111 1.45648906 2.02849490 0.61704200 0.69791931
9   2.13629539 1.83167669 1.67835968 2.35675598 1.18349654 1.11500116
10  2.06419586 1.76999236 1.63109790 2.29239480 1.23847877 1.16550201
11  2.14702468 1.85183204 1.71074417 2.37461984 1.28153948 1.21077373
12  2.05664233 1.74662555 1.58658782 2.27232243 1.07700974 1.00777231
            7          8          9         10         11
2
3
4
5
6
7
8   0.65062566
9   1.28582631 1.76460709
10  1.32063059 1.83517785 0.14090406
11  1.37369662 1.86999431 0.11624471 0.08317570
12  1.17740375 1.66223814 0.10848966 0.19128645 0.20802789
```

The default distance metric used by the `dist()` function is Euclidean distance.

Note that usually you will *not* have to explicitly compute the distance matrix (unless you are inventing your own clustering method). Here I just print it out to show what's going on internally.

First an agglomerative clustering approach attempts to find the two points that are closest together. In other words, we want to find the smallest non-zero entry in the distance matrix.

```
> rdistxy <- as.matrix(dist(dataFrame))
>
> ## Remove the diagonal from consideration
> diag(rdistxy) <- diag(rdistxy) + 100000
>
> # Find the index of the points with minimum distance
> ind <- which(rdistxy == min(rdistxy), arr.ind = TRUE)
> ind
  row col
6   6   5
5   5   6
```

Now we can plot the points and show which two points are closest together according to our distance metric.

```
> plot(x, y, col = "blue", pch = 19, cex = 2)
> text(x + 0.05, y + 0.05, labels = as.character(1:12))
> points(x[ind[1, ]], y[ind[1, ]], col = "orange", pch = 19, cex = 2)
```

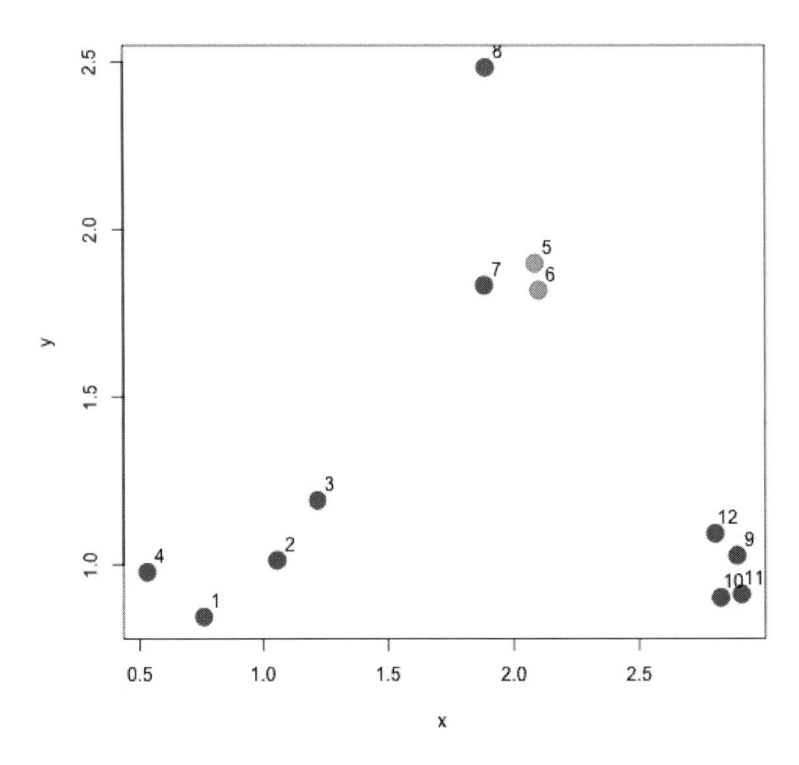

Two closest points

The next step for the algorithm is to start drawing the tree, the first step of which would be to "merge" these two points together.

```
> par(mfrow = c(1, 2))
> plot(x, y, col = "blue", pch = 19, cex = 2, main = "Data")
> text(x + 0.05, y + 0.05, labels = as.character(1:12))
> points(x[ind[1, ]], y[ind[1, ]], col = "orange", pch = 19, cex = 2)
>
> # Make a cluster and cut it at the right height
> library(dplyr)
> hcluster <- dist(dataFrame) %>% hclust
> dendro <- as.dendrogram(hcluster)
> cutDendro <- cut(dendro, h = (hcluster$height[1] + 0.00001))
> plot(cutDendro$lower[[11]], yaxt = "n", main = "Begin building tree")
```

Data

Begin building tree

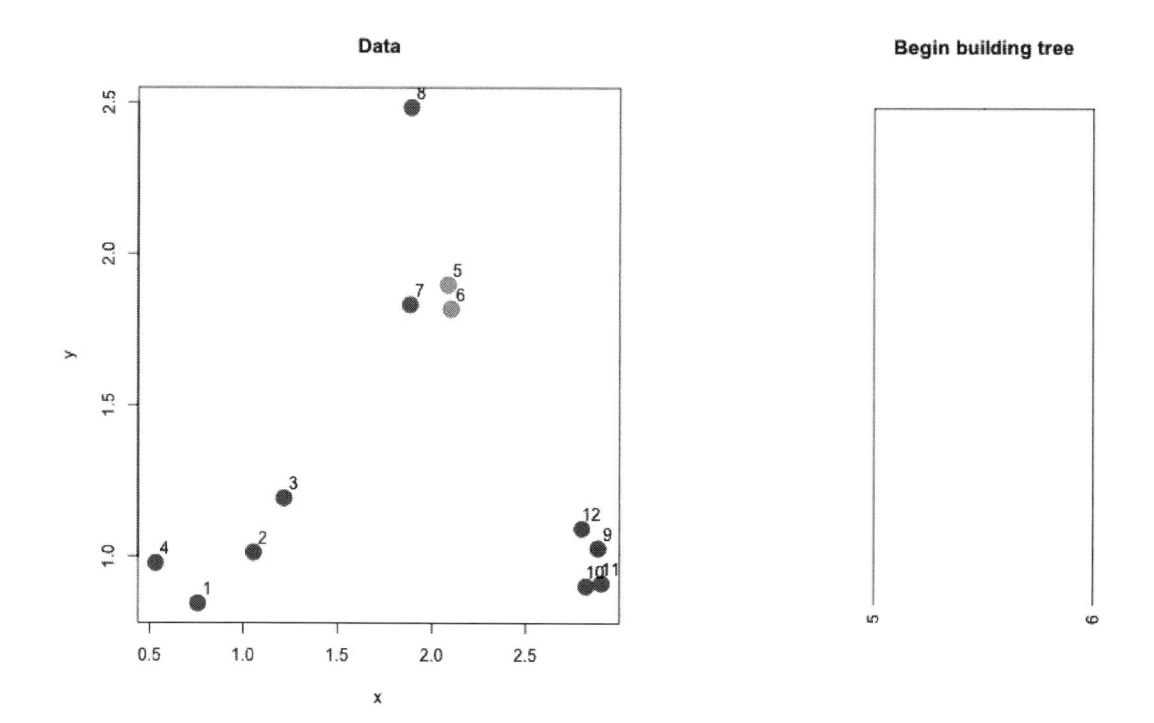

Merging of first two points

Now that we've merged the first two "leaves" of this tree, we can turn the algorithm crank and continue to build the tree. Now, the two points we identified in the previous iteration will get "merged" into a single point, as depicted below.

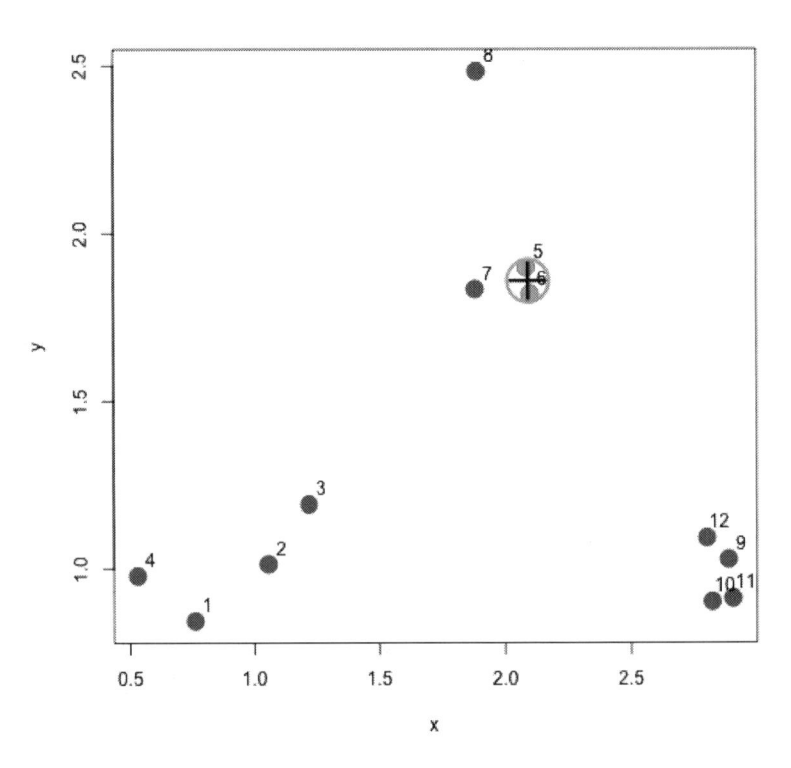

First set of merged points/cluster

We need to search the distance matrix for the *next* two closest points, ignoring the first two that we already merged.

```
> nextmin <- rdistxy[order(rdistxy)][3]
> ind <- which(rdistxy == nextmin,arr.ind=TRUE)
> ind
   row col
11  11  10
10  10  11
```

Now we can plot the data with this next pair of points and the merged tree leaves.

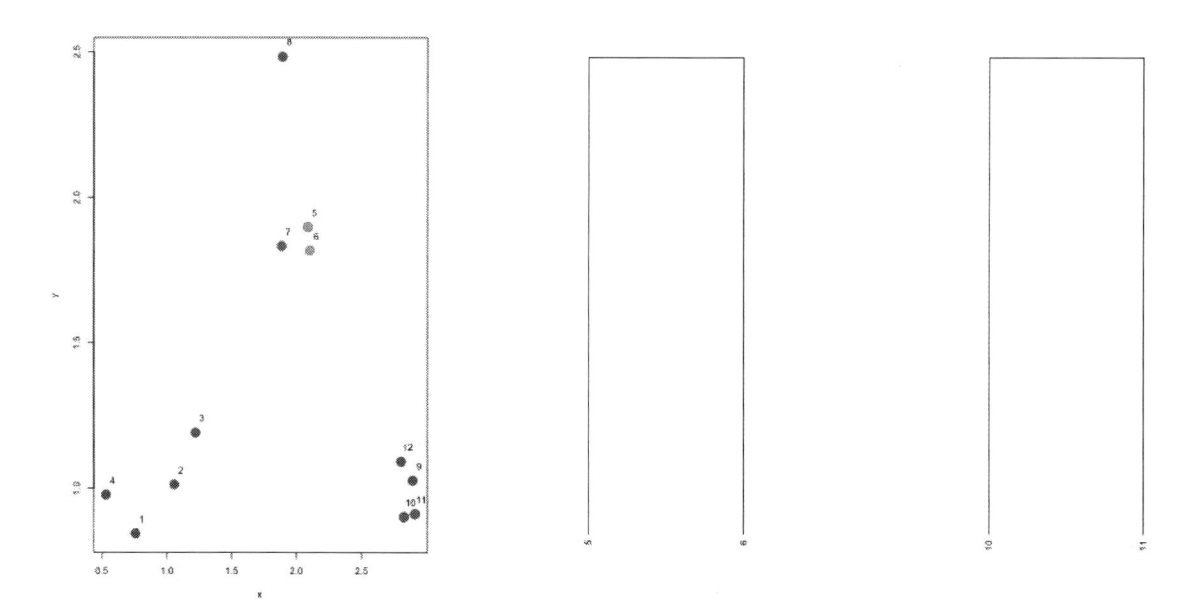

Second set of merged points

And on and on in this manner. If we were to continue in this fashion–identifying the two closest points and merging them, we'd end up with a *dendrogram* that looks like this one. Here, we call the hclust() do run the clustering algorithm.

```
> hClustering <- data.frame(x=x,y=y) %>% dist %>% hclust
> plot(hClustering)
```

Cluster Dendrogram

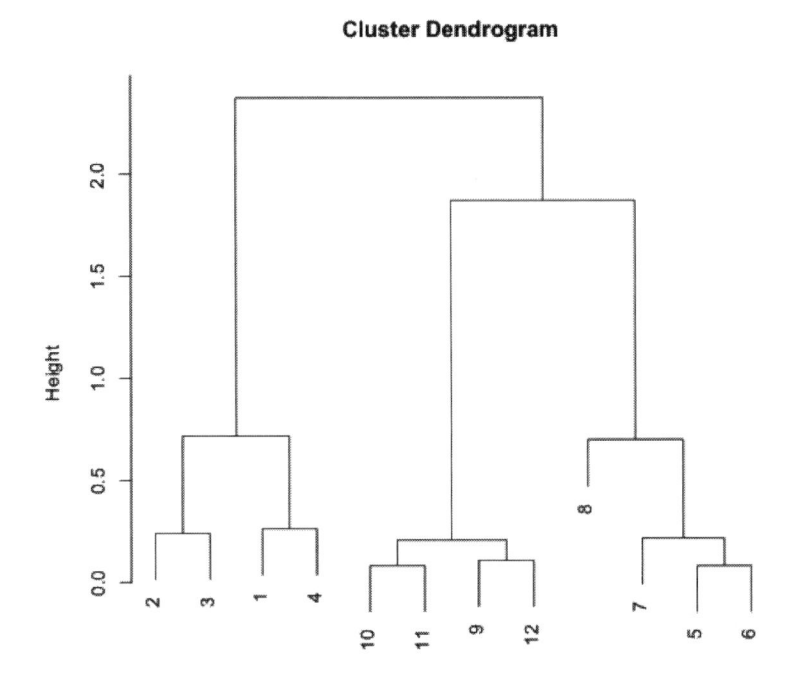

Full hierarchical clustering dendrogram

From the tree/dendrogram it's clear that there are three clusters each with four points.

12.6 Prettier dendrograms

It's possible to make slightly prettier dendrograms with some modification to the usual plotting method for the output of hclust(). Here's a function that takes the output of hclust() and color codes each of the cluster members by their cluster membership.

```
> myplclust <- function(hclust, lab = hclust$labels, lab.col = rep(1, length(hclust$labels)),
+     hang = 0.1, ...) {
+     ## modifiction of plclust for plotting hclust objects *in colour*!  Copyright
+     ## Eva KF Chan 2009 Arguments: hclust: hclust object lab: a character vector
+     ## of labels of the leaves of the tree lab.col: colour for the labels;
+     ## NA=default device foreground colour hang: as in hclust & plclust Side
+     ## effect: A display of hierarchical cluster with coloured leaf labels.
+     y <- rep(hclust$height, 2)
+     x <- as.numeric(hclust$merge)
+     y <- y[which(x < 0)]
+     x <- x[which(x < 0)]
+     x <- abs(x)
+     y <- y[order(x)]
```

```
+       x <- x[order(x)]
+       plot(hclust, labels = FALSE, hang = hang, ...)
+       text(x = x, y = y[hclust$order] - (max(hclust$height) * hang), labels = lab[hclust$order],
+           col = lab.col[hclust$order], srt = 90, adj = c(1, 0.5), xpd = NA, ...)
+ }
```

And here's the output the function produces.

```
> hClustering <- data.frame(x = x, y = y) %>% dist %>% hclust
> myplclust(hClustering, lab = rep(1:3, each = 4), lab.col = rep(1:3, each = 4))
```

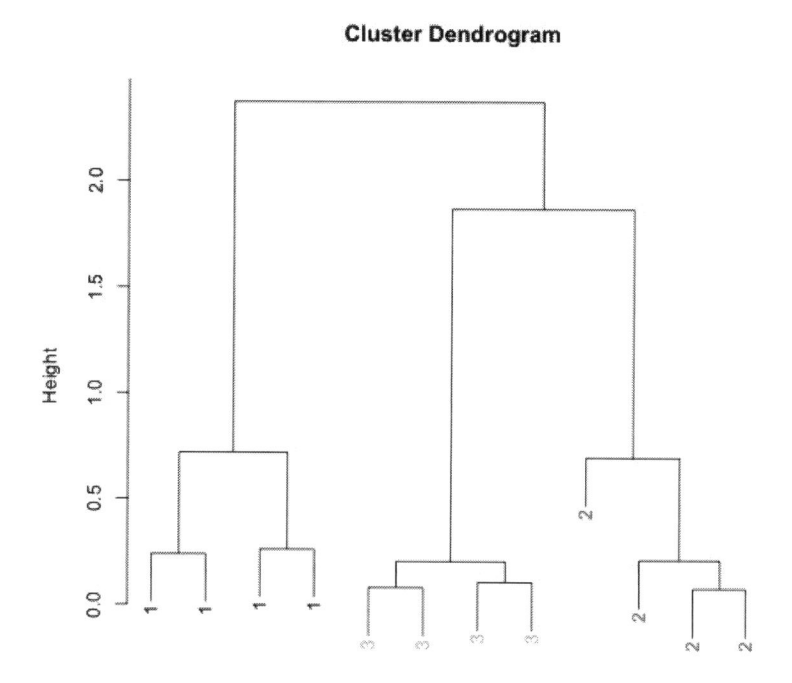

Cluster Dendrogram

hclust (*, "complete")

Prettier dendrogram

12.7 Merging points: Complete

One issue that we haven't discussed yet is how exactly the merging of clusters works. Recall that once we find the two points that are closest together, we "merge" them and then consider the merged pair as a single "point". When we compare this merged "point" with other points, how should we measure the distance from one point to this merged cluster of points?

One method, called "complete" is to measure the distance between two groups of points by the maximun distance between the two groups. That is, take all points in group 1 and all points in group 2 and find the two points that are *furthest* apart–that's the distance between the groups.

Here's what that would look like with our simulated data.

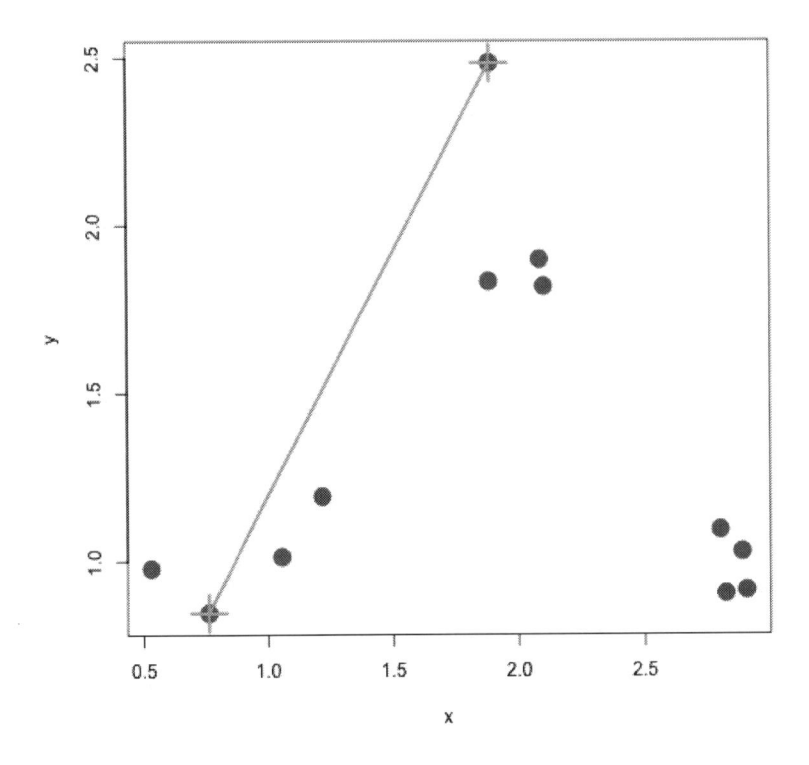

Complete merging

Complete merging is the default method in the hclust() function.

12.8 Merging points: Average

Another approach is average merging, which takes the average of the coordinate values in each group and measures the distance between these two averages. That approach is shown below.

Average merging

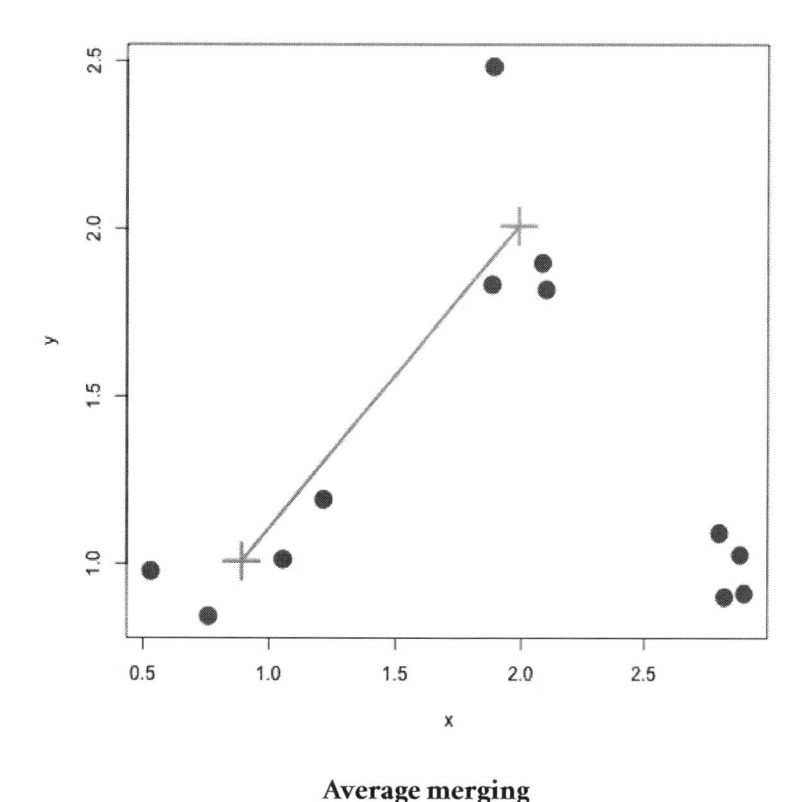

While there's not necessarily a correct merging approach for any given application, it's important to note that the resulting tree/hierarchy that you get can be sensitive to the merging approach that you use.

12.9 Using the `heatmap()` function

The `heatmap()` function is a handy way to visualize matrix data. The basic idea is that `heatmap()` sorts the rows and columns of a matrix according to the clustering determined by a call to `hclust()`. Conceptually, `heatmap()` first treats the rows of a matrix as observations and calls `hclust()` on them, then it treats the columns of a matrix as observations and calls `hclust()` on those values. The end result is that you get a dendrogram associated with both the rows and columns of a matrix, which can help you to spot obvious patterns in the data.

```
> dataMatrix <- data.frame(x=x,y=y) %>% data.matrix
> heatmap(dataMatrix)
```

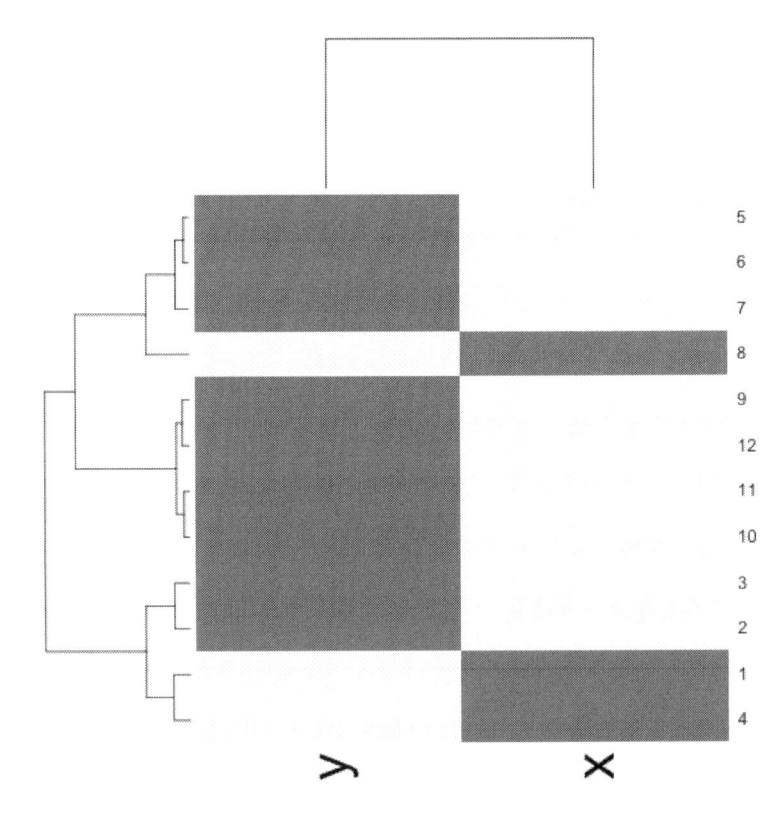

Heatmap with dendrograms on rows and columns

12.10 Notes and further resources

Hierarchical clustering is a really useful tool because it quickly gives you an idea of the relationships between variables/observations. But caution should be used with clustering as often the picture that you produce can be unstable. In particular, it may be sensitive to

- Changing a few points in the dataset
- Having different missing values in some of the observations
- Picking a different distance metric (i.e. Euclidean vs. Manhattan)
- Changing the merging strategy (i.e. complete vs. average)
- Changing the scale of points for one variable

Another issue is that choosing where to "cut" the tree to determine the number of clusters isn't always obvious. In light of some of these limitations, hierarchical clustering should be primarily used for exploration of data. Once major patterns have been identified, it's often best to delve further with other tools and formal modeling.

Some other resources to check out:

- Rafa's Distances and Clustering Video[6]
- Elements of statistical learning[7]

---

[6] http://www.youtube.com/watch?v=wQhVWUcXM0A
[7] http://www-stat.stanford.edu/~tibs/ElemStatLearn/

13. K-Means Clustering

Watch a video of this chapter: Part 1[1] Part 2[2]

The K-means clustering algorithm is another bread-and-butter algorithm in high-dimensional data analysis that dates back many decades now (for a comprehensive examination of clustering algorithms, including the K-means algorithm, a classic text is John Hartigan's book *Clustering Algorithms*).

The K-means approach, like many clustering methods, is highly algorithmic (can't be summarized in a formula) and is iterative. The basic idea is that you are trying to find the centroids of a fixed number of clusters of points in a high-dimensional space. In two dimensions, you can imagine that there are a bunch of clouds of points on the plane and you want to figure out where the centers of each one of those clouds is.

Of course, in two dimensions, you could probably just look at the data and figure out with a high degree of accuracy where the cluster centroids are. But what if the data are in a 100-dimensional space? That's where we need an algorithm.

The K-means approach is a partitioning approach, whereby the data are partitioned into groups at each iteration of the algorithm. One requirement is that you must **pre-specify how many clusters there are**. Of course, this may not be known in advance, but you can guess and just run the algorithm anyway. Afterwards, you can change the number of clusters and run the algorithm again to see if anything changes.

The outline of the algorithm is

1. Fix the number of clusters at some integer greater than or equal to 2
2. Start with the "centroids" of each cluster; initially you might just pick a random set of points as the centroids
3. Assign points to their closest centroid; cluster membership corresponds to the centroid assignment
4. Reclaculate centroid positions and repeat.

This approach, like most clustering methods requires a defined distance metric, a fixed number of clusters, and an initial guess as to the cluster centriods. There's no set approach to determining the initial configuration of centroids, but many algorithms simply randomly select data points from your dataset as the initial centroids.

The K-means algorithm produces

---

[1] https://youtu.be/QGDuvVRUURA
[2] https://youtu.be/XRlYz1jfCqs

13.1 Illustrating the K-means algorithm

We will use an example with simulated data to demonstrate how the K-means algorithm works. Here we simulate some data from three clusters and plot the dataset below.

```
> set.seed(1234)
> x <- rnorm(12, mean = rep(1:3, each = 4), sd = 0.2)
> y <- rnorm(12, mean = rep(c(1, 2, 1), each = 4), sd = 0.2)
> plot(x, y, col = "blue", pch = 19, cex = 2)
> text(x + 0.05, y + 0.05, labels = as.character(1:12))
```

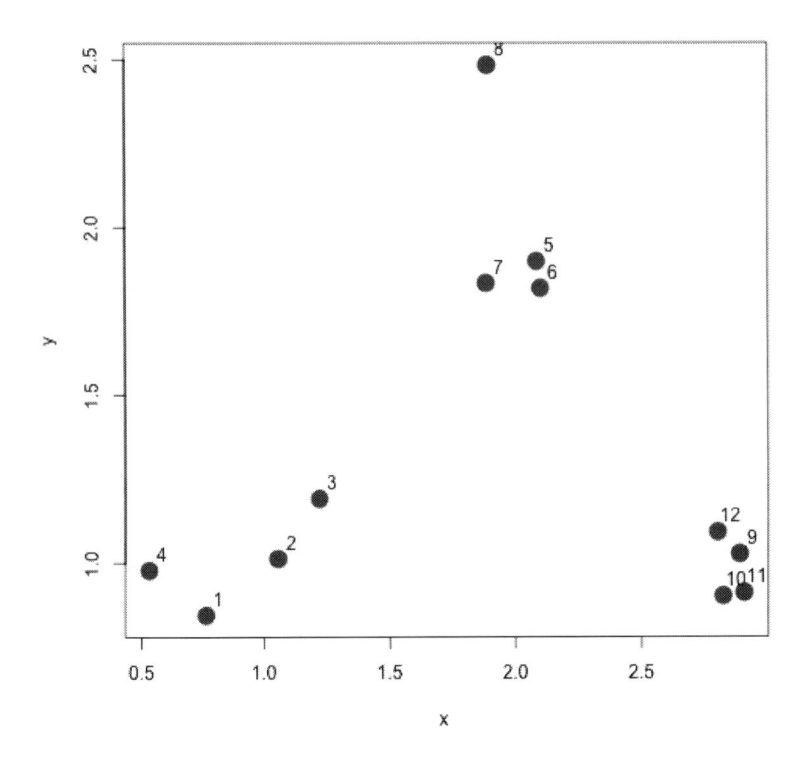

Simulated dataset

The first thing K-means has to do is assign an initial set of centroids. For this example, we will assume that there are three clusters (which also happens to be the truth). We will choose three centroids arbitrarily and show them in the plot below.

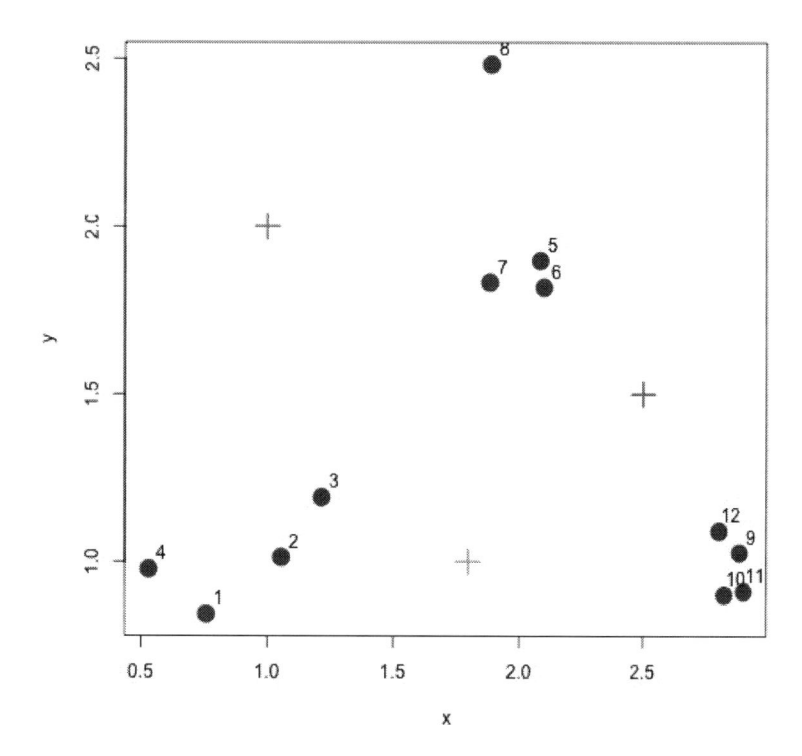

Initialize centroids

The next stage in the algorithm assigns every point in the dataset to the closest centroid. In the plot below, we color each point according to the color of its closest centroid (red, purple, or orange).

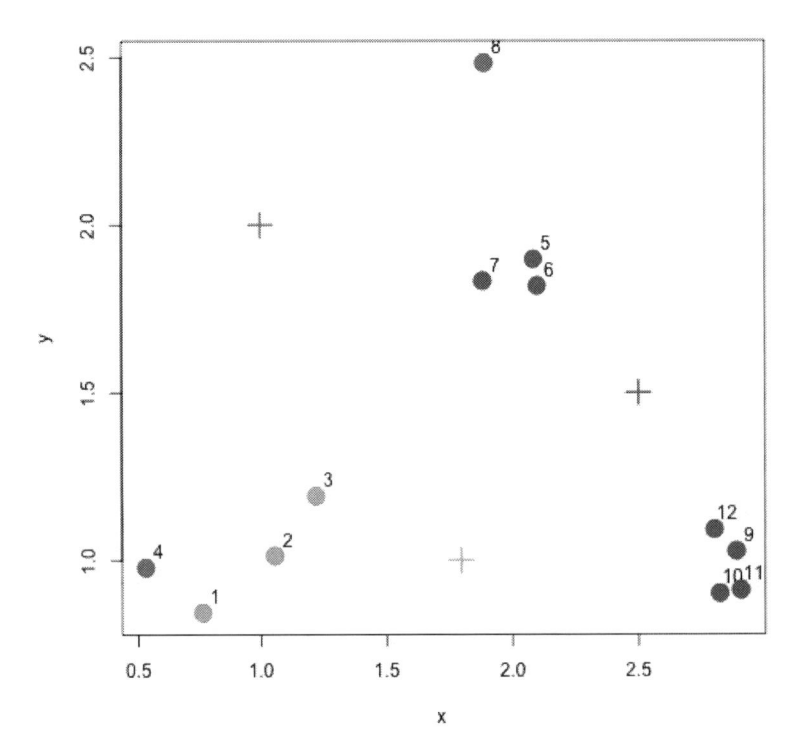

Assign points to nearest centroid

You can see that this initial clustering incorrectly clusters some points that are truly in the same cluster to separate clusters. The hope is that iterating algorithm more times that we will eventually converge on the correct solution.

The next stage is the re-calculate the centroids based on the new cluster assignments of the data points. The new cluster centroids are shown in the plot below.

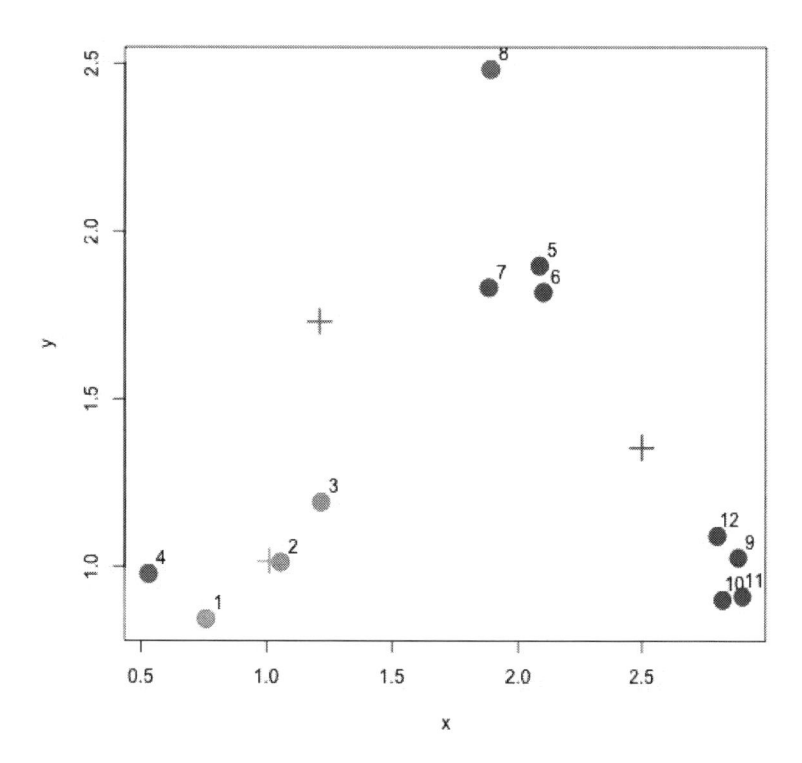

Re-calculate cluster centroids

Now we have completed one full cycle of the algorithm we can continue and re-assign points to their (new) closest cluster centroid.

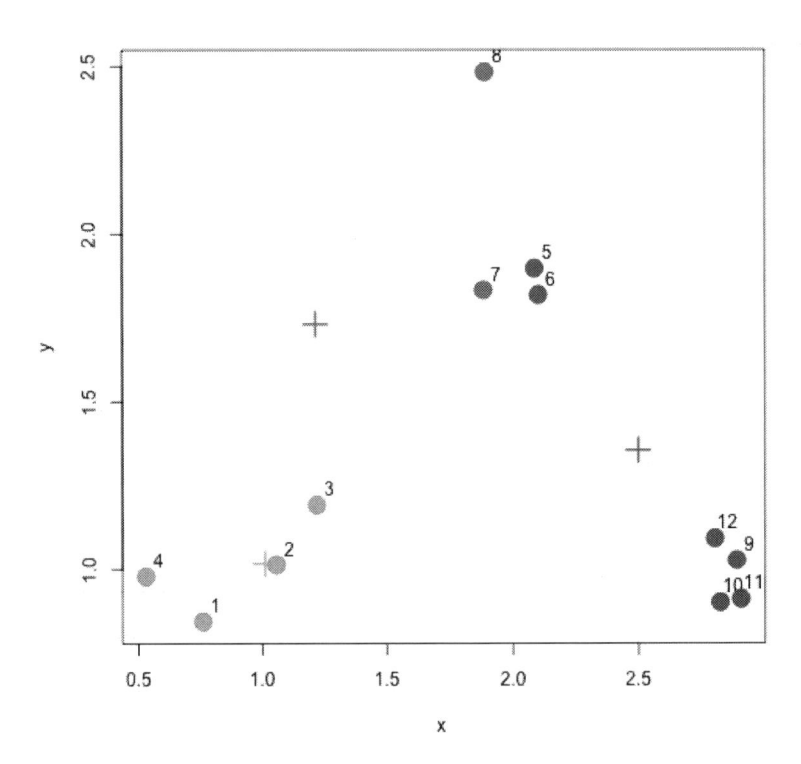

Re-assign points to new cluster centroids

And we can update the centroid positions one more time based on the re-assigned points.

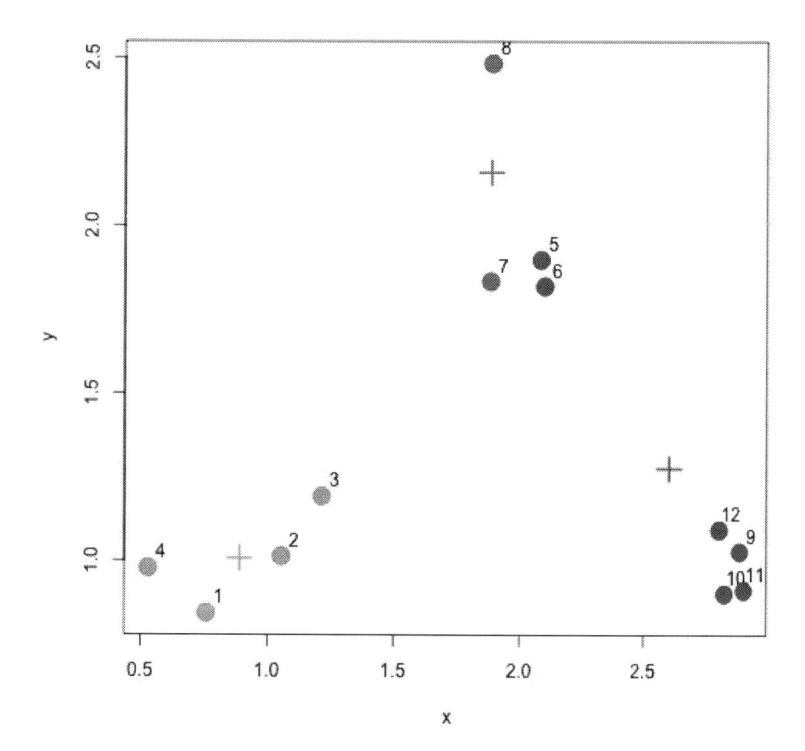

Updated centroid configuration

We can see from this last plot that things are actually pretty close to where they should be. There are just two purple points that have been assigned to the wrong cluster.

13.2 Stopping the algorithm

In practice, we would not know where the actual clusters were, so we wouldn't necessarily know when we were close to the truth. But eventually our algorithm needs to stop, so how do we decide when to stop iterating?

At some point the cluster centroids will stabilize and stop moving with each iteration. You could see that from the first iteration to the second iteration, the cluster centroids moved a lot. But after the second iteration, they moved less. Between each iteration we can keep track of the distance that each centroid moves from one iteration to the next. Once this distance is relatively small, we can stop the algorithm.

13.3 Using the `kmeans()` function

The `kmeans()` function in R implements the K-means algorithm and can be found in the `stats` package, which comes with R and is usually already loaded when you start R. Two key parameters that you have to specify are x, which is a matrix or data frame of data, and centers which is either an integer indicating the number of clusters or a matrix indicating the locations of the initial cluster centroids. The data should be organized so that each row is an observation and each column is a variable or feature of that observation.

```
> dataFrame <- data.frame(x, y)
> kmeansObj <- kmeans(dataFrame, centers = 3)
> names(kmeansObj)
[1] "cluster"      "centers"    "totss"     "withinss"
[5] "tot.withinss" "betweenss"  "size"      "iter"
[9] "ifault"
```

You can see which cluster each data point got assigned to by looking at the cluster element of the list returned by the kmeans() function.

```
> kmeansObj$cluster
 [1] 3 3 3 3 1 1 1 1 2 2 2 2
```

Here is a plot of the K-means clustering solution. Not surprisingly for this simple dataset, K-means was able to identify the true solution.

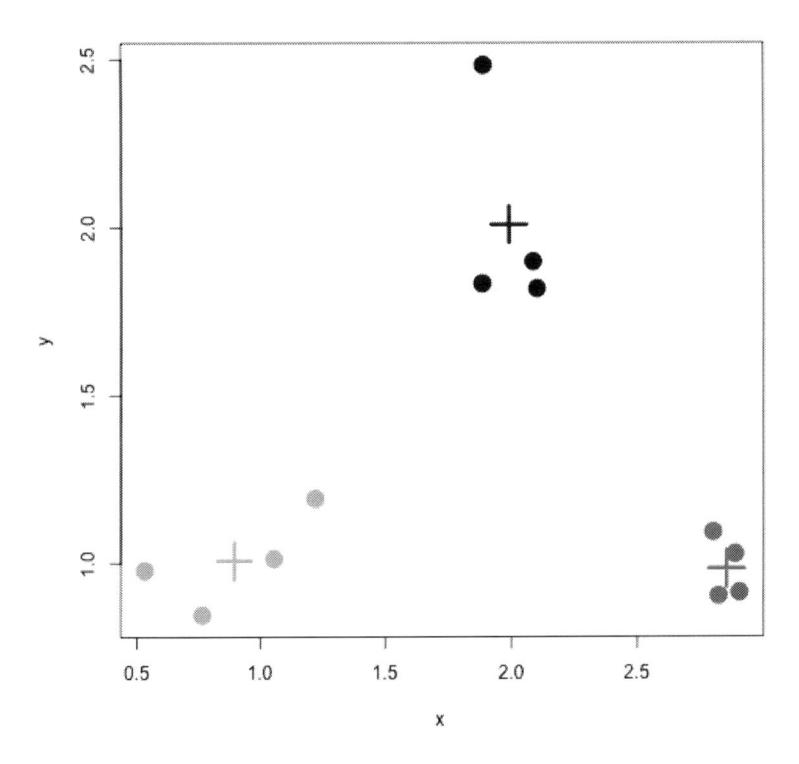

K-means clustering solution

13.4 Building heatmaps from K-means solutions

A heat map or image plot is sometimes a useful way to visualize matrix or array data. The idea is that each cell of the image is colored in a manner proportional to the value in the corresponding matrix element. It take a bit of work to get this to look right in R but the result can be very useful, especially for high-dimensional datasets that can be visualized using the simple plots we used above.

First, we need to find the K-means solution.

```
> set.seed(1234)
> dataMatrix <- as.matrix(dataFrame)[sample(1:12), ]
> kmeansObj <- kmeans(dataMatrix, centers = 3)
```

Then we can make an image plot using the K-means clusters.

```
> par(mfrow = c(1, 2))
> image(t(dataMatrix)[, nrow(dataMatrix):1], yaxt = "n", main = "Original Data")
> image(t(dataMatrix)[, order(kmeansObj$cluster)], yaxt = "n", main = "Clustered Data")
```

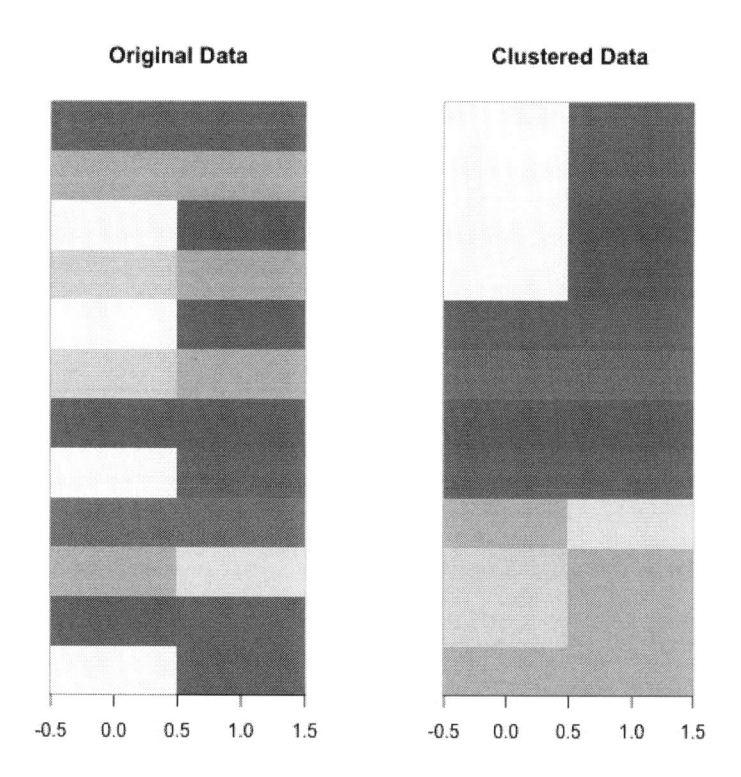

Heatmap of K-means solution

The plot above orders the rows of the matrix/image so that all of the rows in the same cluster are grouped together. You can see this with the more homogeneous nature of the coloring in the clustered version of the image.

13.5 Notes and further resources

- Determining the number of clusters[3]
- Rafael Irizarry's Distances and Clustering Video[4]
- Elements of statistical learning[5]

---
[3] http://en.wikipedia.org/wiki/Determining_the_number_of_clusters_in_a_data_set
[4] http://www.youtube.com/watch?v=wQhVWUcXM0A
[5] http://www-stat.stanford.edu/~tibs/ElemStatLearn/

14. Dimension Reduction

Watch a video of this chapter: Part 1[1] Part 2[2] Part 3[3]

14.1 Matrix data

The key aspect of matrix data is that every element of the matrix is the same type and represents the same kind of measurement. This is in contrast to a data frame, where every column of a data frame can potentially be of a different class.

Matrix data have some special statistical methods that can be applied to them. One category of statistical dimension reduction techniques is commonly called *principal components analysis* (PCA) or the *singular value decomposition* (SVD). These techniques generally are applied in situations where the rows of a matrix represent observations of some sort and the columns of the matrix represent features or variables (but this is by no means a requirement).

In an abstract sense, the SVD or PCA can be thought of as a way to approximate a high-dimensional matrix (i.e. a large number of columns) with a a few low-dimensional matrices. So there's a bit of data compression angle to it. We'll take a look at what's going on in this chapter.

First, we can simulate some matrix data. Here, we simulate some random Normal data in a matrix that has 40 rows and 10 columns.

```
> set.seed(12345)
> dataMatrix <- matrix(rnorm(400), nrow = 40)
> image(1:10, 1:40, t(dataMatrix)[, nrow(dataMatrix):1])
```

---

[1] https://youtu.be/ts6UQnE6E1U
[2] https://youtu.be/BSfw0rpyC2g
[3] https://youtu.be/drNwEvEx3LY

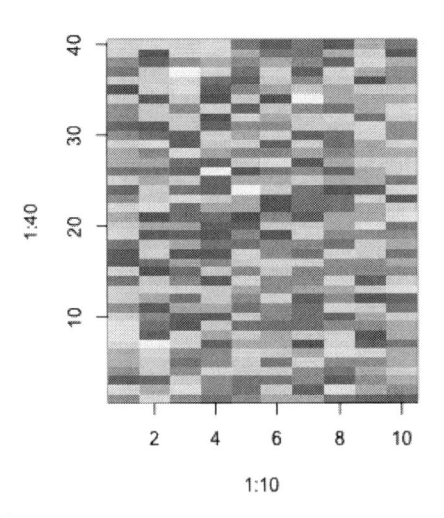

plot of chunk randomData

When confronted with matrix data a quick and easy thing to organize the data a bit is to apply an hierarchical clustering algorithm to it. Such a clustering can be visualized with the `heatmap()` function.

```
> heatmap(dataMatrix)
```

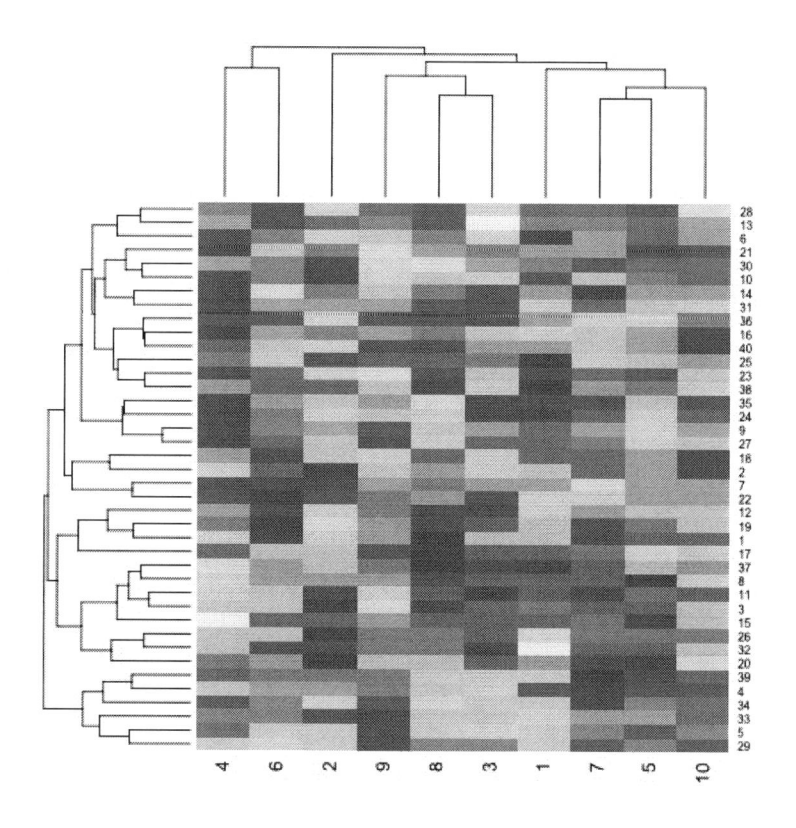

Heatmap of matrix data

Not surprisingly, there aren't really any interesting patterns given that we just simulated random noise. At least it's good to know that the clustering algorithm won't pick up something when there's nothing there!

But now what if there were a pattern in the data? How would we discover it?

Let's first simulate some data that indeed does have a pattern. In the code below, we cycle through all the rows of the matrix and randomly add 3 to the last 5 columns of the matrix.

```
> set.seed(678910)
> for (i in 1:40) {
+     coinFlip <- rbinom(1, size = 1, prob = 0.5)
+     
+     ## If coin is heads add a common pattern to that row
+     if (coinFlip) {
+         dataMatrix[i, ] <- dataMatrix[i, ] + rep(c(0, 3), each = 5)
+     }
+ }
```

Here's what the new data look like.

```
> image(1:10, 1:40, t(dataMatrix)[, nrow(dataMatrix):1])
```

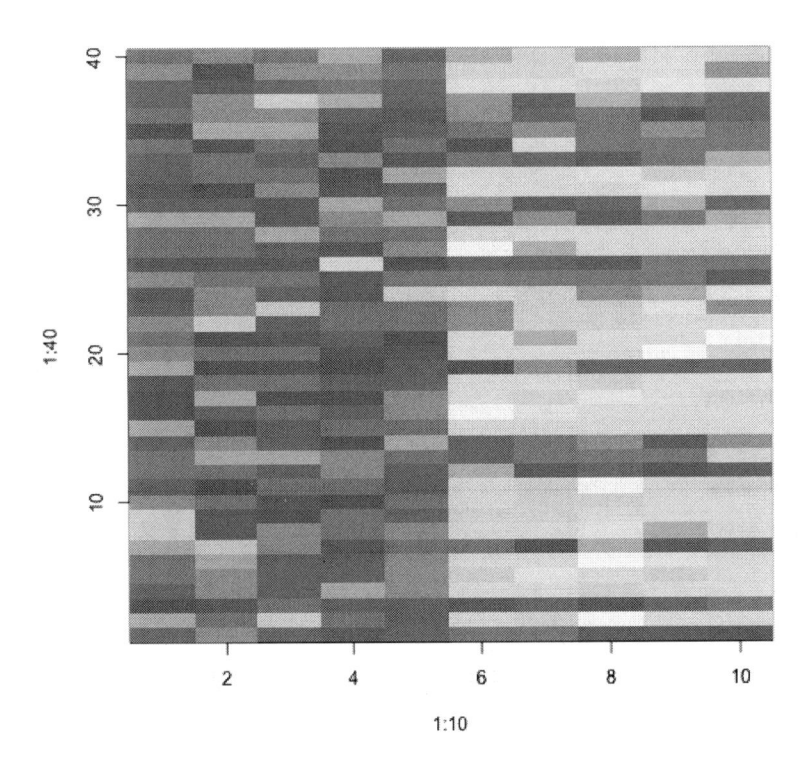

Matrix data with a pattern

You can see that some of the rows on the right side of the matrix have higher values than on the left side.

Now what happens if we cluster the data?

```
> heatmap(dataMatrix)
```

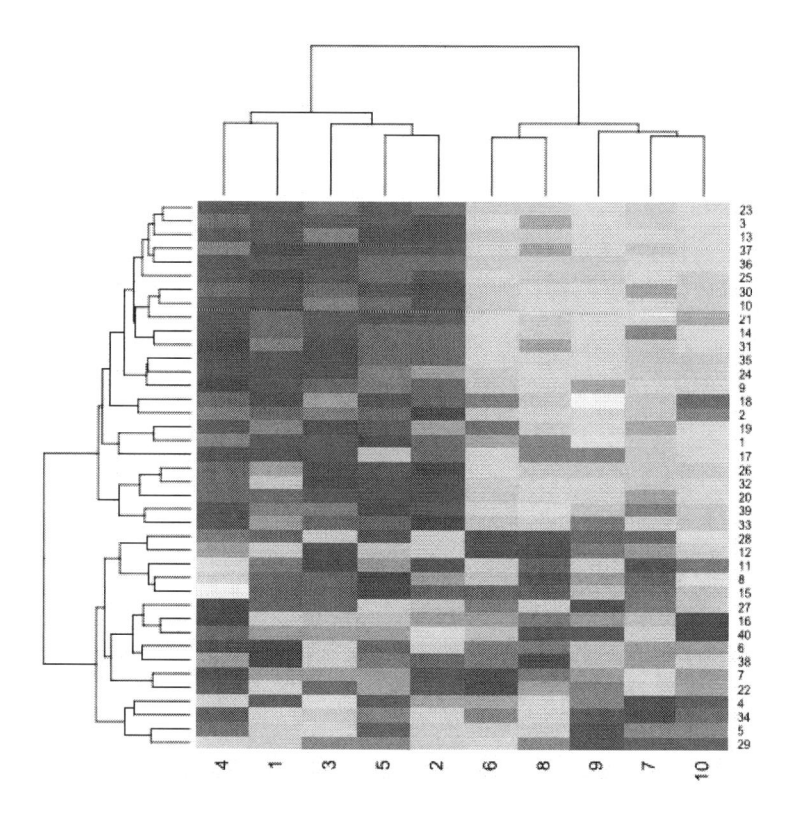

Clustered data with pattern

We can see from the dendrogram on top of the matrix (for the columns) that the columns pretty clearly split into two clusters, which is what we'd expect.

14.2 Patterns in rows and columns

In general, with matrix data, there may be patterns that occur accross the rows and columns of the matrix. In the example above, we shifted the mean of some of the observations in columns 5 through 10. We can display this a bit more explicitly by looking at the row and column means of the data.

```r
> library(dplyr)
> hh <- dist(dataMatrix) %>% hclust
> dataMatrixOrdered <- dataMatrix[hh$order, ]
> par(mfrow = c(1, 3))
>
> ## Complete data
> image(t(dataMatrixOrdered)[, nrow(dataMatrixOrdered):1])
>
> ## Show the row means
> plot(rowMeans(dataMatrixOrdered), 40:1, , xlab = "Row Mean", ylab = "Row", pch = 19)
>
> ## Show the column means
> plot(colMeans(dataMatrixOrdered), xlab = "Column", ylab = "Column Mean", pch = 19)
```

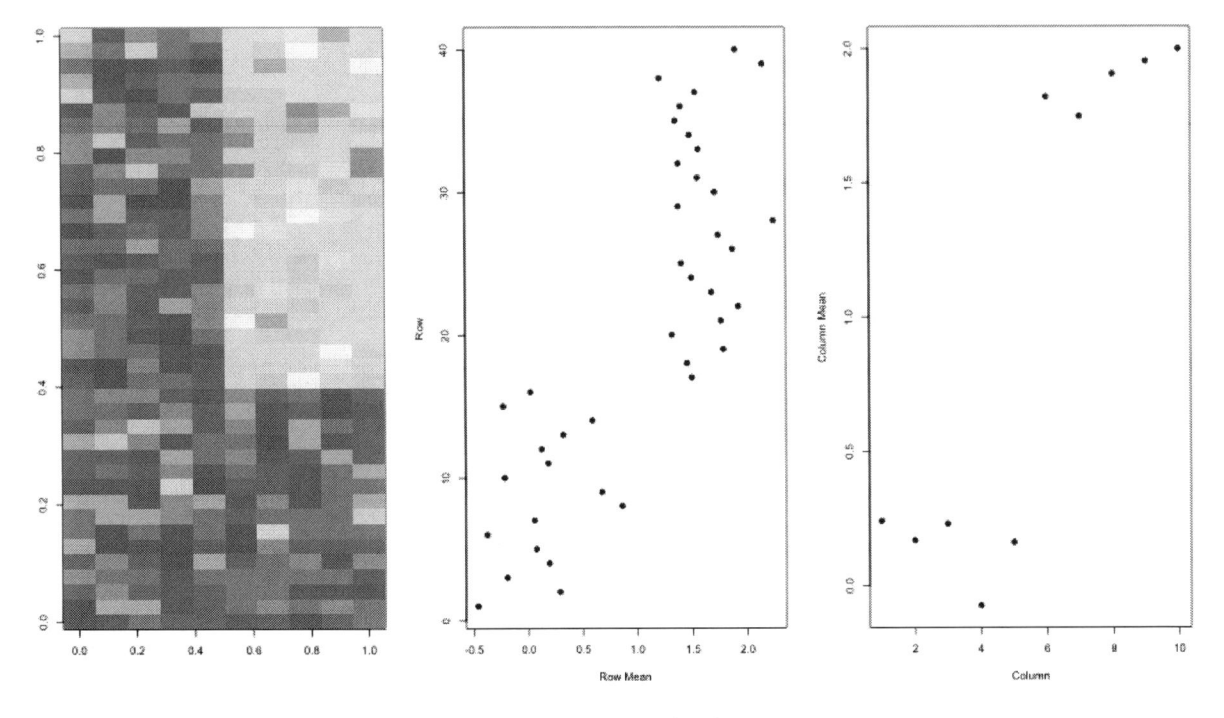

Pattern in rows and columns

However, there may be other patterns beyond a simple mean shift and so more sophisticated methods will be needed. Futhermore, there may be multiple patterns layered on top of each other so we need a method that can distangle these patterns.

14.3 Related problem

Here's another way to formulate the problem that matrix data present. Suppose you have multivariate observations

$$X_1, \ldots, X_n$$

so that each of the n observations has m features,

$$X_1 = (X_{11}, \ldots, X_{1m})$$

Given this setup, the goal is to find a new set of variables/features that are uncorrelated and explain as much variance in the data as possible. Put another way, if you were to put all these multivariate observations together in one matrix, find the *best* matrix created with fewer variables (lower rank) that explains the original data.

The first goal is *statistical* in nature and the second goal is perhaps better characterized as *lossy data compression*.

14.4 SVD and PCA

If X is a matrix with each variable in a column and each observation in a row then the SVD is a matrix decomposition that represents X as a matrix product of three matrices:

$$X = UDV'$$

where the columns of U (left singular vectors) are orthogonal, the columns of V (right singular vectors) are orthogonal and D is a diagonal matrix of singular values.

Principal components analysis (PCA) is simply an application of the SVD. The *principal components* are equal to the right singular values if you first scale the data by subtracting the column mean and dividing each column by its standard deviation (that can be done with the `scale()` function).

14.5 Unpacking the SVD: *u* and *v*

The SVD can be computed in R using the `svd()` function. Here, we scale our original matrix data with the pattern in it and apply the svd.

```
> svd1 <- svd(scale(dataMatrixOrdered))
```

The `svd()` function returns a list containing three components named u, d, and v. The u and v components correspond to the matrices of left and right singular vectors, respectively, while the d component is a vector of singular values, corresponding to the diagonal of the matrix D described above.

Below we plot the first left and right singular vectors along with the original data.

```
> par(mfrow = c(1, 3))
> image(t(dataMatrixOrdered)[, nrow(dataMatrixOrdered):1], main = "Original Data")
> plot(svd1$u[, 1], 40:1, , ylab = "Row", xlab = "First left singular vector",
+      pch = 19)
> plot(svd1$v[, 1], xlab = "Column", ylab = "First right singular vector", pch = 19)
```

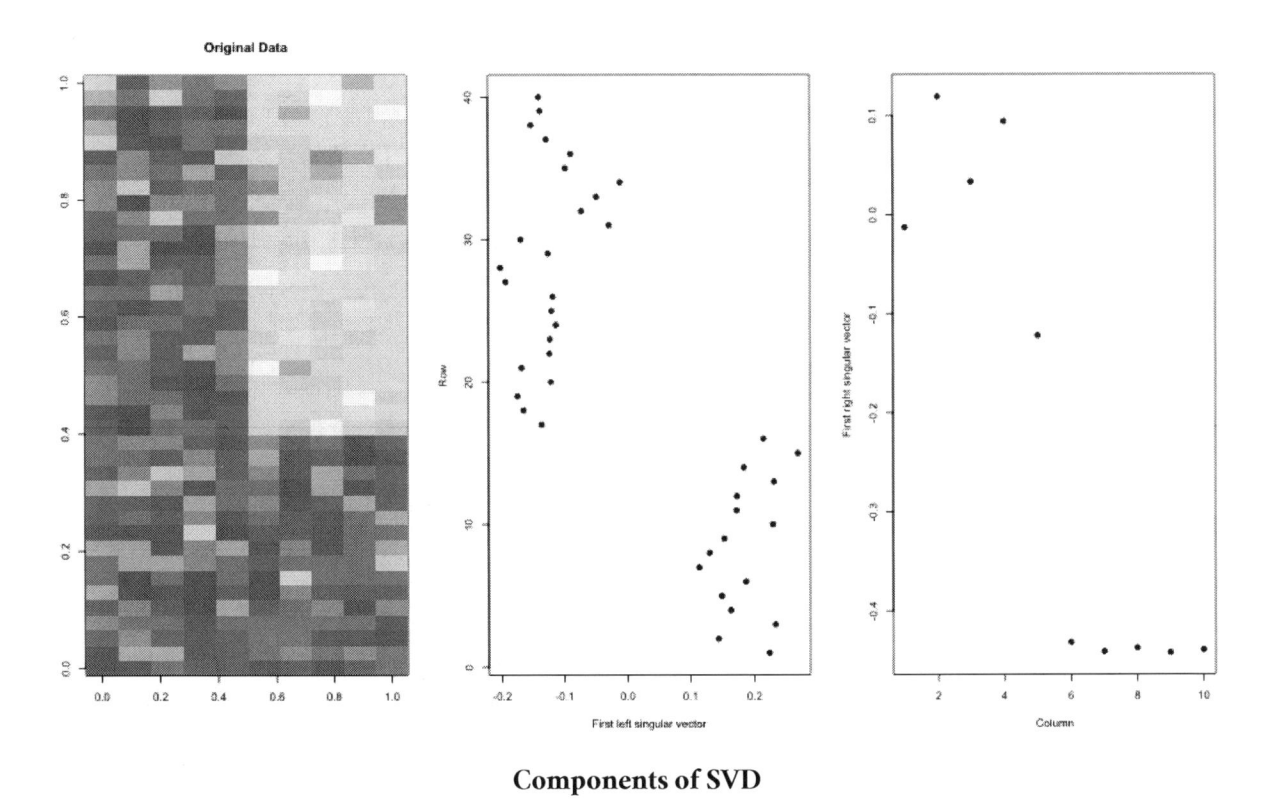

Components of SVD

You can see how the first left and right singular vectors pick up the mean shift in both the rows and columns of the matrix.

14.6 SVD for data compression

If we believed that the first left and right singular vectors, call them u1 and v1, captured all of the variation in the data, then we could approximate the original data matrix with

$$X \approx u_1 v_1'$$

Thus, we would reduce 400 numbers in the original matrix to 40 + 10 = 50 numbers in the compressed matrix, a nearly 90% reduction in information. Here's what the original data and the approximation would look like.

```
> ## Approximate original data with outer product of first singular vectors
> approx <- with(svd1, outer(u[, 1], v[, 1]))
>
> ## Plot original data and approximated data
> par(mfrow = c(1, 2))
> image(t(dataMatrixOrdered)[, nrow(dataMatrixOrdered):1], main = "Original Matrix")
> image(t(approx)[, nrow(approx):1], main = "Approximated Matrix")
```

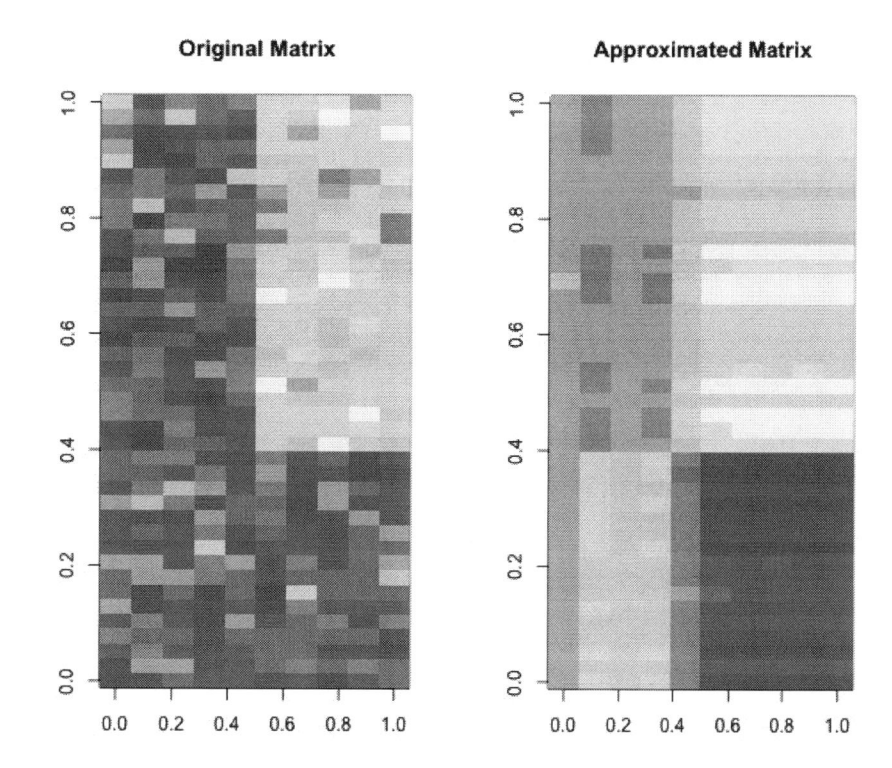

Approximating a matrix

Obviously, the two matrices are not identical, but the approximation seems reasonable in this case. This is not surprising given that there was only one real feature in the original data.

14.7 Components of the SVD - Variance explained

The statistical interpretation of singular values is in the form of variance in the data explained by the various components. The singular values produced by the svd() are in order from largest to smallest and when squared are proportional the amount of variance explained by a given singular vector.

To show how this works, here's a very simple example. First, we'll simulate a "dataset" that just takes two values, 0 and 1.

138 Dimension Reduction

```
> constantMatrix <- dataMatrixOrdered * 0
> for (i in 1:dim(dataMatrixOrdered)[1]) {
+     constantMatrix[i, ] <- rep(c(0, 1), each = 5)
+ }
```

Then we can take the SVD of this matrix and show the singular values as well as the proportion of variance explained.

```
> svd1 <- svd(constantMatrix)
> par(mfrow = c(1, 3))
> image(t(constantMatrix)[, nrow(constantMatrix):1], main = "Original Data")
> plot(svd1$d, xlab = "Column", ylab = "Singular value", pch = 19)
> plot(svd1$d^2/sum(svd1$d^2), xlab = "Column", ylab = "Prop. of variance explained",
+     pch = 19)
```

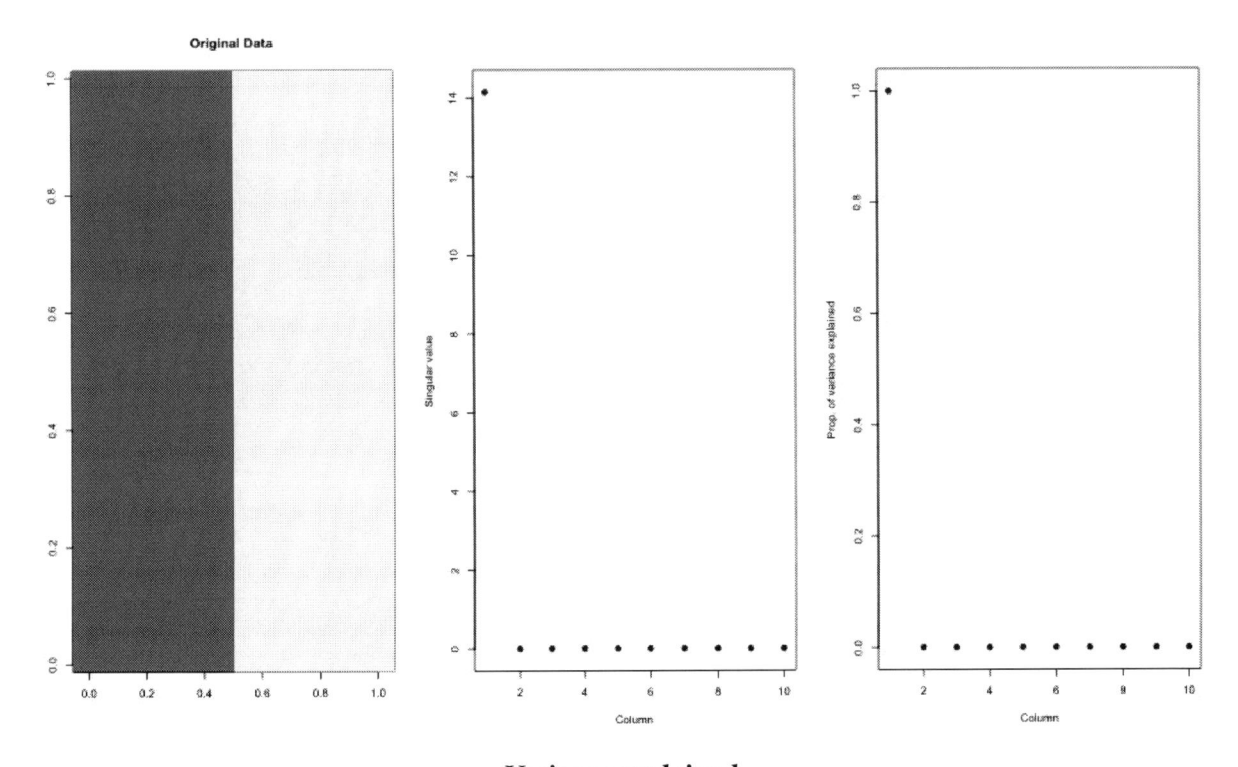

Variance explained

As we can see from the right-most plot, 100% of the variation in this "dataset" can be explained by the first singular value. Or, all of the variation in this dataset occurs in a single dimension. This is clear because all of the variation in the data occurs as you go from left to right across the columns. Otherwise, the values of the data are constant.

In the plot below, we plot the singular values (left) and the proportion of variance explained for the slightly more complex dataset that we'd been using previously.

```
> par(mfrow = c(1, 2))
> svd1 <- svd(scale(dataMatrixOrdered))
> plot(svd1$d, xlab = "Column", ylab = "Singular value", pch = 19)
> plot(svd1$d^2/sum(svd1$d^2), xlab = "Column", ylab = "Prop. of variance explained",
+      pch = 19)
```

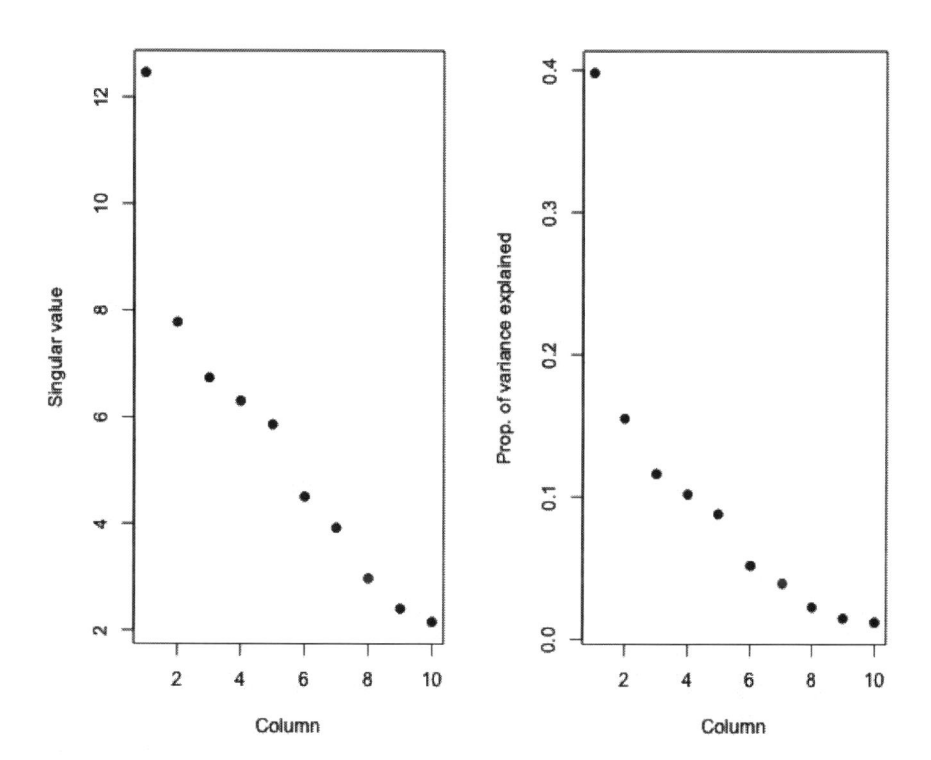

Variance explained by singular vectors

We can see that the first component explains about 40% of all the variation in the data. In other words, even though there are 10 dimensions in the data, 40% of the variation in the data can be explained by a single dimension. That suggests that the data could be simplified quite a bit, a phenomenon we observed in the last section where it appeared the data could be reasonably approximated by the first left and right singular vectors.

14.8 Relationship to principal components

As we mentioned above, the SVD has a close connection to principal components analysis (PCA). PCA can be applied to the data by calling the prcomp() function in R. Here, we show that the first right singular vector from the SVD is equal to the first principal component vector returned by PCA.

```
> svd1 <- svd(scale(dataMatrixOrdered))
> pca1 <- prcomp(dataMatrixOrdered, scale = TRUE)
> plot(pca1$rotation[, 1], svd1$v[, 1], pch = 19, xlab = "Principal Component 1",
+      ylab = "Right Singular Vector 1")
> abline(c(0, 1))
```

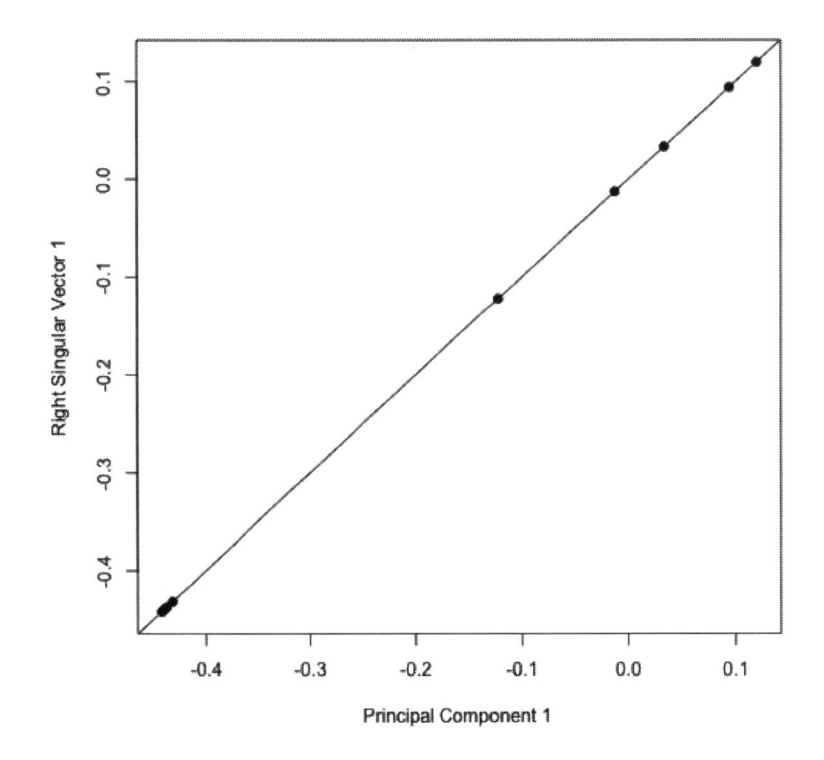

Singular vectors and principal components

Whether you call this procedure SVD or PCA really just depends on who you talk to. Statisticians and people with that kind of background will typically call it PCA while engineers and mathematicians will tend to call it SVD.

14.9 What if we add a second pattern?

Tracking a single patter in a matrix is relatively straightforward, but typically there will be multiple layered patterns in a matrix of data. Here we add two patterns to a simulated dataset. One pattern simple adds a constant to the last 5 columns of data, while the other pattern adds an alternating pattern (every other column).

```
> set.seed(678910)
> for (i in 1:40) {
+     coinFlip1 <- rbinom(1, size = 1, prob = 0.5)
+     coinFlip2 <- rbinom(1, size = 1, prob = 0.5)
+     if (coinFlip1) {
+         ## Pattern 1
+         dataMatrix[i, ] <- dataMatrix[i, ] + rep(c(0, 5), each = 5)
+     }
+     if (coinFlip2) {
+         ## Pattern 2
+         dataMatrix[i, ] <- dataMatrix[i, ] + rep(c(0, 5), 5)
+     }
+ }
> hh <- hclust(dist(dataMatrix))
> dataMatrixOrdered <- dataMatrix[hh$order, ]
```

Here is a plot of this new dataset along with the two different patterns.

```
> svd2 <- svd(scale(dataMatrixOrdered))
> par(mfrow = c(1, 3))
> image(t(dataMatrixOrdered)[, nrow(dataMatrixOrdered):1], main = "Data")
> plot(rep(c(0, 1), each = 5), pch = 19, xlab = "Column", ylab = "Pattern 1",
+     main = "Block pattern")
> plot(rep(c(0, 1), 5), pch = 19, xlab = "Column", ylab = "Pattern 2", main = "Alternating pattern")
```

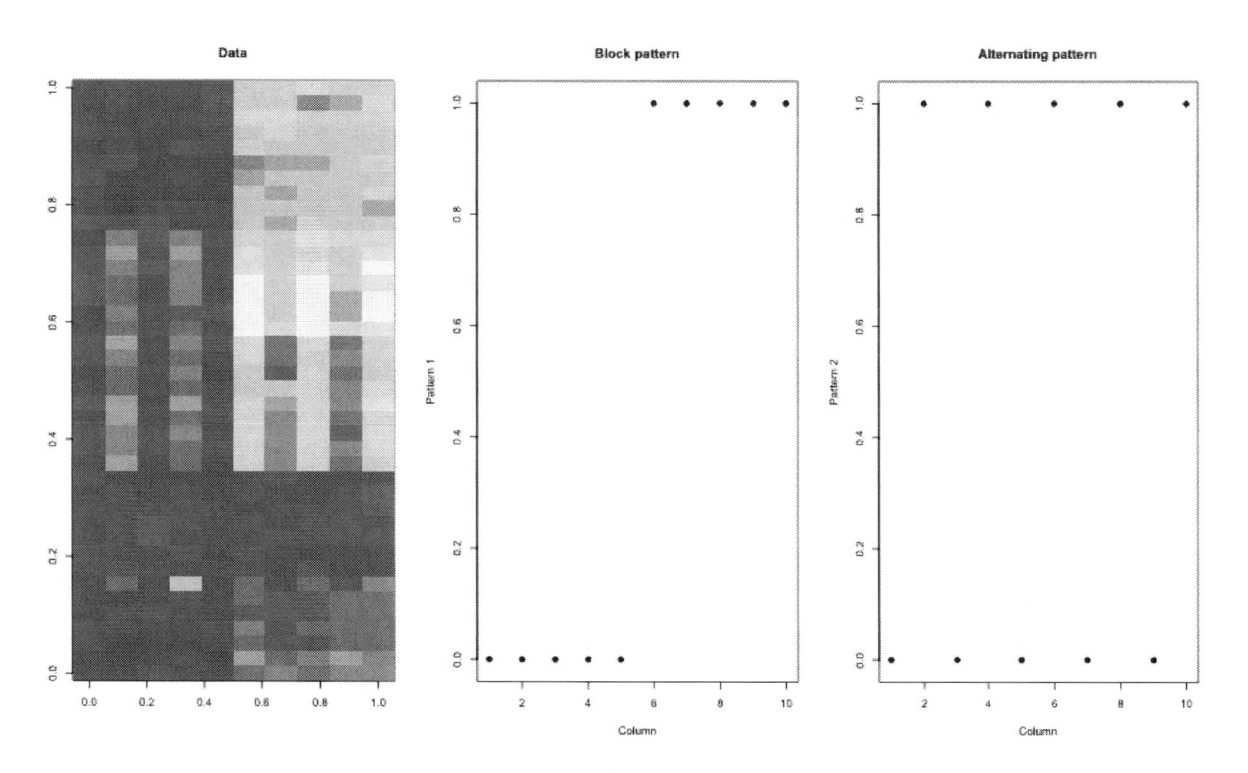

Dataset with two patterns

142   Dimension Reduction

Now, of course the plot above shows the truth, which in general we will not know. We can apply the SVD/PCA to this matrix and see how well the patterns are picked up.

```
> svd2 <- svd(scale(dataMatrixOrdered))
> par(mfrow = c(1, 3))
> image(t(dataMatrixOrdered)[, nrow(dataMatrixOrdered):1])
> plot(svd2$v[, 1], pch = 19, xlab = "Column", ylab = "First right singular vector")
> plot(svd2$v[, 2], pch = 19, xlab = "Column", ylab = "Second right singular vector")
```

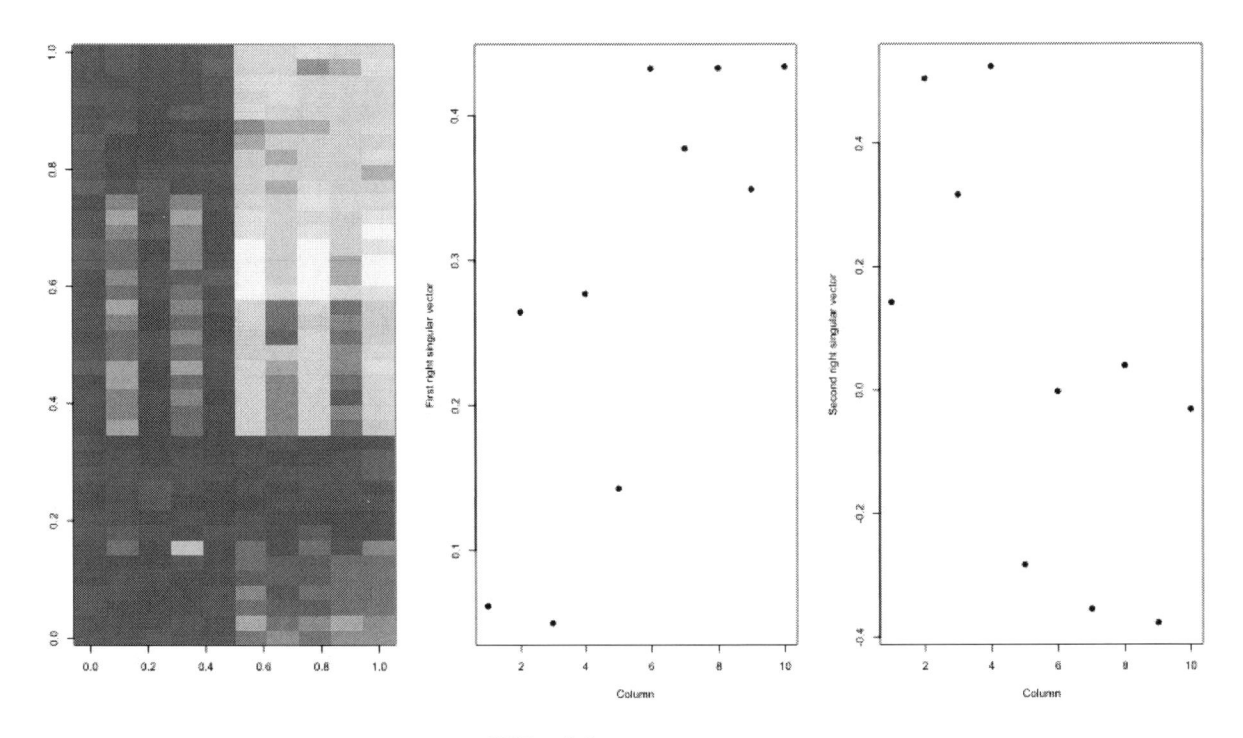

SVD with two patterns

We can see that the first right singular vector seems to pick up both the alternating pattern as well as the block/step pattern in the data. The second right singular vector seems to pick up a similar pattern.

When we look at the variance explained, we can see that the first singular vector picks up a little more than 50% of the variation in the data.

```
> svd1 <- svd(scale(dataMatrixOrdered))
> par(mfrow = c(1, 2))
> plot(svd1$d, xlab = "Column", ylab = "Singular value", pch = 19)
> plot(svd1$d^2/sum(svd1$d^2), xlab = "Column", ylab = "Percent of variance explained",
+       pch = 19)
```

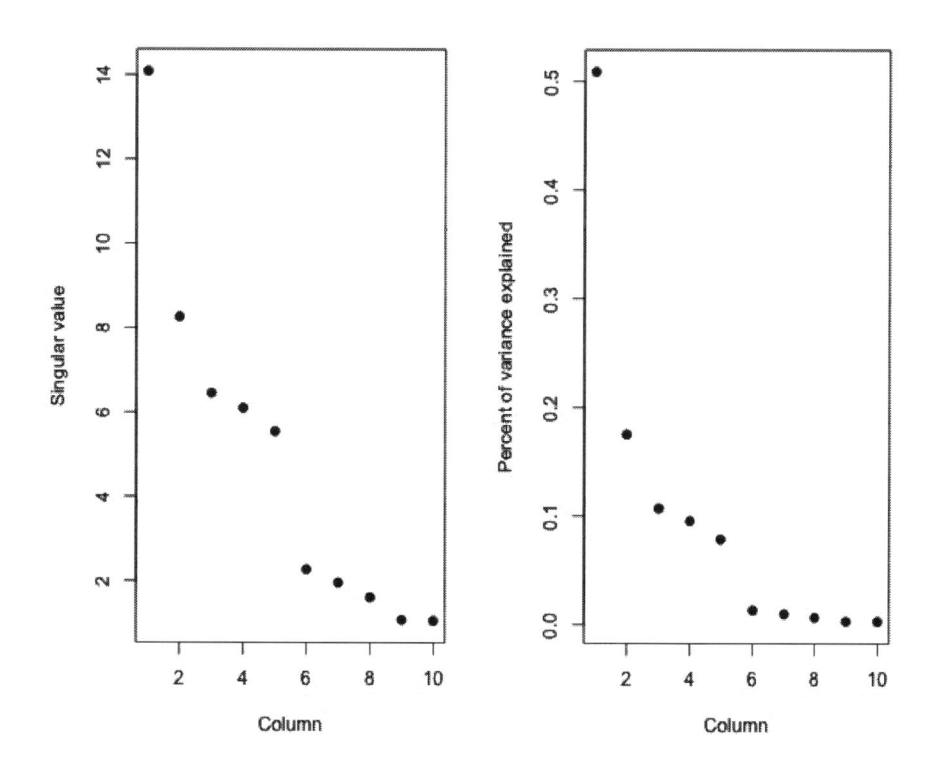

Variation explained by singular vectors

14.10 Dealing with missing values

Missing values are a problem that plagues any data analysis and the analysis of matrix data is no exception. Most SVD and PCA routines simply cannot be applied if there are missing values in the dataset. In the event of missing data, there are typically a series of questions that should be asked:

- Determine the reason for the missing data; what is the *process* that lead to the data being missing?
- Is the proportion of missing values so high as to invalidate any sort of analysis?
- Is there information in the dataset that would allow you to predict/infer the values of the missing data?

In the example below, we take our dataset and randomly insert some missing data.

```
> dataMatrix2 <- dataMatrixOrdered
> ## Randomly insert some missing data
> dataMatrix2[sample(1:100, size = 40, replace = FALSE)] <- NA
```

If we try to apply the SVD on this matrix it won't work.

```
> svd1 <- svd(scale(dataMatrix2))
Error in svd(scale(dataMatrix2)): infinite or missing values in 'x'
```

Since in this case we know that the missing data appeared completely randomly in the data, it would make sense to try to impute the values so that we can run the SVD. Here, we use the `impute` package to do a k-nearest-neighbors imputation of the missing data. The `impute` package is available from the Bioconductor project[4].

```
> library(impute)
> dataMatrix2 <- impute.knn(dataMatrix2)$data
```

Now we can compare how the SVD performs on the original dataset (no missing data) and the imputed dataset. Here, we plot the first right singular vector.

```
> svd1 <- svd(scale(dataMatrixOrdered))
> svd2 <- svd(scale(dataMatrix2))
> par(mfrow = c(1, 2))
> plot(svd1$v[, 1], pch = 19, main = "Original dataset")
> plot(svd2$v[, 1], pch = 19, main = "Imputed dataset")
```

---

[4]http://bioconductor.org

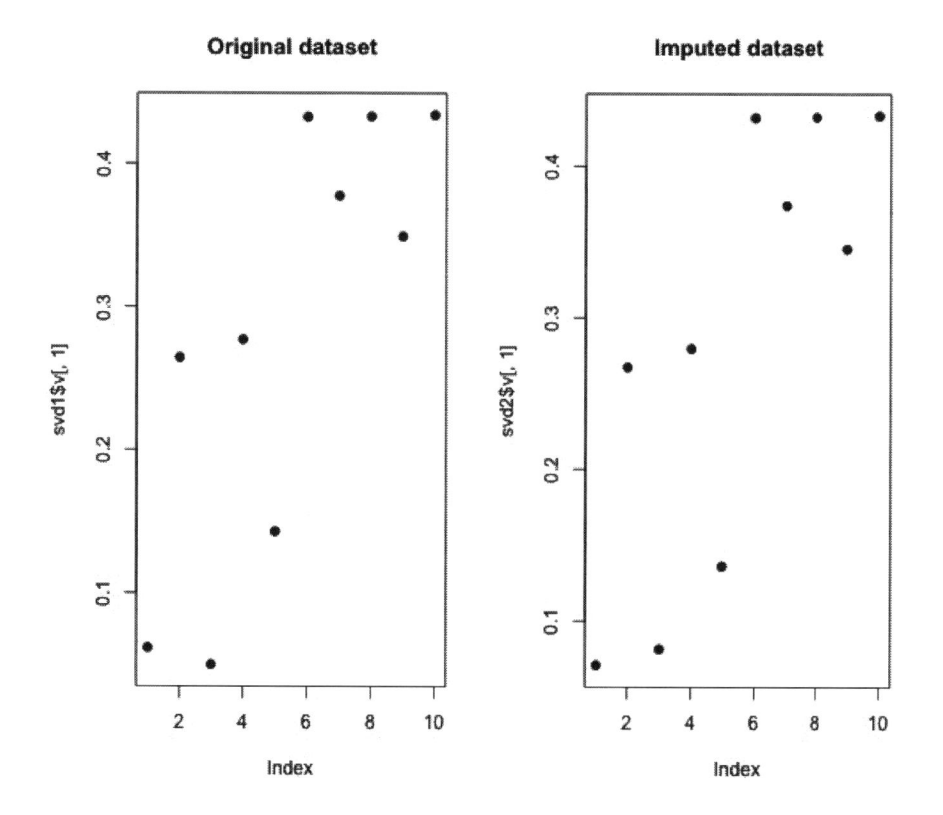

SVD on original and imputed data

We can see that the results are not identical but they are pretty close. Obviously, the missing data process was pretty simple in this case and is likely to be more complex in other situations.

14.11 Example: Face data

In this example, we use some data that make up an image of a face and show how the SVD can be used to produce varying approximations to this "dataset". Here is the original data.

```
> load("data/face.rda")
> image(t(faceData)[, nrow(faceData):1])
```

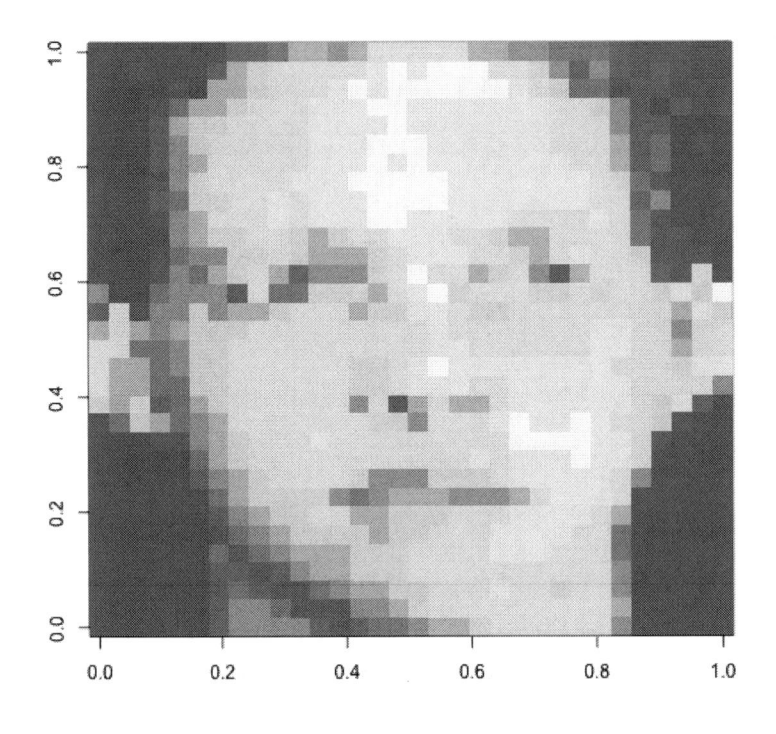

Face data

If we take the SVD and plot the squared and normalized singular values, we can see that the data can be explained by just a few singular vectors, maybe 4 or 5.

```
> svd1 <- svd(scale(faceData))
> plot(svd1$d^2/sum(svd1$d^2), pch = 19, xlab = "Singular vector", ylab = "Variance explained")
```

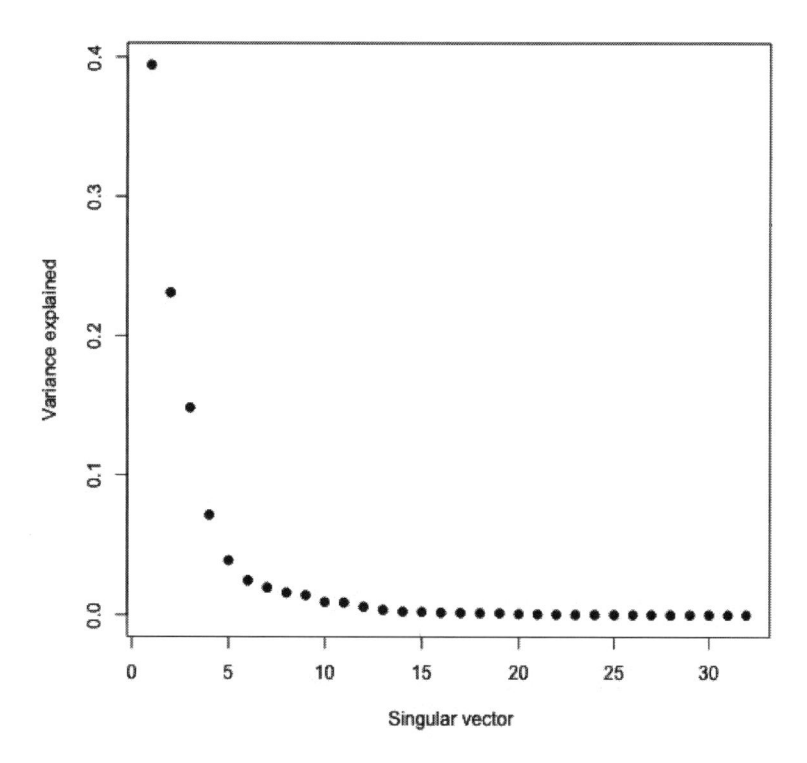

Proportion of variance explained

Now we can start constructing approximations to the data using the left and right singular vectors. Here we create one using just the first left and right singular vectors.

```
> ## Note that %*% is matrix multiplication Here svd1$d[1] is a constant
> approx1 <- svd1$u[, 1] %*% t(svd1$v[, 1]) * svd1$d[1]
```

We can also create ones using 5 and 10 singular vectors, which presumably would be better approximations.

```
> # In these examples we need to make the diagonal matrix out of d
> approx5 <- svd1$u[, 1:5] %*% diag(svd1$d[1:5]) %*% t(svd1$v[, 1:5])
> approx10 <- svd1$u[, 1:10] %*% diag(svd1$d[1:10]) %*% t(svd1$v[, 1:10])
```

Now we can plot each one of these approximations along with the original data.

```
> par(mfrow = c(1, 4))
> image(t(approx1)[, nrow(approx1):1], main = "1 vector")
> image(t(approx5)[, nrow(approx5):1], main = "5 vectors")
> image(t(approx10)[, nrow(approx10):1], main = "10 vectors")
> image(t(faceData)[, nrow(faceData):1], main = "Original data")
```

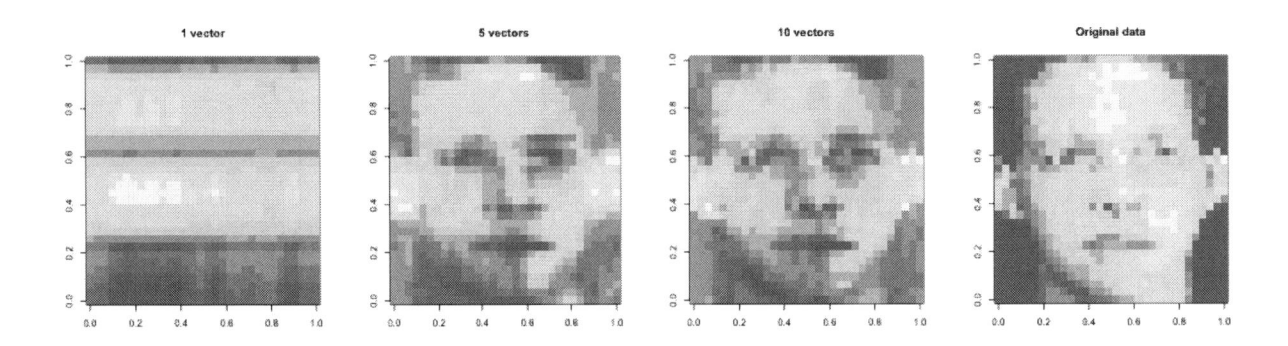

plot of chunk unnamed-chunk-26

Here, the approximation using 1 singular vector is pretty poor, but using 5 gets us pretty close to the truth. Using 10 vectors doesn't seem to add much to the features, maybe just a few highlights. So 5 singular vectors is a reasonable approximation in this case.

14.12 Notes and further resources

- For PCA/SVD, the scale/units of the data matters
- PC's/SV's may mix real patterns, as we saw in the example with two overlayed patterns
- SVD can be computationally intensive for very large matrices
- Advanced data analysis from an elementary point of view[5]
- Elements of statistical learning[6]
- Alternatives and variations
    - Factor analysis[7]
    - Independent components analysis[8]
    - Latent semantic analysis[9]

---
[5] http://www.stat.cmu.edu/~cshalizi/ADAfaEPoV/ADAfaEPoV.pdf
[6] http://www-stat.stanford.edu/~tibs/ElemStatLearn/
[7] http://en.wikipedia.org/wiki/Factor_analysis
[8] http://en.wikipedia.org/wiki/Independent_component_analysis
[9] http://en.wikipedia.org/wiki/Latent_semantic_analysis

15. The ggplot2 Plotting System: Part 1

The `ggplot2` package in R is an implementation of *The Grammar of Graphics* as described by Leland Wilkinson in his book. The package was originally written by Hadley Wickham while he was a graduate student at Iowa State University (he still actively maintains the packgae). The package implements what might be considered a third graphics system for R (along with `base` graphics and `lattice`). The package is available from CRAN[1] via `install.packages()`; the latest version of the source can be found on the package's GitHub Repository[2]. Documentation of the package can be found at http://docs.ggplot2.org/current/[3]

The grammar of graphics represents an abstraction of graphics ideas and objects. You can think of this as developing the verbs, nouns, and adjectives for data graphics. Developing such a grammar allows for a "theory" of graphics on which to build new graphics and graphics objects. To quote from Hadley Wickham's book on `ggplot2`, we want to "shorten the distance from mind to page". In summary,

> "...the grammar tells us that a statistical graphic is a **mapping** from data to **aesthetic** attributes (colour, shape, size) of **geometric** objects (points, lines, bars). The plot may also contain statistical transformations of the data and is drawn on a specific coordinate system" – from *ggplot2* book

You might ask yourself "Why do we need a grammar of graphics?" Well, for much the same reasons that having a grammar is useful for spoken languages. The grammer allows for a more compact summary of the base components of a language, and it allows us to extend the language and to handle situations that we have not before seen.

If you think about making a plot with the base graphics system, the plot is constructed by calling a series of functions that either create or annotate a plot. There's no convenient agreed-upon way to describe the plot, except to just recite the series of R functions that were called to create the thing in the first place. In a previous chapter, we described the base plotting system as a kind of "artist's palette" model, where you start with blank "canvas" and build up from there.

For example, consider the following plot made using base graphics.

---
[1] http://cran.r-project.org/package=ggplot2
[2] https://github.com/hadley/ggplot2
[3]

```
with(airquality, {
        plot(Temp, Ozone)
        lines(loess.smooth(Temp, Ozone))
})
```

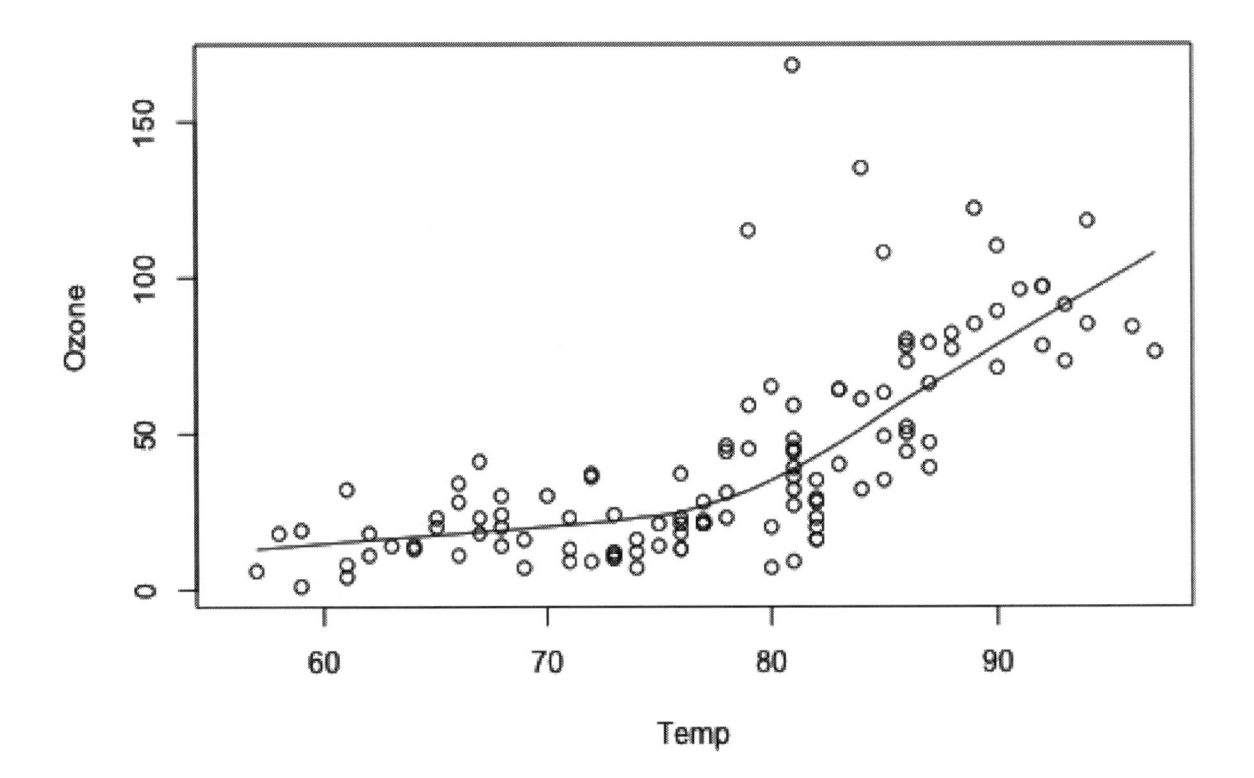

Scatterplot of Temperature and Ozone in New York (base graphics)

How would one describe the creation of this plot? Well, we could say that we called the `plot()` function and then added a loess smoother by calling the `lines()` function on the output of `loess.smooth()`.

The base plotting system is convenient and it often mirrors how we think of building plots and analyzing data. But a key drawback is that you can't go back once plot has started (e.g. to adjust margins), so there is in fact a need to plan in advance. Furthermore, it is difficult to "translate" a plot to others because there's no formal graphical language; each plot is just a series of R commands.

Here's the same plot made using `ggplot2`.

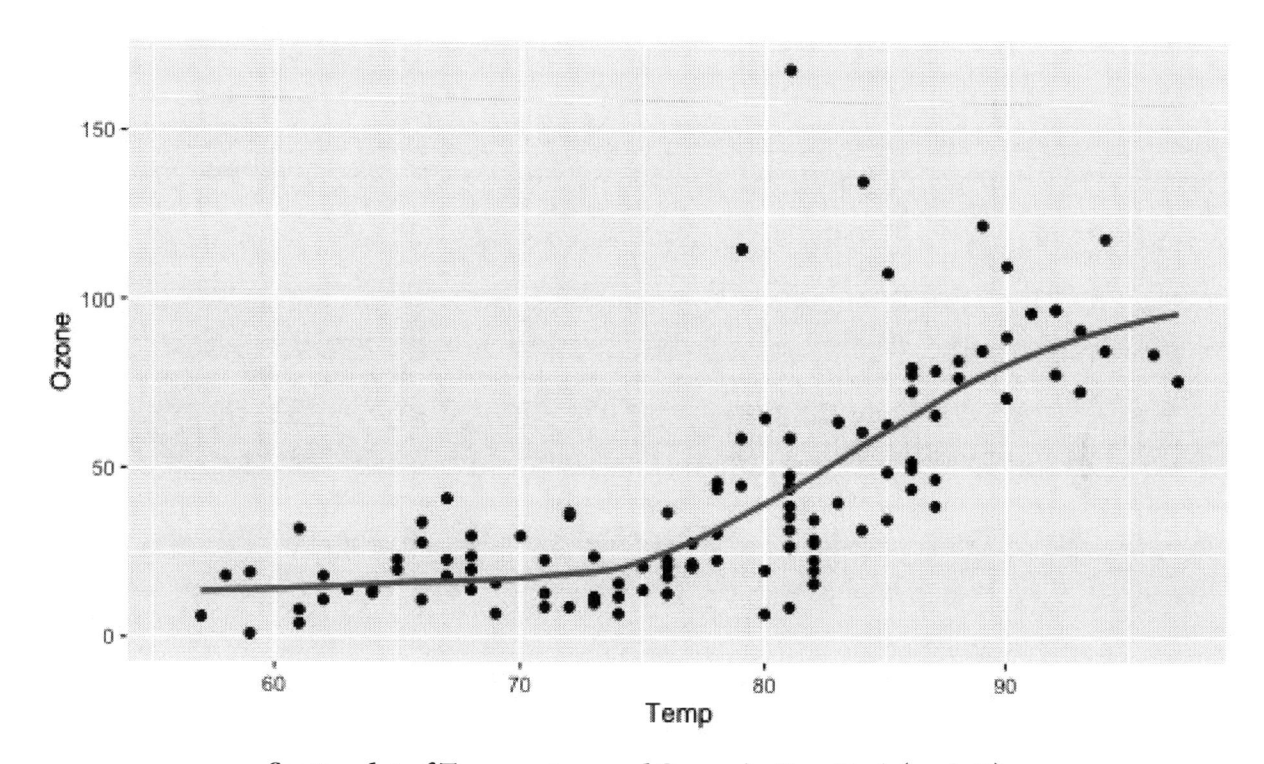

```
library(ggplot2)
ggplot(airquality, aes(Temp, Ozone)) +
        geom_point() +
        geom_smooth(method = "loess", se = FALSE)
```

Scatterplot of Temperature and Ozone in New York (ggplot2)

Note that the output is roughly equivalent, and the amount of code is similar, but ggplot2 allows for a more elegant way of expressing the components of the plot. In this case, the plot is a *dataset* (airquality) with *aesthetic mappings* derived from the Temp and Ozone variables, a set of *points*, and a *smoother*. In a sense, the ggplot2 system takes many of the cues from the base plotting system and formalizes them a bit.

The ggplot2 system also takes some cues from lattice. With the lattice system, plots are created with a single function call (xyplot, bwplot, etc.). Things like margins and spacing are set automatically because the entire plot is specified at once. The lattice system is most useful for conditioning types of plots and is good for putting many many plots on a screen. That said, it is sometimes awkward to specify an entire plot in a single function call because many different options have to be specified at once. Furthermore, annotation in plots is not intuitive and the use of panel functions and subscripts is difficult to wield and requires intense preparation.

The ggplot2 system essentially takes the good parts of both the base graphics and lattice graphics system. It automatically handles things like margins and spacing, and also has the concept of "themes" which provide a default set of plotting symbols and colors. While ggplot2 bears a superficial similarity to lattice, ggplot2 is generally easier and more intuitive to use. The default thems makes many choices for you, but you can customize the presentation if you want.

15.1 The Basics: `qplot()`

The `qplot()` function in ggplot2 is meant to get you going *quickly*. It works much like the `plot()` function in base graphics system. It looks for variables to plot within a data frame, similar to lattice, or in the parent environment. In general, it's good to get used to putting your data in a data frame and then passing it to `qplot()`.

Plots are made up of *aesthetics* (size, shape, color) and *geoms* (points, lines). Factors play an important role for indicating subsets of the data (if they are to have different properties) so they should be **labeled** properly. The `qplot()` hides much of what goes on underneath, which is okay for most operations, `ggplot()` is the core function and is very flexible for doing things `qplot()` cannot do.

15.2 Before You Start: Label Your Data

One thing that is always true, but is particularly useful when using ggplot2, is that you should always use informative and descriptive labels on your data. More generally, your data should have appropriate *metadata* so that you can quickly look at a dataset and know

- what the variables are
- what the values of each variable mean

This means that each column of a data frame should have a meaningful (but concise) variable name that accurately reflects the data stored in that column. Also, non-numeric or categorical variables should be coded as factor variables and have meaningful labels for each level of the factor. For example, it's common to code a binary variable as a "0" or a "1", but the problem is that from quickly looking at the data, it's impossible to know whether which level of that variable is represented by a "0" or a "1". Much better to simply label each observation as what they are. If a variable represents temperature categories, it might be better to use "cold", "mild", and "hot" rather than "1", "2", and "3".

While it's sometimes a pain to make sure all of your data are properly labelled, this investment in time can pay dividends down the road when you're trying to figure out what you were plotting. In other words, including the proper metadata can make your exploratory plots essentially self-documenting.

15.3 ggplot2 "Hello, world!"

This example dataset comes with the `ggplot2` package and contains data on the fuel economy of 38 popular models of car from 1999 to 2008.

```
library(ggplot2)
str(mpg)
```

```
Classes 'tbl_df', 'tbl' and 'data.frame':        234 obs. of  11 variables:
 $ manufacturer: chr  "audi" "audi" "audi" "audi" ...
 $ model       : chr  "a4" "a4" "a4" "a4" ...
 $ displ       : num  1.8 1.8 2 2 2.8 2.8 3.1 1.8 1.8 2 ...
 $ year        : int  1999 1999 2008 2008 1999 1999 2008 1999 1999 2008 ...
 $ cyl         : int  4 4 4 4 6 6 6 4 4 4 ...
 $ trans       : chr  "auto(l5)" "manual(m5)" "manual(m6)" "auto(av)" ...
 $ drv         : chr  "f" "f" "f" "f" ...
 $ cty         : int  18 21 20 21 16 18 18 18 16 20 ...
 $ hwy         : int  29 29 31 30 26 26 27 26 25 28 ...
 $ fl          : chr  "p" "p" "p" "p" ...
 $ class       : chr  "compact" "compact" "compact" "compact" ...
```

You can see from the `str()` output that all of the factor variables are appropriately coded with meaningful labels. This will come in handy when `qplot()` has to label different aspects of a plot. Also note that all of the columns/variables have meaningful (if sometimes abbreviated) names, rather than names like "X1", and "X2", etc.

We can make a quick scatterplot of the engine displacement (`displ`) and the highway miles per gallon (`hwy`).

```
qplot(displ, hwy, data = mpg)
```

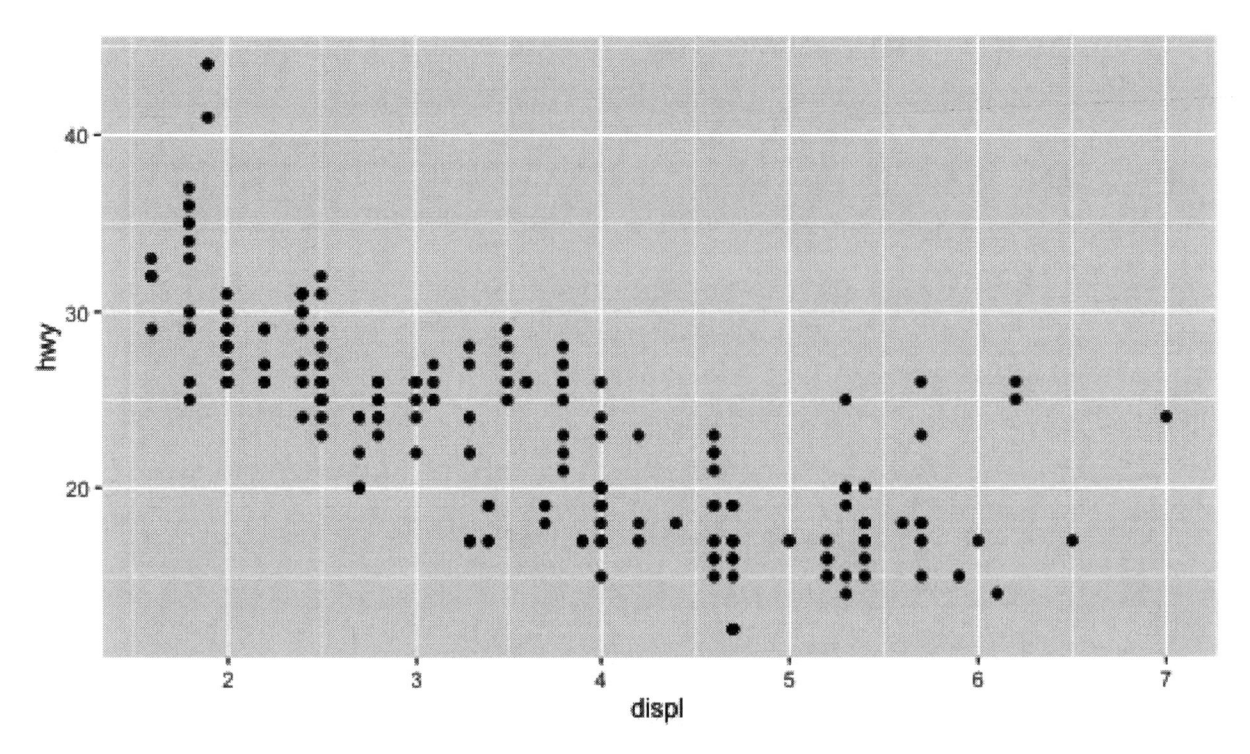

Plot of engine displacement and highway mileage

Note that in the call to qplot() you must specify the data argument so that qplot() knows where to look up the variables.

15.4 Modifying aesthetics

We can introduce a third variable into the plot by modifying the color of the points based on the value of that third variable. Color is an aesthetic and the color of each point can be mapped to a variable. Note that the x-coordinates and y-coordinates are aesthetics too, and they got mapped to the displ and hwy variables, respectively. In this case we will map the color to the drv variable which indicates whether a car is front wheel drive, rear wheel drive, or 4-wheel drive.

```
qplot(displ, hwy, data = mpg, color = drv)
```

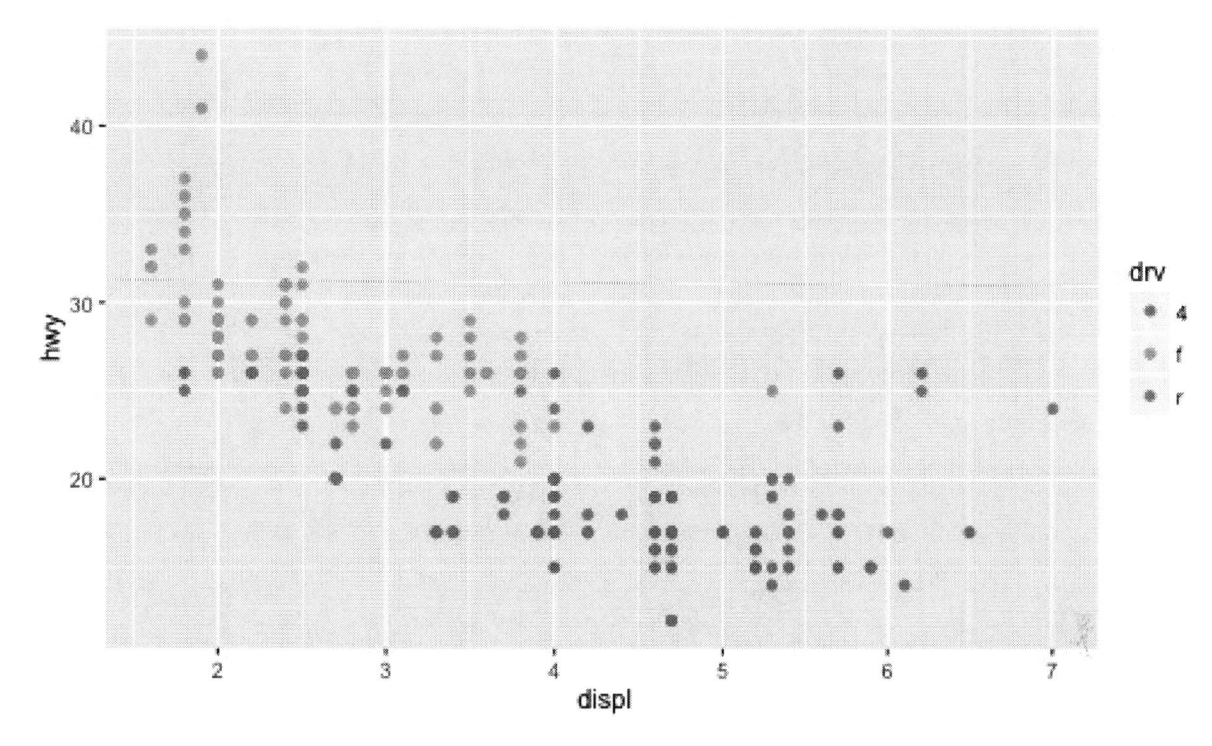

Engine displacement and highway mileage by drive class

Now we can see that the front wheel drive cars tend to have lower displacement relative to the 4-wheel or rear wheel drive cars. Also, it's clear that the 4-wheel drive cars have the lowest highway gas mileage.

15.5 Adding a geom

Sometimes it's nice to add a smoother to a scatterplot ot highlight any trends. Trends can be difficult to see if the data are very noisy or there are many data points obscuring the view. A smooth is a "geom" that you can add along with your data points.

```
qplot(displ, hwy, data = mpg, geom = c("point", "smooth"))
```

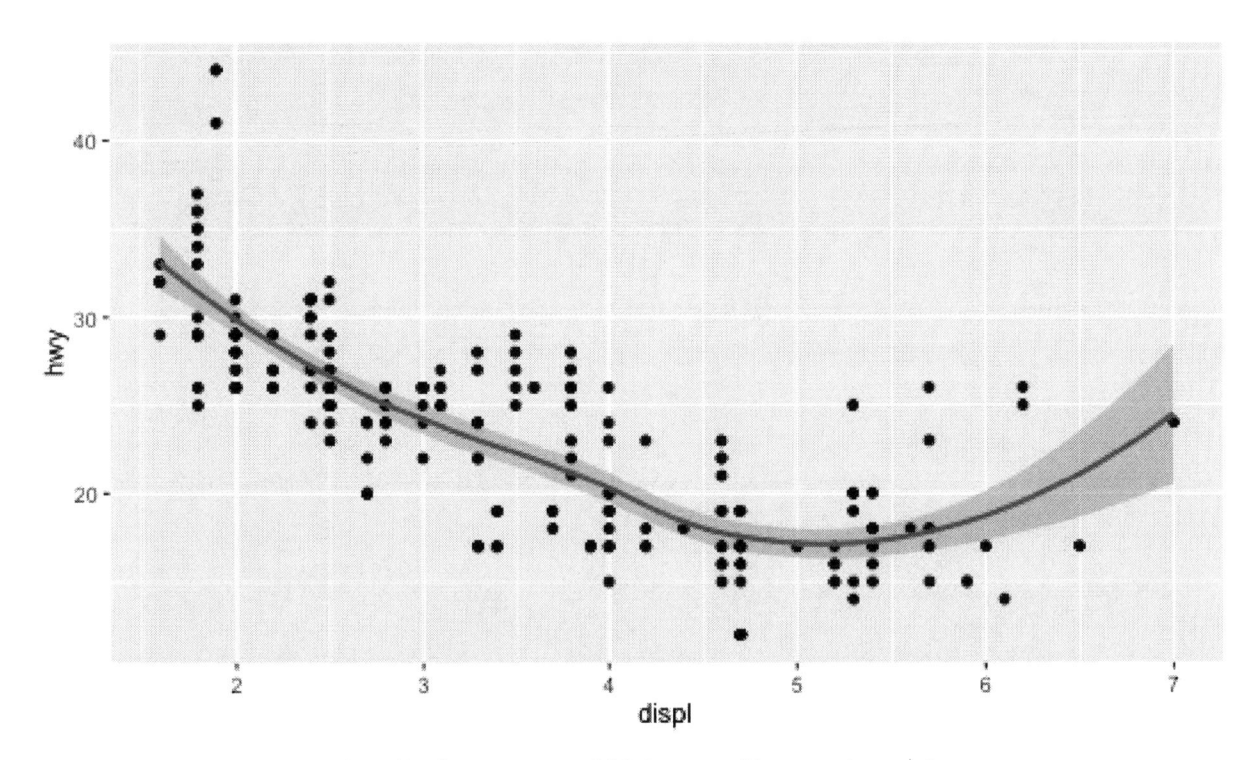

Engine displacement and highway mileage w/smoother

Note that previously, we didn't have to specify `geom = "point"` because that was done automatically. But if you want the smoother overlayed with the points, then you need to specify both explicitly.

Here it seems that engine displacement and highway mileage have a nonlinear U-shaped relationship, but from the previous plot we know that this is largely due to confounding by the drive class of the car.

15.6 Histograms

The `qplot()` function can be used to be used to plot 1-dimensional data too. By specifying a single variable, `qplot()` will by default make a histogram. Here we make a histogram if the highway mileage data and stratify on the drive class. So technically this is three histograms overlayed on top of each other.

```
qplot(hwy, data = mpg, fill = drv, binwidth = 2)
```

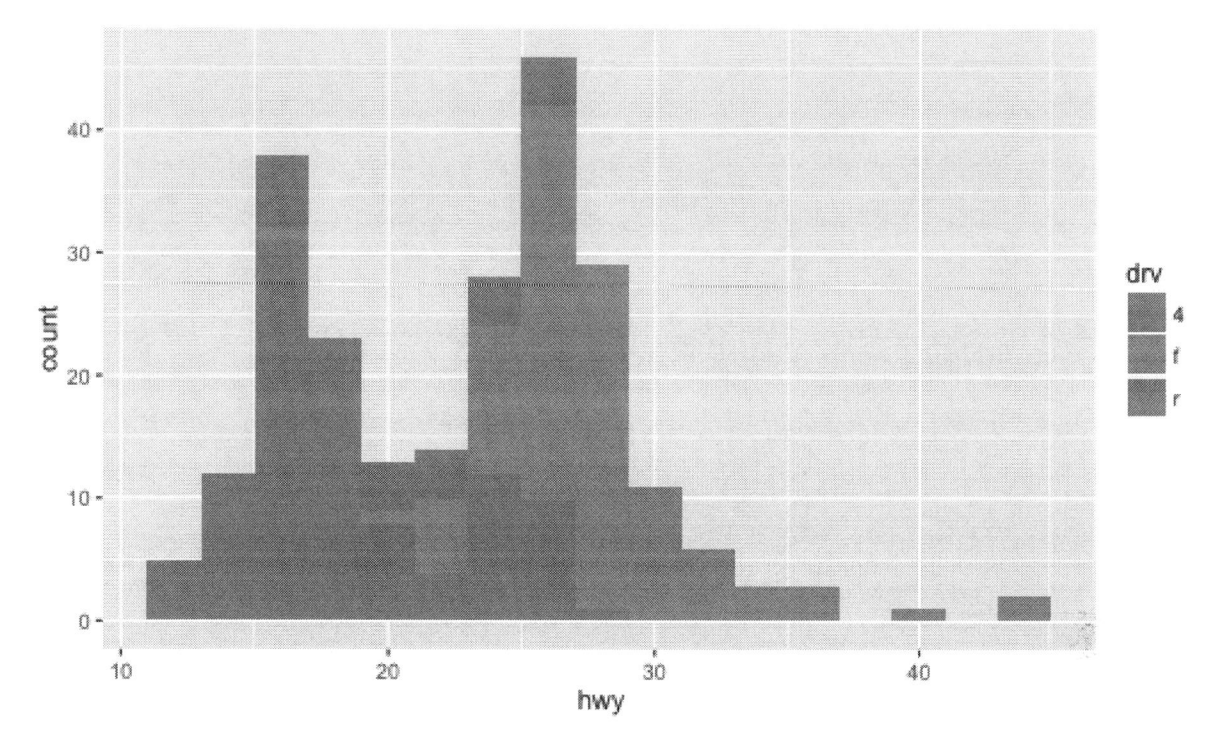

Histogram of highway mileage by drive class

Having the different colors for each drive class is nice, but the three histograms can be a bit difficult to separate out. Side-by-side boxplots is one solution to this problem.

```
qplot(drv, hwy, data = mpg, geom = "boxplot")
```

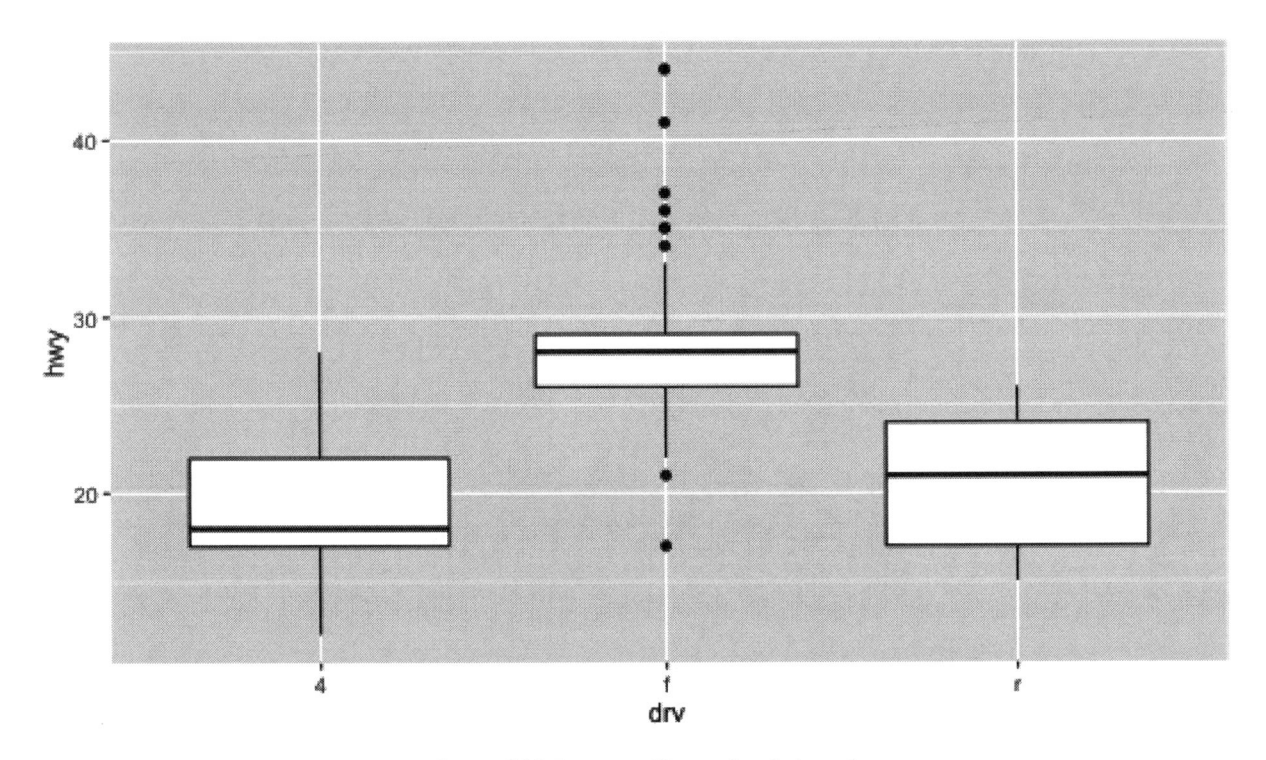

Boxplots of highway mileage by drive class

Another solution is to plot the histograms in separate panels using facets.

15.7 Facets

Facets are a way to create multiple panels of plots based on the levels of categorical variable. Here, we want to see a histogram of the highway mileages and the categorical variable is the drive class variable. We can do that using the `facets` argument to `qplot()`.

The `facets` argument expects a formula type of input, with a ~ separating the left hand side variable and the right hand side variable. The left hand side variable indicates how the rows of the panels should be divided and the right hand side variable indicates how the columns of the panels should be divided. Here, we just want three rows of histograms (and just one column), one for each drive class, so we specify `drv` on the left hand side and . on the right hand side indicating that there's no variable there (it's empty).

```
qplot(hwy, data = mpg, facets = drv ~ ., binwidth = 2)
```

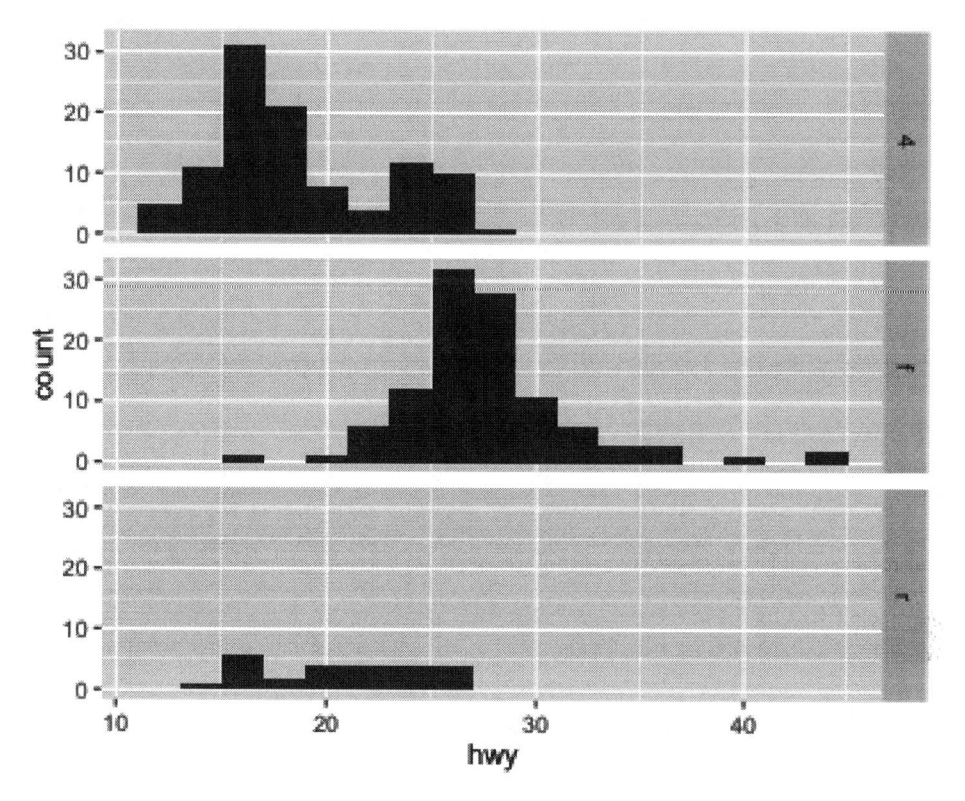

Histogram of highway mileage by drive class

We could also look at more data using facets, so instead of histograms we could look at scatterplots of engine displacement and highway mileage by drive class. Here we put the `drv` variable on the right hand side to indicate that we want a column for each drive class (as opposed to splitting by rows like we did above).

```
qplot(displ, hwy, data = mpg, facets = . ~ drv)
```

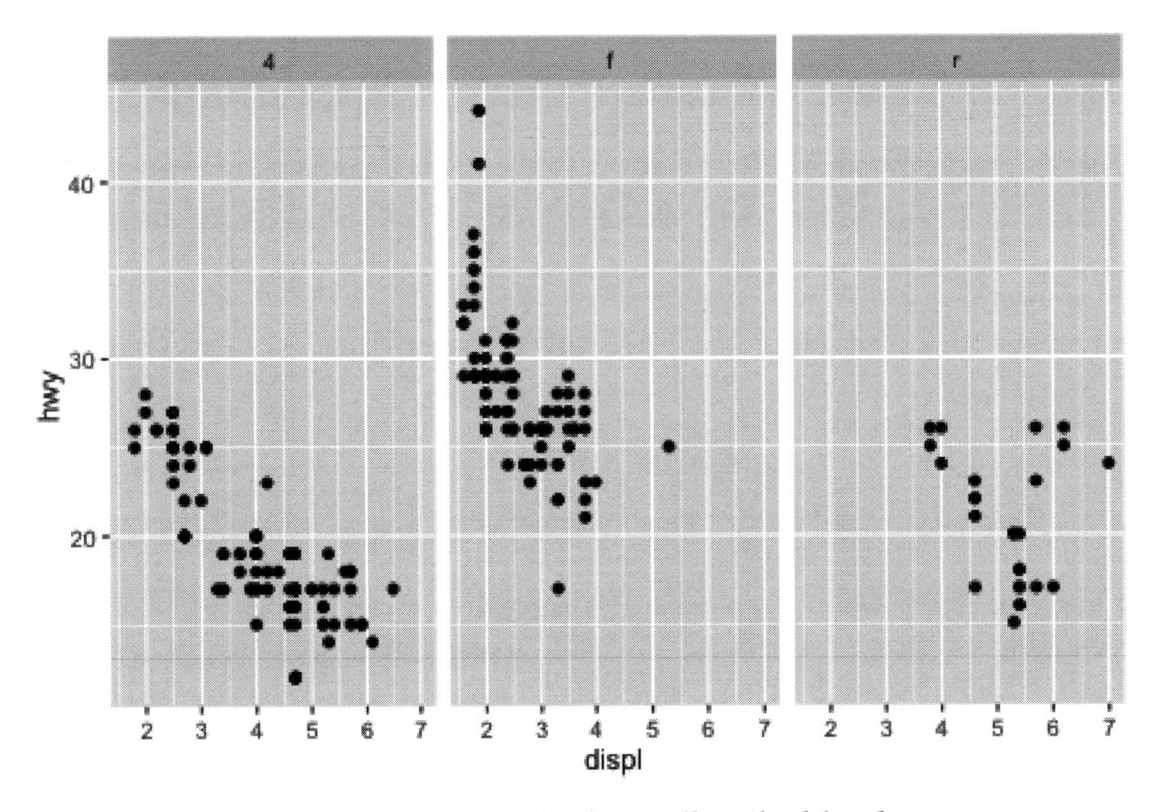

Engine displacement and highway mileage by drive class

What if you wanted to add a smoother to each one of those panels? Simple, you literally just add the smoother as another geom.

```
qplot(displ, hwy, data = mpg, facets = . ~ drv) + geom_smooth()
```

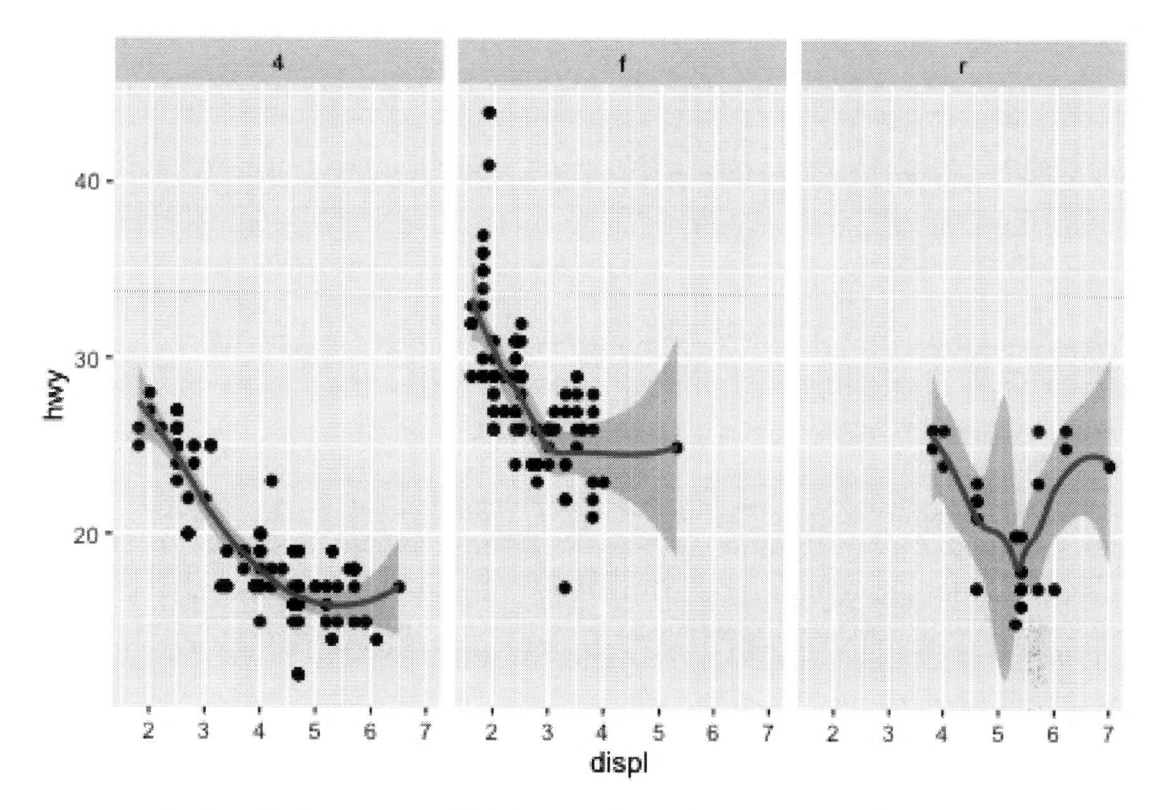

Engine displacement and highway mileage by drive class w/smoother

You could have also used the "geom" argument to `qplot()`, as in

```
qplot(displ, hwy, data = mpg, facets = . ~ drv, geom = c("point", "smooth"))
```

There's more than one way to do it.

15.8 Case Study: MAACS Cohort

This case study will use data based on the Mouse Allergen and Asthma Cohort Study (MAACS). This study was aimed at characterizing the indoor (home) environment and its relationship with asthma morbidity amongst children aged 5–17 living in Baltimore, MD. The children all had persistent asthma, defined as having had an exacerbation in the past year. A representative publication of results from this study can be found in this paper by Lu, et al.[4]

NOTE: Because the individual-level data for this study are protected by various U.S. privacy laws, we cannot make those data available. For the purposes of this chapter, we have simulated data that share many of the same features of the original data, but do not contain any of the actual measurements or values contained in the original dataset.

---

[4]http://goo.gl/WqE9j8

```
'data.frame':      750 obs. of  4 variables:
 $ id   : int  1 2 3 4 5 6 7 8 9 10 ...
 $ mopos: Factor w/ 2 levels "no","yes": 2 1 2 1 1 1 2 2 2 2 ...
 $ pm25 : num  6.01 25.17 21.77 13.44 49.39 ...
 $ eno  : num  28.8 17.7 43.6 288.3 7.6 ...
```

The key variables are:

- `mopos`: an indicator of whether the subject is allergic to mouse allergen (yes/no)
- `pm25`: average level of PM2.5 over the course of 7 days (micrograms per cubic meter)
- `eno`: exhaled nitric oxide

The outcome of interest for this analysis will be exhaled nitric oxide (eNO), which is a measure of pulmonary inflamation. We can get a sense of how eNO is distributed in this population by making a quick histogram of the variable. Here, we take the log of eNO because some right-skew in the data.

```
qplot(log(eno), data = maacs)
```

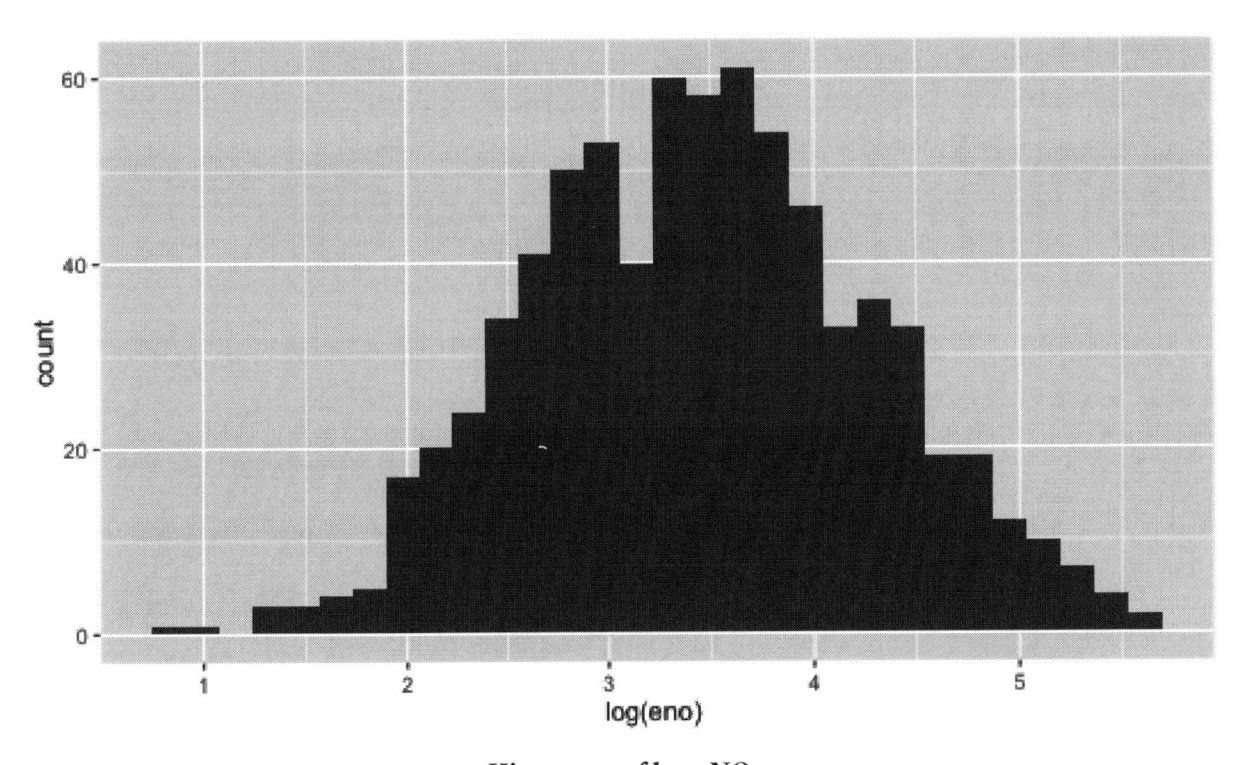

Histogram of log eNO

A quick glance suggests that the histogram is a bit "fat", suggesting that there might be multiple groups of people being lumped together. We can stratify the histogram by whether they are allergic to mouse.

```
qplot(log(eno), data = maacs, fill = mopos)
```

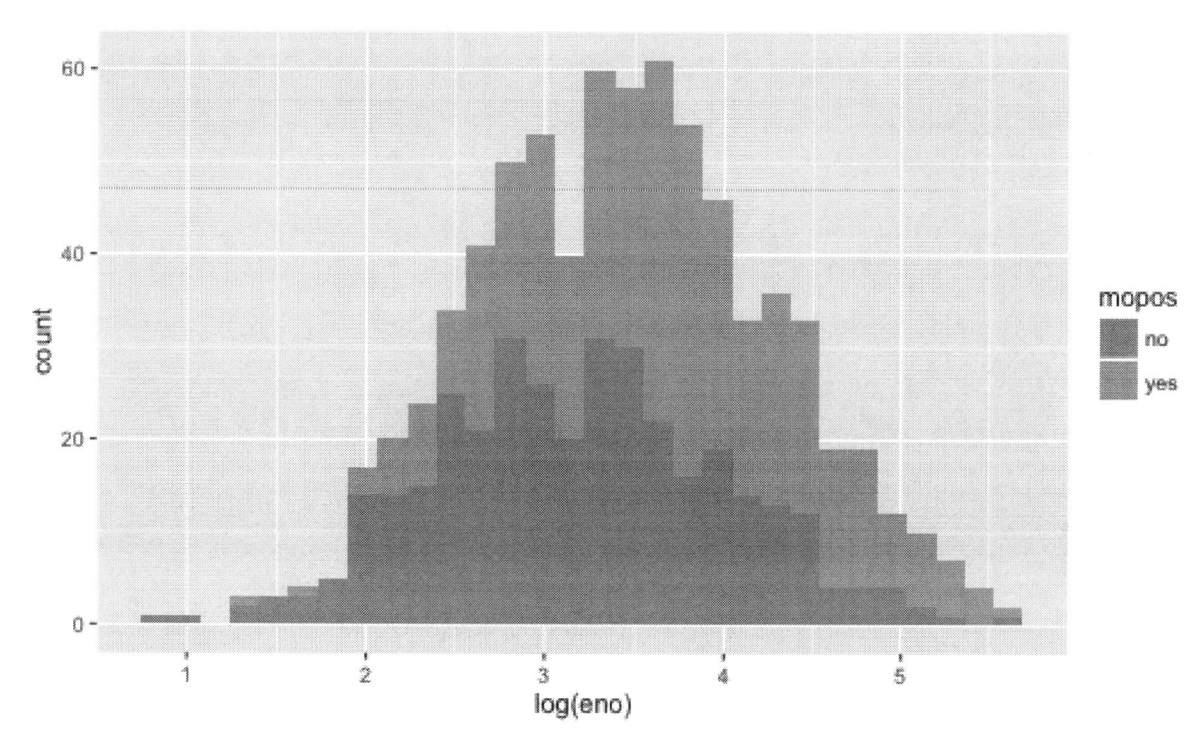

Histogram of log eNO by mouse allergic status

We can see from this plot that the non-allergic subjects are shifted slightly to the left, indicating a lower eNO and less pulmonary inflammation. That said, there is significant overlap between the two groups.

An alternative to histograms is a density smoother, which sometimes can be easier to visualize when there are multiple groups. Here is a density smooth of the entire study population.

```
qplot(log(eno), data = maacs, geom = "density")
```

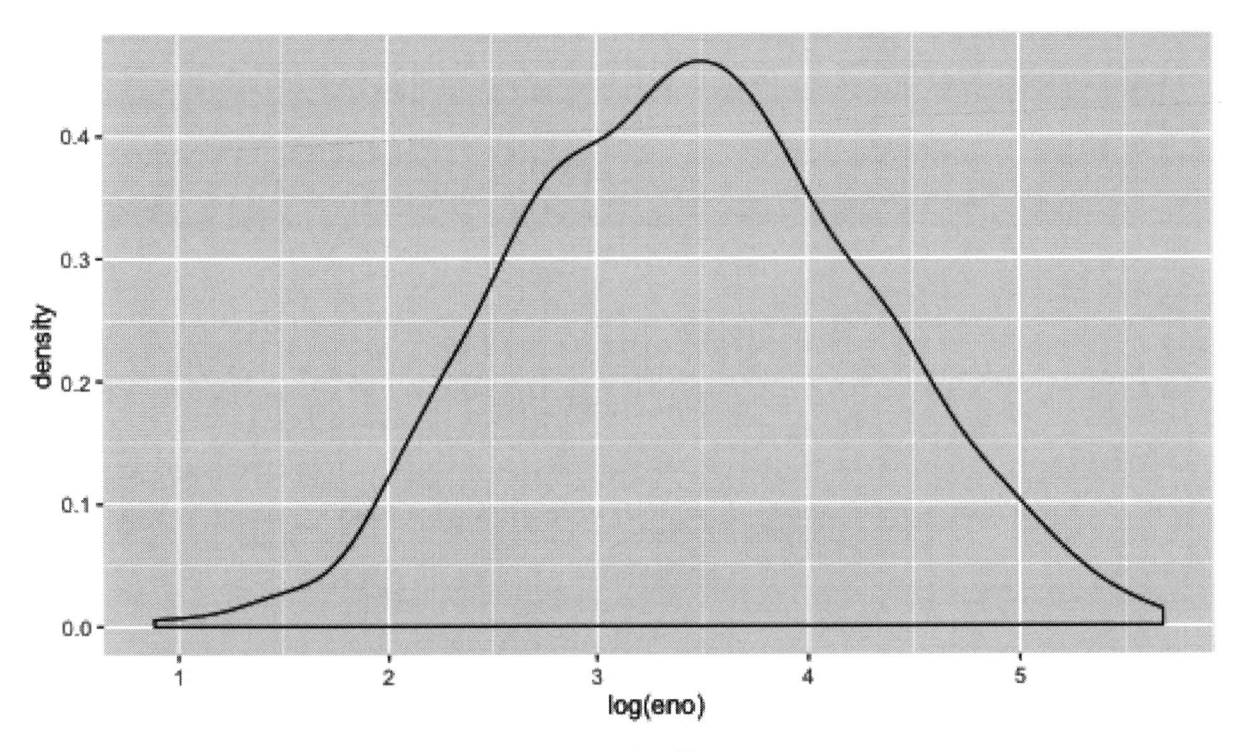

Density smooth of log eNO

And here are the densities straitified by allergic status. We can map the color aesthetic to the mopos variable.

```
qplot(log(eno), data = maacs, geom = "density", color = mopos)
```

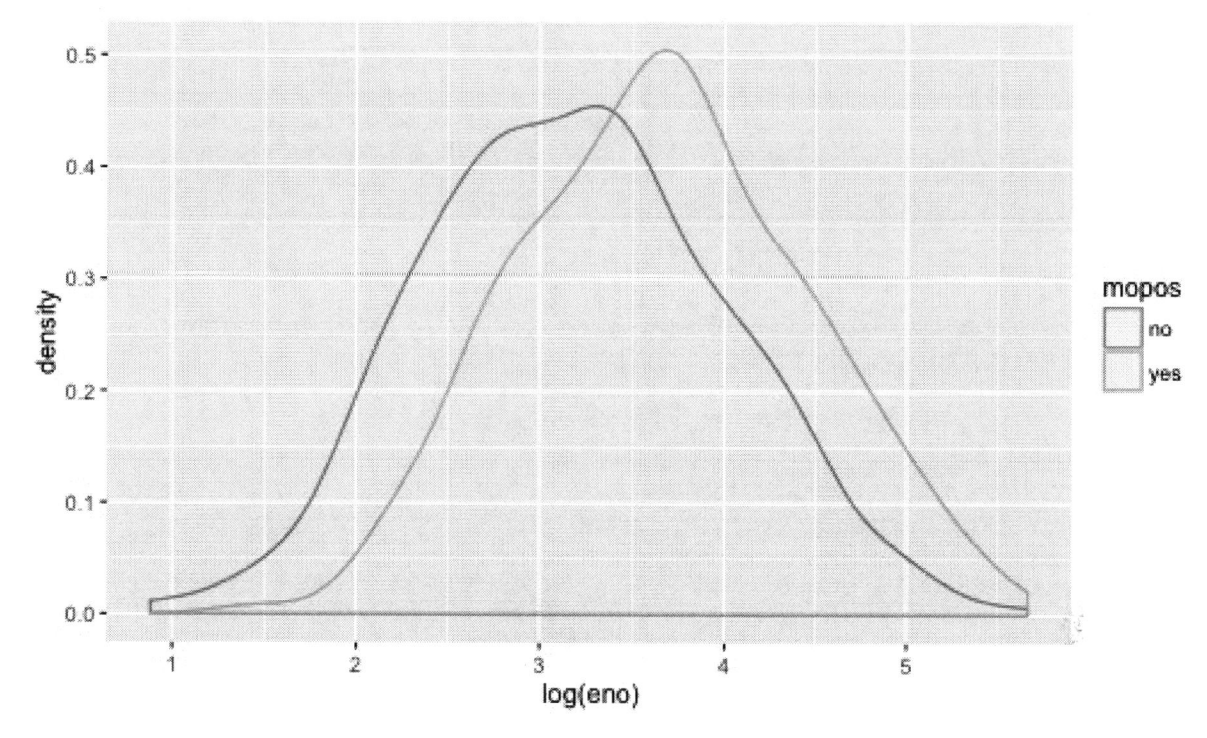

Density smooth of log eNO by mouse allergic status

These tell the same story as the stratified histograms, which sould come as no surprise.

Now we can examine the indoor environment and its relationship to eNO. Here, we use the level of indoor PM2.5 as a measure of indoor environment air quality. We can make a simple scatterplot of PM2.5 and eNO.

```
qplot(log(pm25), log(eno), data = maacs, geom = c("point", "smooth"))
```

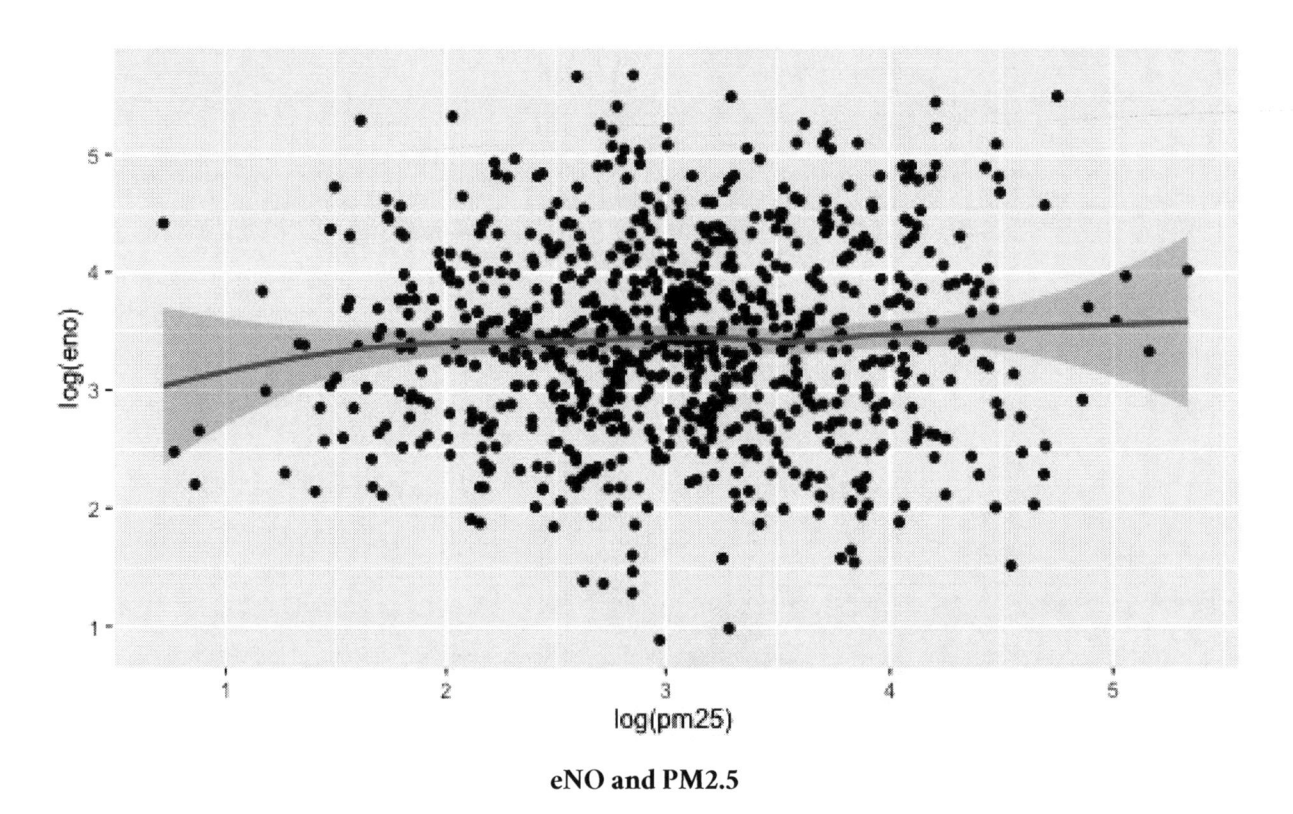

eNO and PM2.5

The relationship appears modest at best, as there is substantial noise in the data. However, one question that we might be interested in is whether allergic individuals are prehaps more sensitive to PM2.5 inhalation than non-allergic individuals. To examine that question we can stratify the data into two groups.

This first plot uses different plot symbols for the two groups and overlays them on a single canvas. We can do this by mapping the `mopos` variable to the `shape` aesthetic.

```
qplot(log(pm25), log(eno), data = maacs, shape = mopos)
```

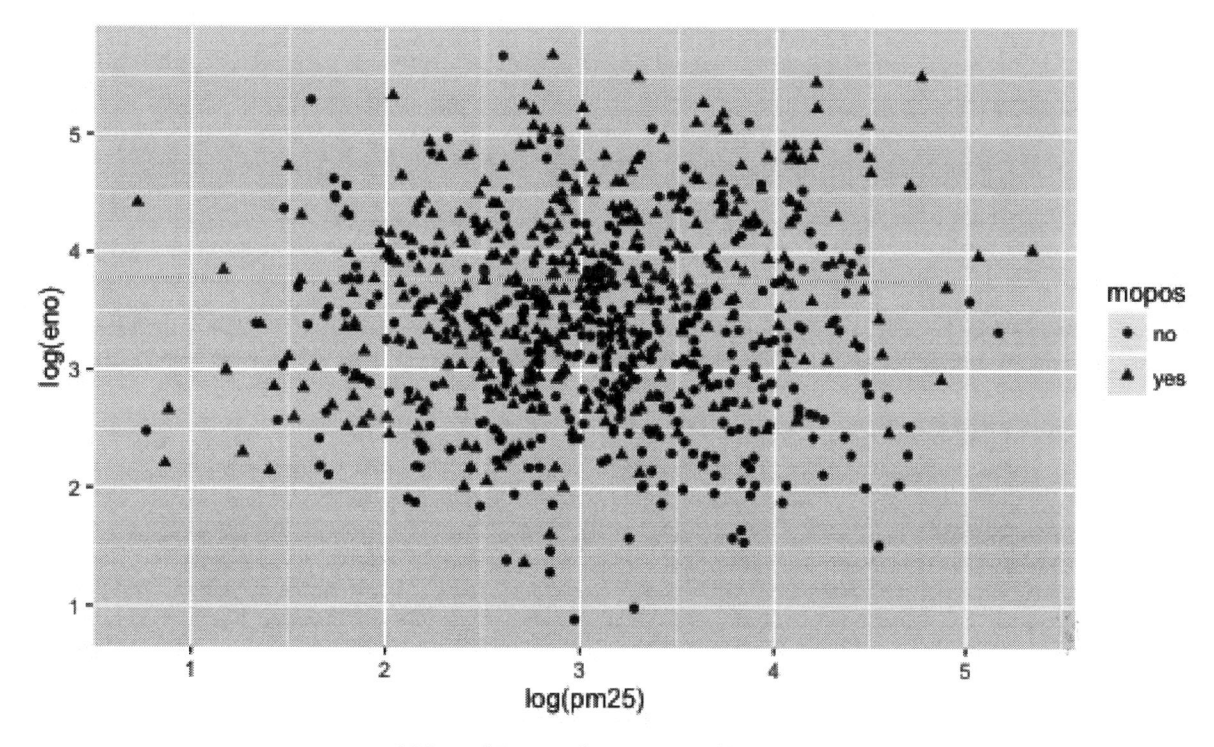

eNO and PM2.5 by mouse allergic status

Because there is substantial overlap in the data it is a bit challenging to discern the circles from the triangles. Part of the reason might be that all of the symbols are the same color (black).

We can plot each group a different color to see if that helps.

```
qplot(log(pm25), log(eno), data = maacs, color = mopos)
```

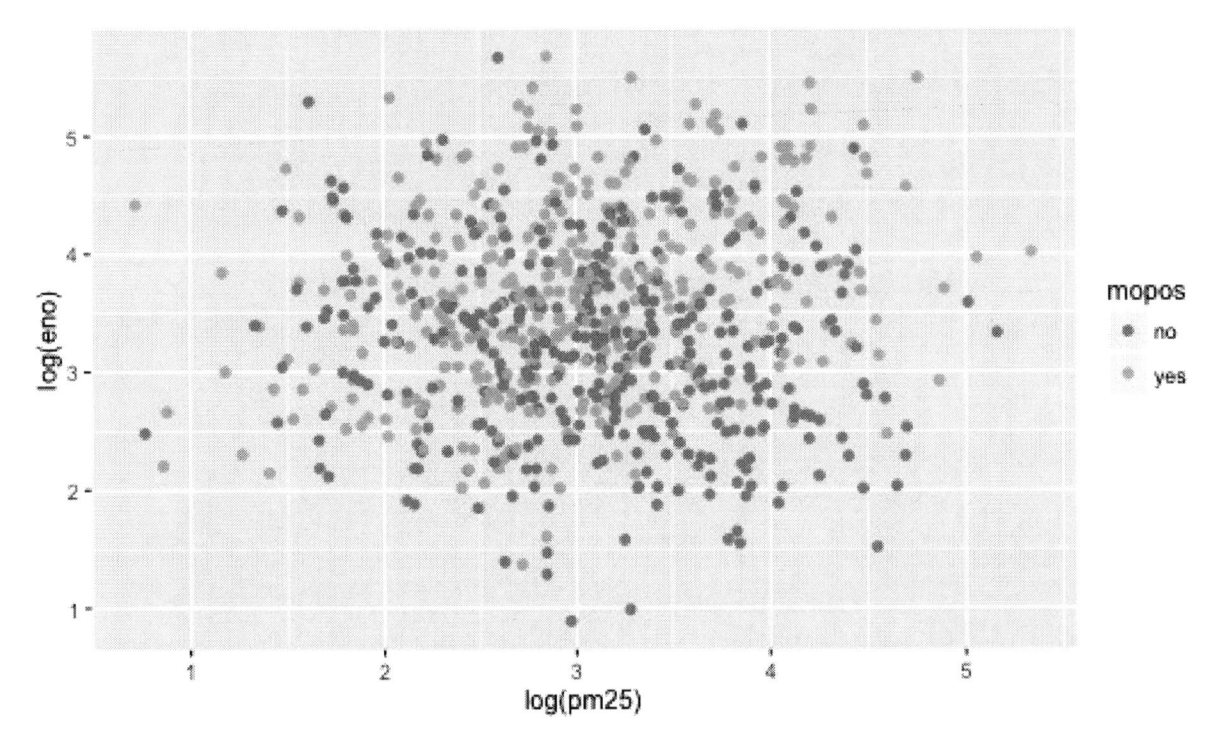

![Scatter plot of log(eno) vs log(pm25) colored by mopos (no/yes)]

eNO and PM2.5 by mouse allergic status

This is slightly better but the substantial overlap makes it difficult to discern any trends in the data. For this we need to add a smoother of some sort. Here we add a linear regression line (a type of smoother) to each group to see if there's any difference.

```
qplot(log(pm25), log(eno), data = maacs, color = mopos) + geom_smooth(method = "lm")
```

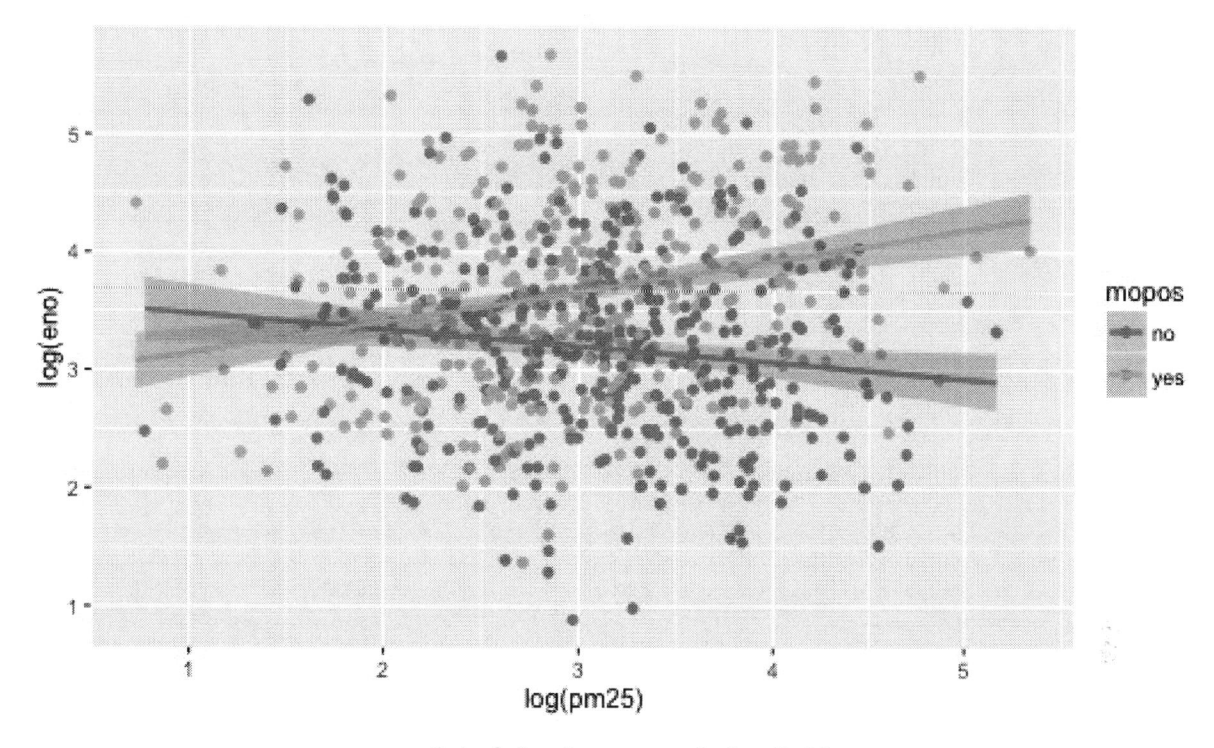

plot of chunk unnamed-chunk-21

Here we see quite clearly that the red group and the green group exhibit rather different relationships between PM2.5 and eNO. For the non-allergic individuals, there appears to be a slightly negative relationship between PM2.5 and eNO and for the allergic individuals, there is a positive relationship. This suggests a strong interaction between PM2.5 and allergic status, an hypothesis perhaps worth following up on in greater detail than this brief exploratory analysis.

Another, and perhaps more clear, way to visualize this interaction is to use separate panels for the non-allergic and allergic individuals using the `facets` argument to `qplot()`.

```
qplot(log(pm25), log(eno), data = maacs, facets = . ~ mopos) + geom_smooth(method = "lm")
```

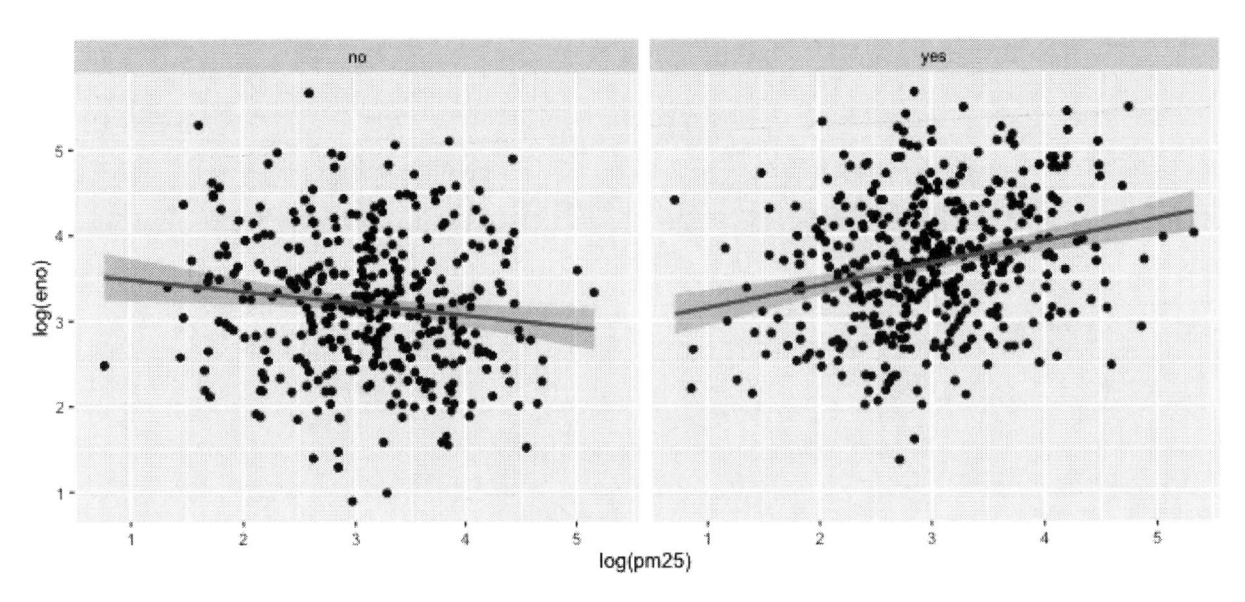

plot of chunk unnamed-chunk-22

15.9 Summary of qplot()

The `qplot()` function in `ggplot2` is the analog of `plot()` in base graphics but with many built-in features that the traditionaly `plot()` does not provide. The syntax is somewhere in between the base and lattice graphics system. The `qplot()` function is useful for quickly putting data on the page/screen, but for ultimate customization, it may make more sense to use some of the lower level functions that we discuss later in the next chapter.

16. The ggplot2 Plotting System: Part 2

In this chapter we'll get into a little more of the nitty gritty of how ggplot2 builds plots and how you can customize various aspects of any plot. In the previous chapter we used the qplot() function to quickly put points on a page. The qplot() function's syntax is very similar to that of the plot() function in base graphics so for those switching over, it makes for an easy transition. But it's worth knowing the underlying details of how ggplot2 works so that you can really exploit its power.

16.1 Basic Components of a ggplot2 Plot

A ggplot2 plot consists of a number of key components. Here are a few of the more commonly used ones.

- A *data frame*: stores all of the data that will be displayed on the plot
- *aesthetic mappings*: describe how data are mapped to color, size, shape, location
- *geoms*: geometric objects like points, lines, shapes.
- *facets*: describes how conditional/panel plots should be constructed
- *stats*: statistical transformations like binning, quantiles, smoothing.
- *scales*: what scale an aesthetic map uses (example: male = red, female = blue).
- *coordinate system*: describes the system in which the locations of the geoms will be drawn

It's essential that you properly organize your data into a data frame before you start with ggplot2. In particular, it's important that you provide all of the appropriate metadata so that your data frame is self-describing and your plots will be self-documenting.

When building plots in ggplot2 (rather than using qplot()) the "artist's palette"' model may be the closest analogy. Essentially, you start with some raw data, and then you gradually add bits and pieces to it to create a plot. Plots are built up in layers, with the typically ordering being

1. Plot the data
2. Overlay a summary
3. Add metadata and annotation

For quick exploratory plots you may not get past step 1.

16.2 Example: BMI, PM2.5, Asthma

To demonstrate the various pieces of `ggplot2` we will use a running example from the Mouse Allergen and Asthma Cohort Study (MAACS), which was described in the previous chapter. Here, the question we are interested in is

> "Are overweight individuals, as measured by body mass index (BMI), more susceptible than normal weight individuals to the harmful effects of PM2.5 on asthma symptoms?"

There is a suggestion that overweight individuals may be more susceptible to the negative effects of inhaling PM2.5. This would suggest that increases in PM2.5 exposure in the home of an overweight child would be more deleterious to his/her asthma symptoms than they would be in the home of a normal weight child. We want to see if we can see that difference in the data from MAACS.

NOTE: Because the individual-level data for this study are protected by various U.S. privacy laws, we cannot make those data available. For the purposes of this chapter, we have simulated data that share many of the same features of the original data, but do not contain any of the actual measurements or values contained in the original dataset.

We can look at the data quickly with `str()`.

```
maacs <- read.csv("data/bmi_pm25_no2_sim.csv")
str(maacs)
```

```
'data.frame':    517 obs. of  4 variables:
 $ logpm25       : num  1.248 1.122 1.93 1.368 0.775 ...
 $ logno2_new    : num  1.184 1.552 1.432 1.774 0.765 ...
 $ bmicat        : Factor w/ 2 levels "normal weight",..: 1 2 1 2 1 1 1 1 1 2 ...
 $ NocturnalSympt: int  1 0 0 2 0 0 0 0 0 3 ...
```

The outcome we will look at here, `NocturnalSymp`, is the number of days in the past 2 weeks where the child experienced asthma symptoms (e.g. coughing, wheezing) while sleeping.

16.3 Building Up in Layers

First we can create a `ggplot` object that stores the dataset and the basic aesthetics for mapping the x- and y-coordinates for the plot. Here we will eventually be plotting the log of PM2.5 and `NocturnalSymp` variable.

```
head(maacs)
```

```
    logpm25 logno2_new       bmicat NocturnalSympt
1 1.2476997  1.1837987 normal weight              1
2 1.1216476  1.5515362    overweight              0
3 1.9300429  1.4323519 normal weight              0
4 1.3679246  1.7736804    overweight              2
5 0.7753367  0.7654826 normal weight              0
6 1.4872785  1.1127378 normal weight              0
```

```
g <- ggplot(maacs, aes(logpm25, NocturnalSympt))
summary(g)
```

```
data: logpm25, logno2_new, bmicat, NocturnalSympt [517x4]
mapping:  x = logpm25, y = NocturnalSympt
faceting: facet_null()
```

```
class(g)
```

```
[1] "gg"      "ggplot"
```

You can see above that the object g contains the dataset maacs and the mappings.

Now, normally if you were to print() a ggplot object a plot would appear on the plot device, however, our object g actually doesn't contain enough information to make a plot yet.

```
g <- ggplot(maacs, aes(logpm25, NocturnalSympt))
print(g)
```

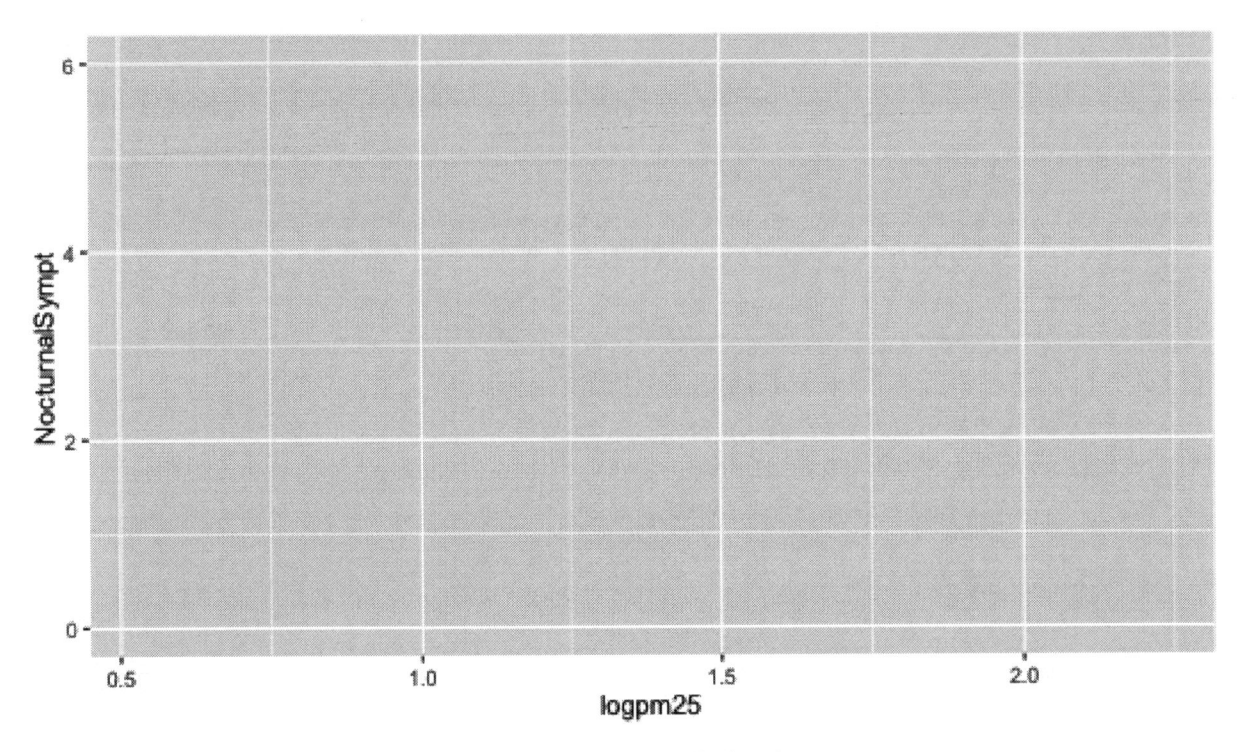

plot of chunk unnamed-chunk-25

16.4 First Plot with Point Layer

To make a scatterplot we need add at least one *geom*, such as points. Here we add the `geom_point()` function to create a traditional scatterplot.

```
g <- ggplot(maacs, aes(logpm25, NocturnalSympt))
g + geom_point()
```

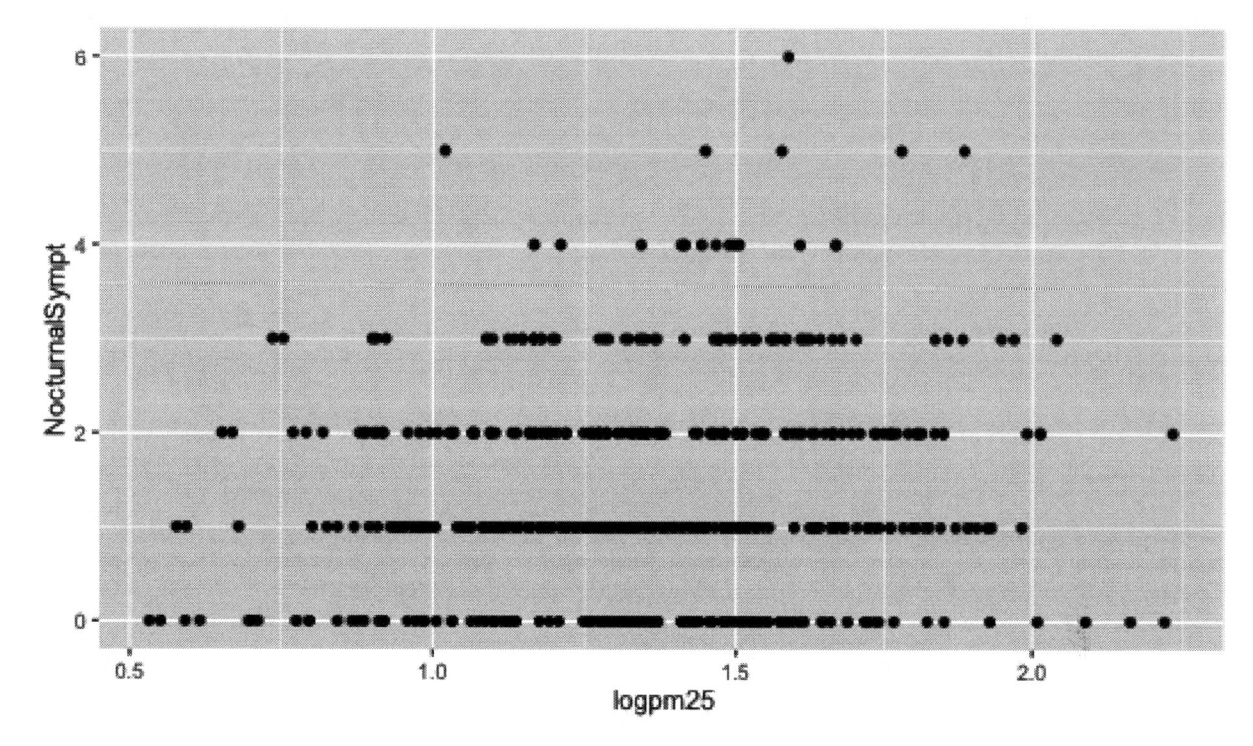

plot of chunk Scatterplot of PM2.5 and days with nocturnal symptoms

16.5 Adding More Layers: Smooth

Because the data appear rather noisy, it might be better if we added a smoother on top of the points to see if there is a trend in the data with PM2.5.

```
g + geom_point() + geom_smooth()
```

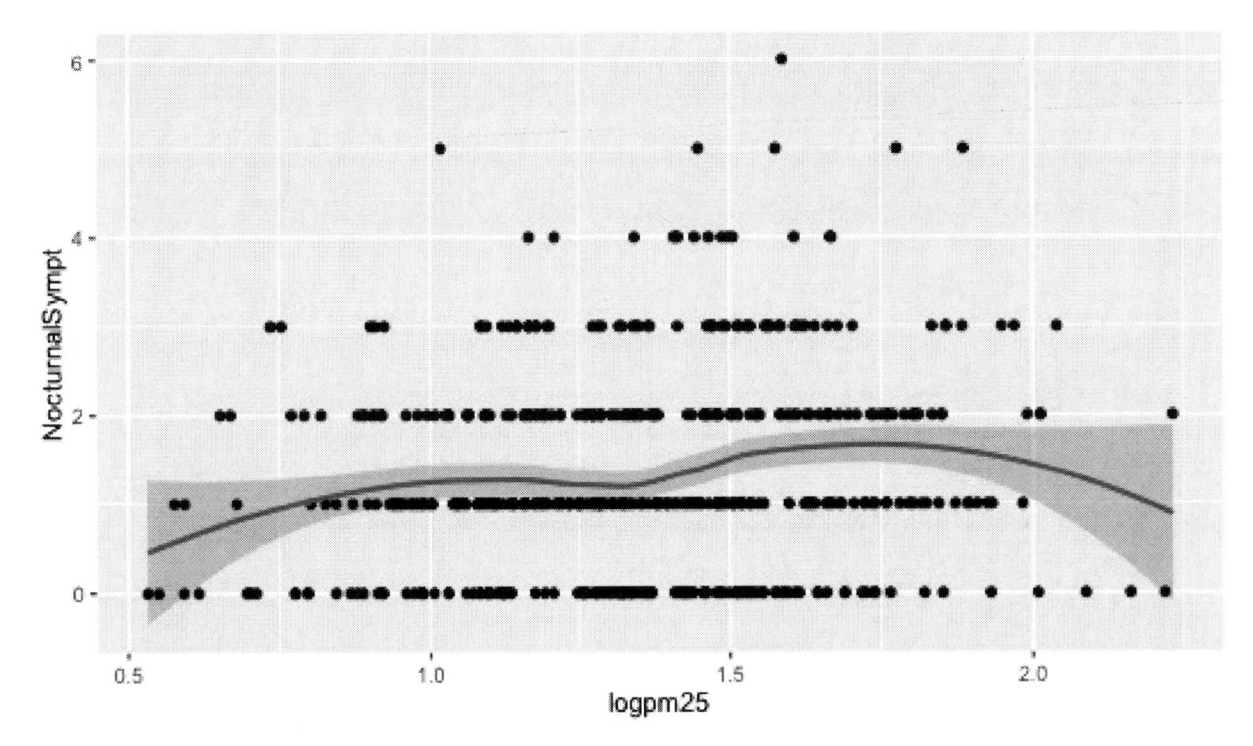

Scatterplot with smoother

The default smoother is a loess smoother, which is flexible and nonparametric but might be too flexible for our purposes. Perhaps we'd prefer a simple linear regression line to highlight any first order trends. We can do this by specifying method = "lm" to geom_-smooth().

```
g + geom_point() + geom_smooth(method = "lm")
```

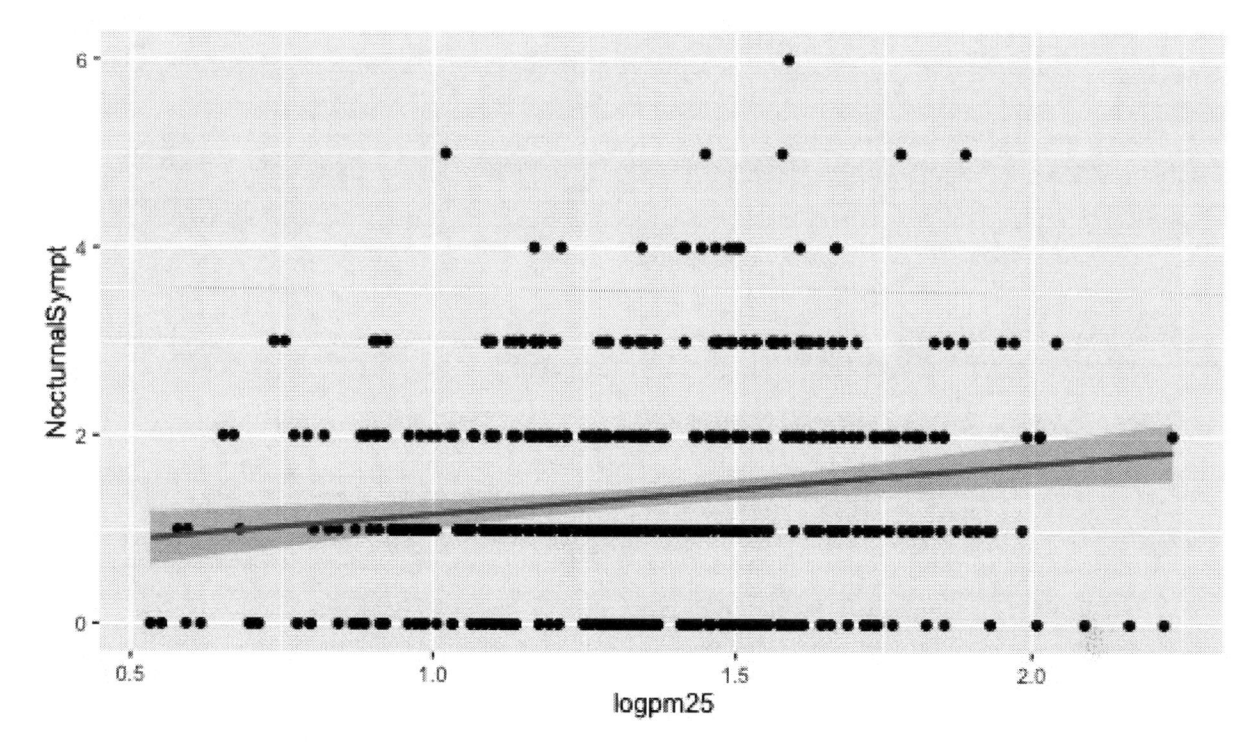

Scatterplot with linear regression line

Here, we can see there appears to be a slight increasing trend, suggesting that higher levels of PM2.5 are assocuated with increased days with nocturnal symptoms.

16.6 Adding More Layers: Facets

Because our primary question involves comparing overweight individuals to normal weight individuals, we can stratify the scatterplot of PM2.5 and nocturnal symptoms by the BMI category (bmicat) variable, which indicates whether an individual is overweight or now. To visualize this we can add a facet_grid(), which takes a formula argument. Here we want one row and two columns, one column for each weight category. So we specify bmicat on the right hand side of the forumla passed to facet_grid().

```
g + geom_point() +
        geom_smooth(method = "lm") +
        facet_grid(. ~ bmicat)
```

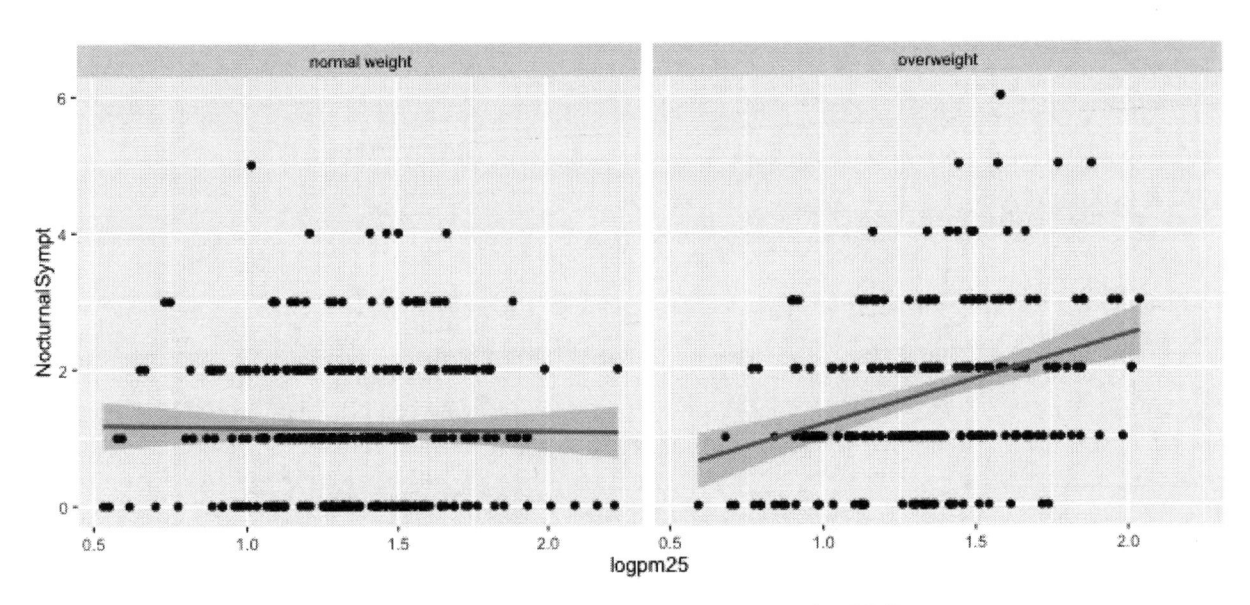

Scatterplot of PM2.5 and nocturnal symptoms by BMI category

Now it seems clear that the relationship between PM2.5 and nocturnal symptoms is relatively flat amongst normal weight individuals, while the relationship is increasing amongst overweight individuals. This plot suggests that overweight individuals may be more susceptible to the effects of PM2.5.

There are a variety of annotations you can add to a plot, including different kinds of labels. You can use `xlab()` for x-axis labels, `ylab()` for y-axis labels, and `ggtitle()` for specifying plot titles. The `labs()` function is generic and can be used to modify multiple types of labels at once.

For things that only make sense globally, use `theme()`, i.e. `theme(legend.position = "none")`. Two standard appearance themes are included

- `theme_gray()`: The default theme (gray background)
- `theme_bw()`: More stark/plain

16.7 Modifying Geom Properties

You can modify properties of geoms by specifying options to their respective `geom_*` functions. For example, here we modify the points in the scatterplot to make the color "steelblue", the size larger, and the alpha transparency greater.

```
g + geom_point(color = "steelblue", size = 4, alpha = 1/2)
```

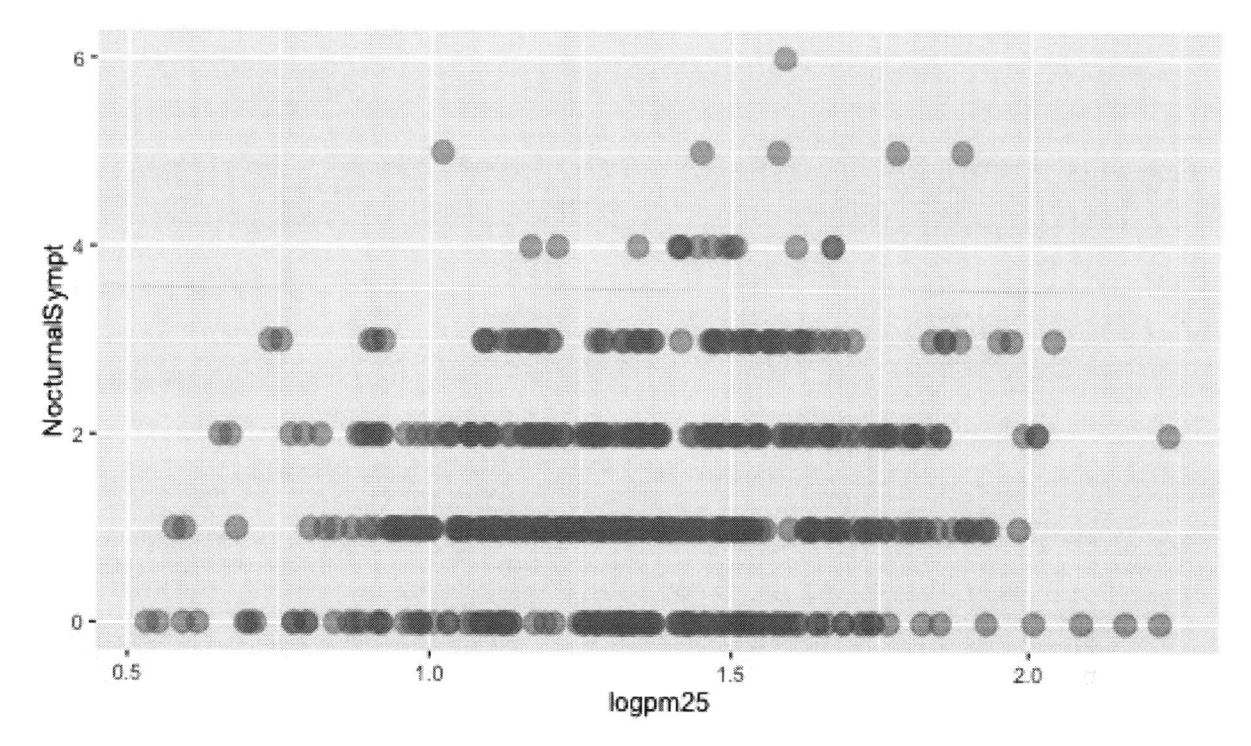

Modifying point color with a constant

In addition to setting specific geom attributes to constants, we can map aesthetics to variables. So, here, we map the color aesthetic `color` to the variable `bmicat`, so the points will be colored according to the levels of `bmicat`. We use the `aes()` function to indicate this difference from the plot above.

```
g + geom_point(aes(color = bmicat), size = 4, alpha = 1/2)
```

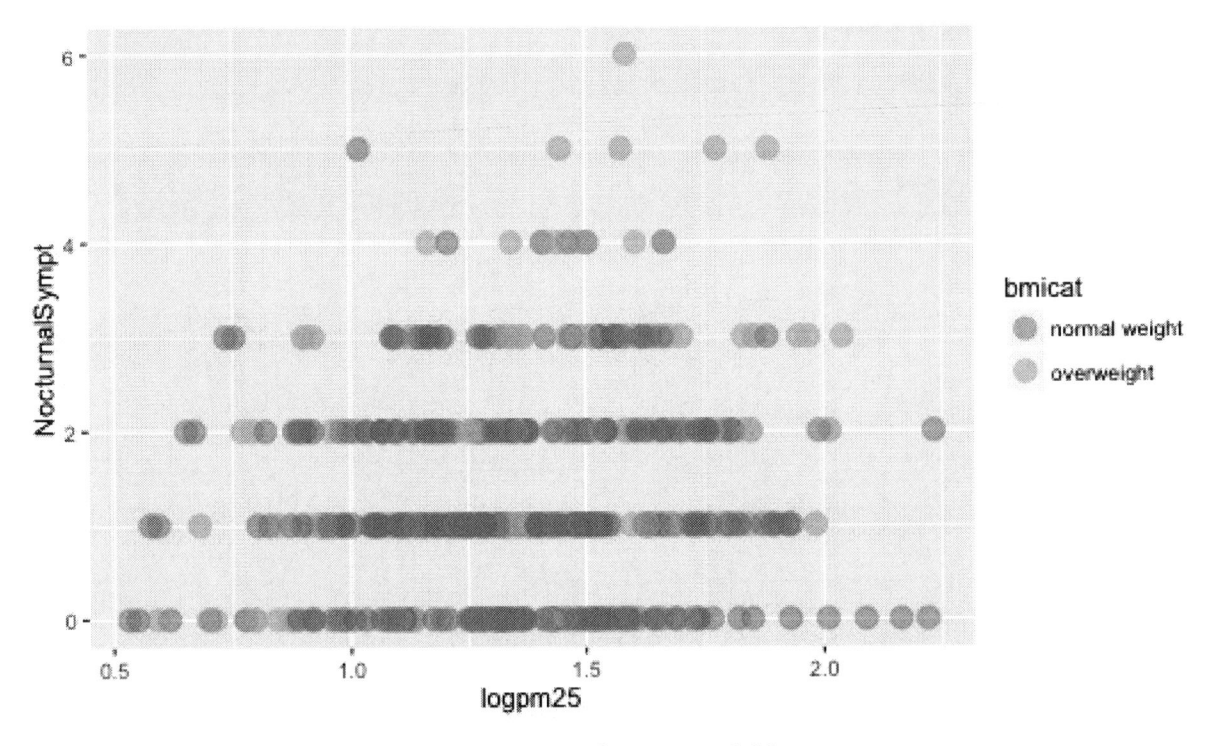

Mapping color to a variable

16.8 Modifying Labels

Here is an example of modifying the title and the x and y labels to make the plot a bit more informative.

```
g + geom_point(aes(color = bmicat)) + 
        labs(title = "MAACS Cohort") + 
        labs(x = expression("log " * PM[2.5]), y = "Nocturnal Symptoms")
```

MAACS Cohort

Modifying plot labels

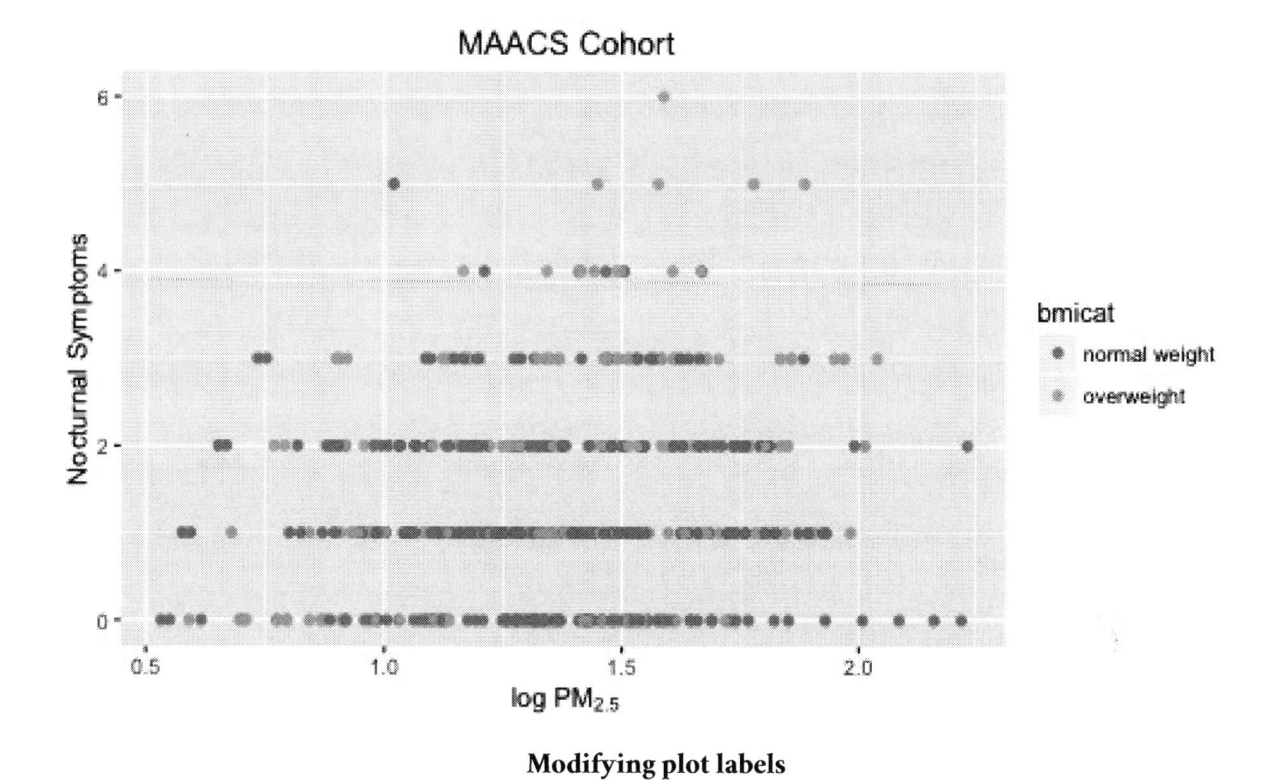

16.9 Customizing the Smooth

We can also customize aspects of the smoother that we overlay on the points with geom_smooth(). Here we change the line type and increase the size from the default. We also remove the shaded standard error from the line.

```
g + geom_point(aes(color = bmicat), size = 2, alpha = 1/2) +
    geom_smooth(size = 4, linetype = 3, method = "lm", se = FALSE)
```

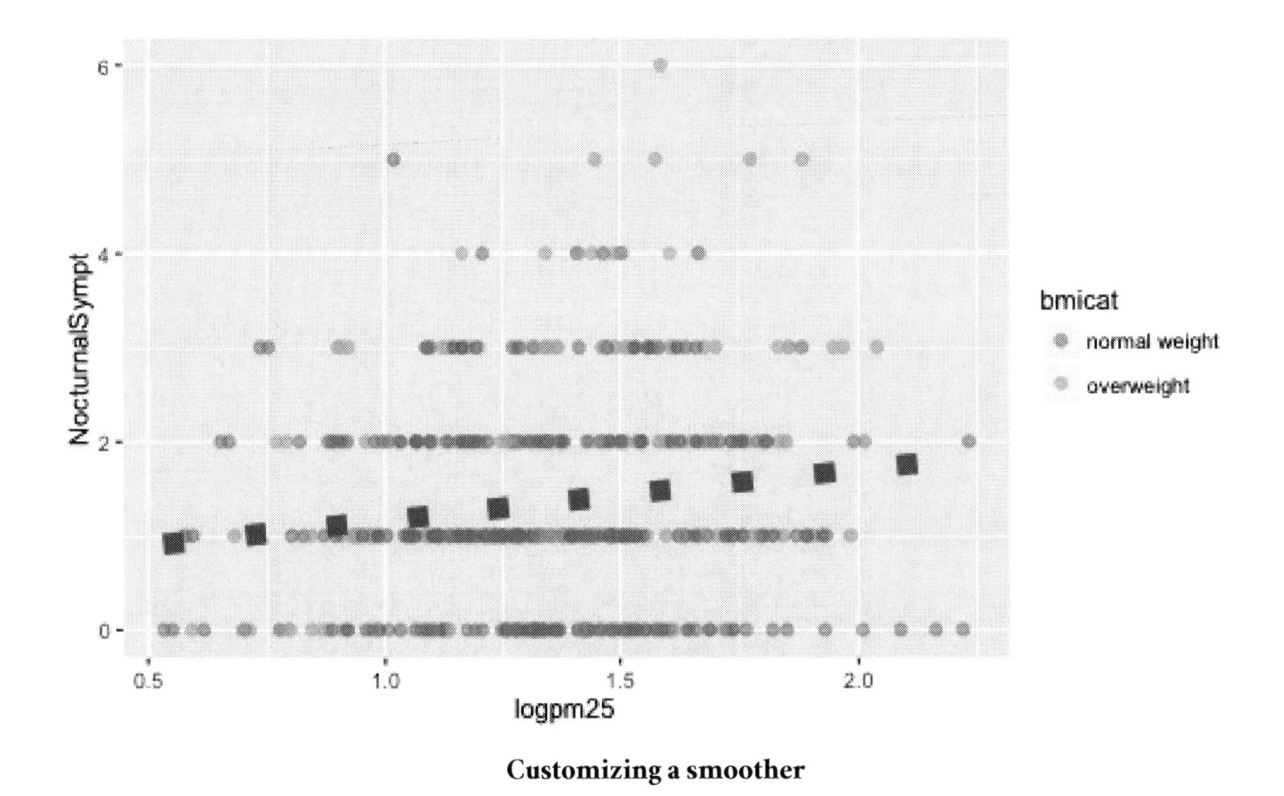

Customizing a smoother

16.10 Changing the Theme

The default theme for `ggplot2` uses the gray background with white grid lines. If you don't find this suitable, you can use the black and white theme by using the `theme_bw()` function. The `theme_bw()` function also allows you to set the typeface for the plot, in case you don't want the default Helvetica. Here we change the typeface to Times.

```
g + geom_point(aes(color = bmicat)) + theme_bw(base_family = "Times")
```

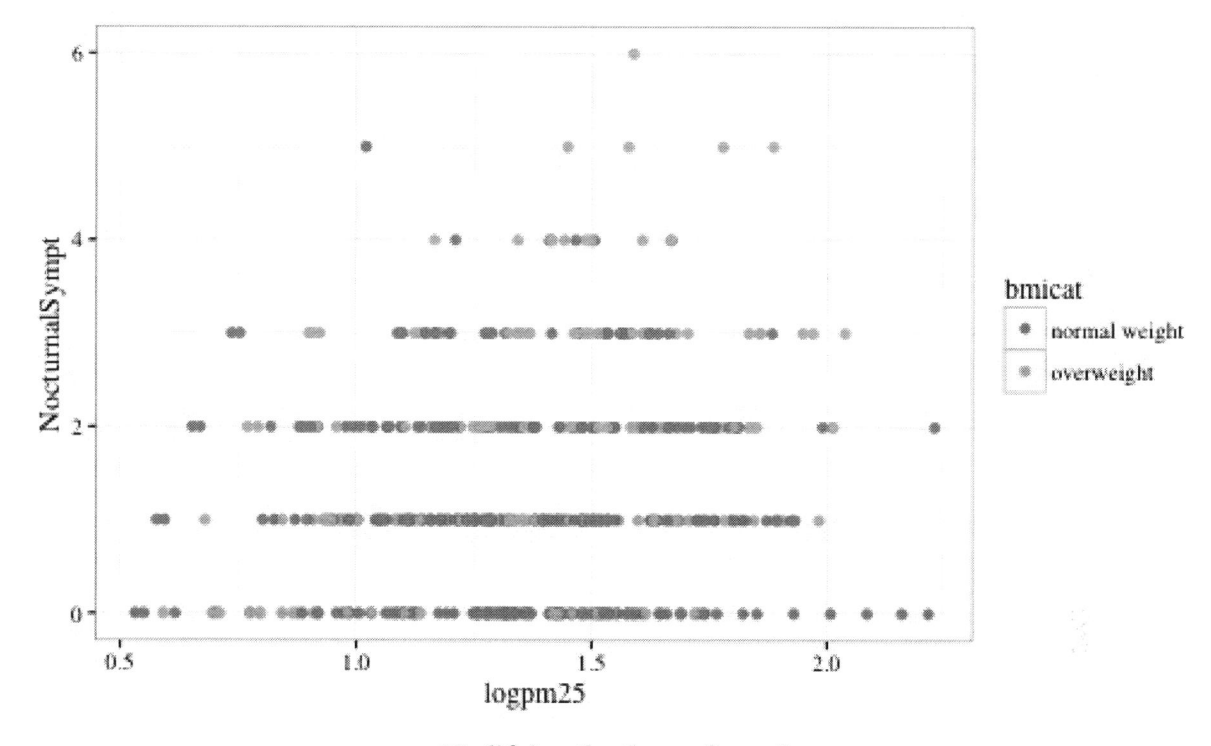

Modifying the theme for a plot

16.11 More Complex Example

Now you get the sense that plots in the `ggplot2` system are constructed by successively adding components to the plot, starting with the base dataset and maybe a scatterplot. In this section we will show a slightly more complicated example with an additional variable. Now, we will ask the question

> How does the relationship between PM2.5 and nocturnal symptoms vary by BMI category and nitrogen dioxide (NO2)?

Unlike our previous BMI variable, NO2 is continuous, and so we need to make NO2 categorical so we can condition on it in the plotting. We can use the `cut()` function for this purpose. We will divide the NO2 variable into tertiles.

First we need to calculate the tertiles with the `quantile()` function.

```
cutpoints <- quantile(maacs$logno2_new, seq(0, 1, length = 4), na.rm = TRUE)
```

Then we need to divide the original `logno2_new` variable into the ranges defined by the cut points computed above.

```
maacs$no2tert <- cut(maacs$logno2_new, cutpoints)
```

The `not2tert` variable is now a categorical factor variable containing 3 levels, indicating the ranges of NO2 (on the log scale).

```
## See the levels of the newly created factor variable
levels(maacs$no2tert)
```

```
[1] "(0.342,1.23]" "(1.23,1.47]"  "(1.47,2.17]"
```

The final plot shows the relationship between PM2.5 and nocturnal symptoms by BMI category and NO2 tertile.

```
## Setup ggplot with data frame
g <- ggplot(maacs, aes(logpm25, NocturnalSympt))

## Add layers
g + geom_point(alpha = 1/3) + 
  facet_wrap(bmicat ~ no2tert, nrow = 2, ncol = 4) + 
  geom_smooth(method="lm", se=FALSE, col="steelblue") + 
  theme_bw(base_family = "Avenir", base_size = 10) + 
  labs(x = expression("log " * PM[2.5])) + 
  labs(y = "Nocturnal Symptoms") + 
  labs(title = "MAACS Cohort")
```

PM2.5 and nocturnal symptoms by BMI category and NO2 tertile

16.12 A Quick Aside about Axis Limits

One quick quirk about `ggplot2` that caught me up when I first started using the package can be displayed in the following example. I make a lot of time series plots and I often want to restrict the range of the y-axis while still plotting all the data. In the base graphics system you can do that as follows.

```
testdat <- data.frame(x = 1:100, y = rnorm(100))
testdat[50,2] <- 100   ## Outlier!
plot(testdat$x, testdat$y, type = "l", ylim = c(-3,3))
```

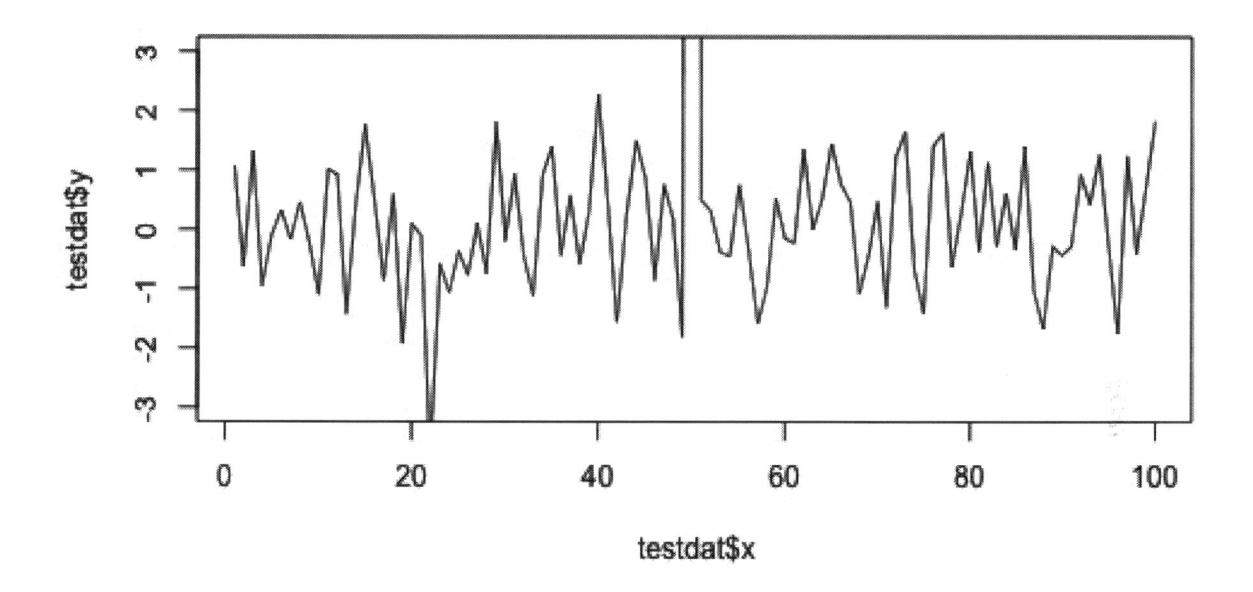

Time series plot with base graphics

Here I've restricted the y-axis range to be between -3 and 3, even though there is a clear outlier in the data.

With `ggplot2` the default settings will give you this.

```
g <- ggplot(testdat, aes(x = x, y = y))
g + geom_line()
```

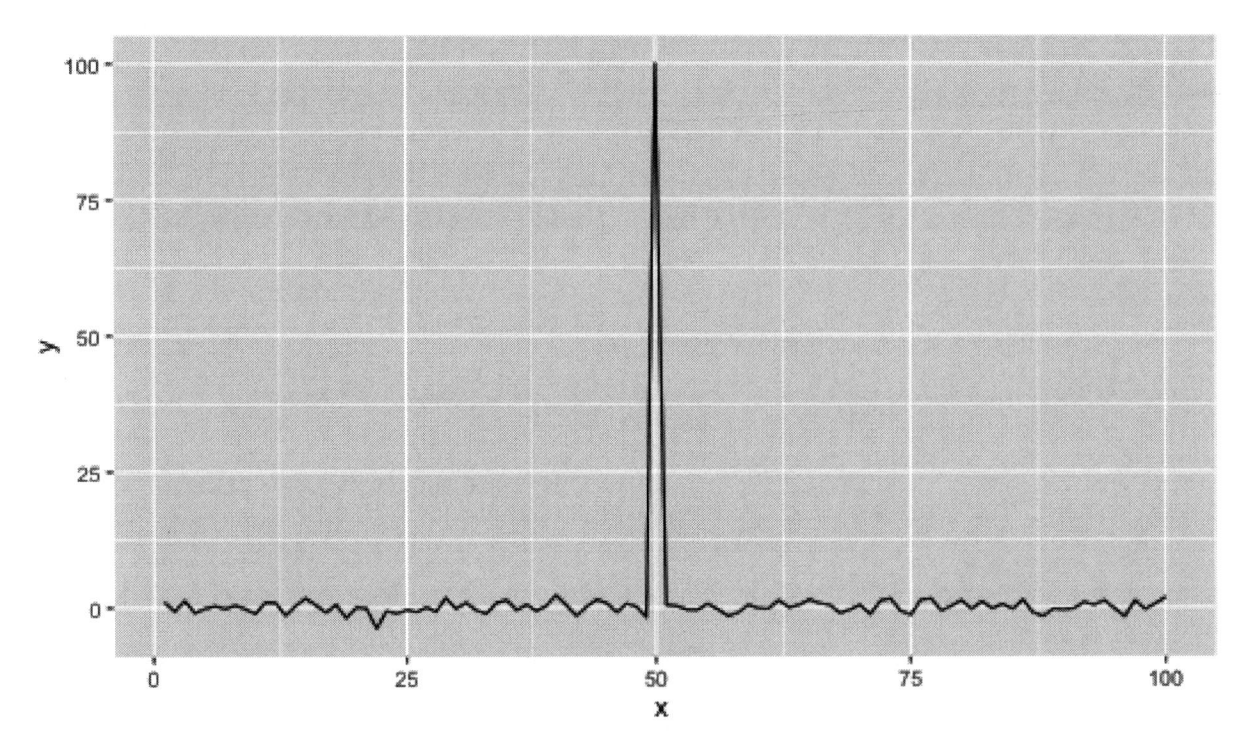

Time series plot with default settings

Modifying the `ylim()` attribute would seem to give you the same thing as the base plot, but it doesn't.

```
g + geom_line() + ylim(-3, 3)
```

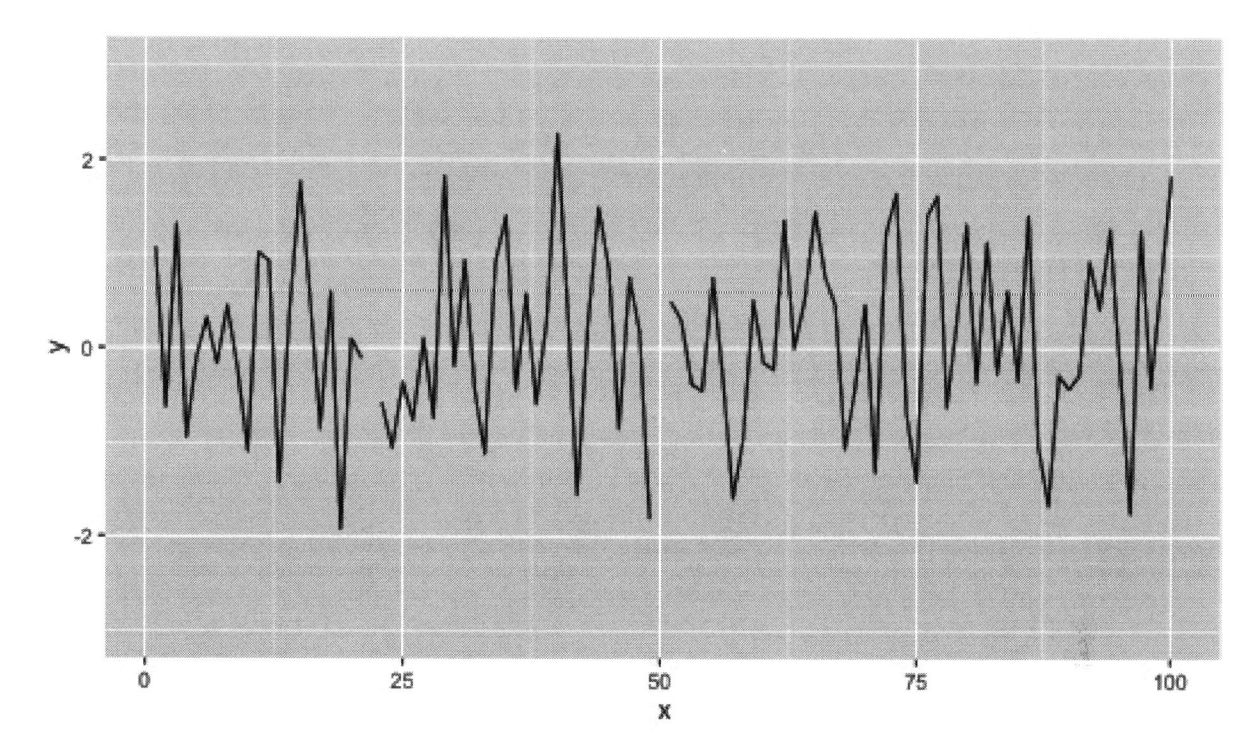

Time series plot with modified ylim

Effectively, what this does is subset the data so that only observations between -3 and 3 are included, then plot the data.

To plot the data without subsetting it first and still get the restricted range, you have to do the following.

```
g + geom_line() + coord_cartesian(ylim = c(-3, 3))
```

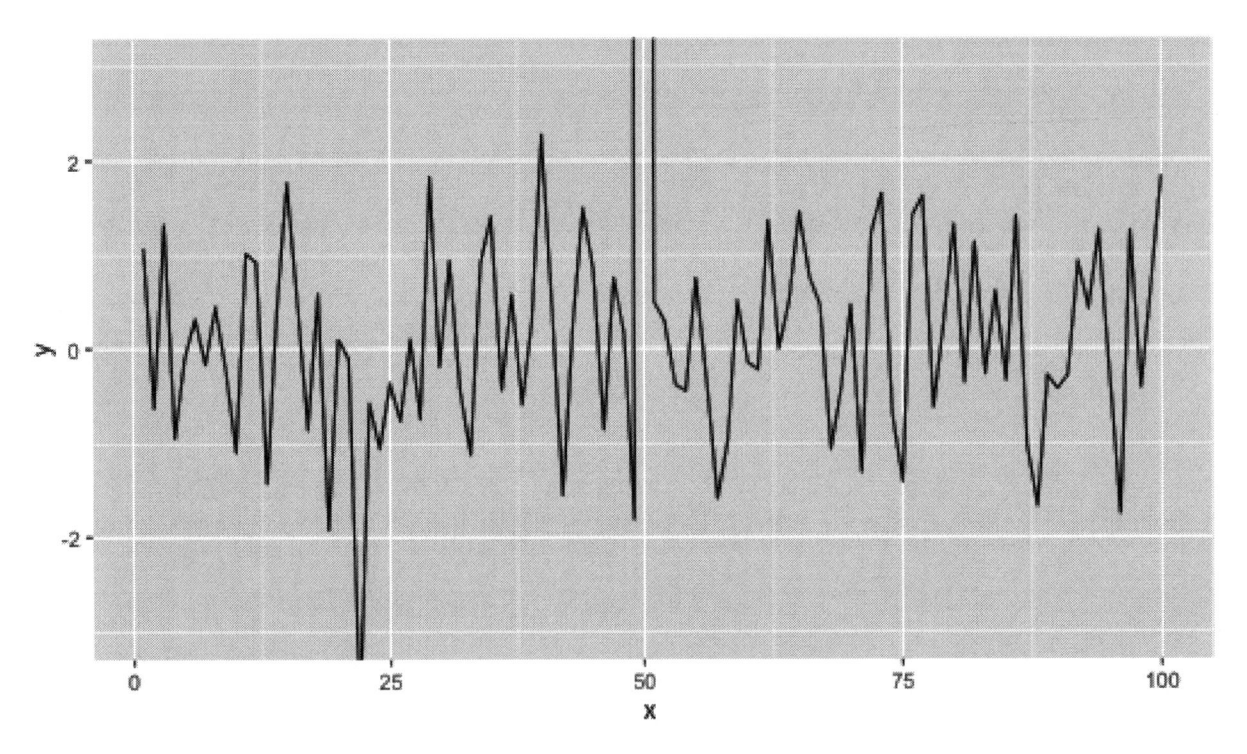

Time series plot with restricted y-axis range

And now you know!

16.13 Resources

- The *ggplot2* book by Hadley Wickham
- The *R Graphics Cookbook* by Winston Chang (examples in base plots and in ggplot2)
- ggplot2 web site (http://ggplot2.org)
- ggplot2 mailing list (http://goo.gl/OdW3uB), primarily for developers

17. Data Analysis Case Study: Changes in Fine Particle Air Pollution in the U.S.

This chapter presents an example data analysis looking at changes in fine particulate matter (PM) air pollution in the United States using the Environmental Protection Agencies freely available national monitoring data. The purpose of the chapter is to just show how the various tools that we have covered in this book can be used to read, manipulate, and summarize data so that you can develop statistical evidence for relevant real-world questions.

Watch a video of this chapter[1]. Note that this video differs slightly from this chapter in the code that is implemented. In particular, the video version focuses on using base graphics plots. However, the general analysis is the same.

17.1 Synopsis

In this chapter we aim to describe the changes in fine particle (PM2.5) outdoor air pollution in the United States between the years 1999 and 2012. Our overall hypothesis is that out door PM2.5 has decreased on average across the U.S. due to nationwide regulatory requirements arising from the Clean Air Act. To investigate this hypothesis, we obtained PM2.5 data from the U.S. Environmental Protection Agency which is collected from monitors sited across the U.S. We specifically obtained data for the years 1999 and 2012 (the most recent complete year available). From these data, we found that, on average across the U.S., levels of PM2.5 have decreased between 1999 and 2012. At one individual monitor, we found that levels have decreased and that the variability of PM2.5 has decreased. Most individual states also experienced decreases in PM2.5, although some states saw increases.

17.2 Loading and Processing the Raw Data

From the EPA Air Quality System[2] we obtained data on fine particulate matter air pollution (PM2.5) that is monitored across the U.S. as part of the nationwide PM monitoring network. We obtained the files for the years 1999 and 2012.

---

[1] https://youtu.be/VE-6bQvyfTQ
[2] http://www.epa.gov/ttn/airs/airsaqs/detaildata/downloadaqsdata.htm

Data Analysis Case Study: Changes in Fine Particle Air Pollution in the U.S.

Reading in the 1999 data

We first read in the 1999 data from the raw text file included in the zip archive. The data is a delimited file were fields are delimited with the | character adn missing values are coded as blank fields. We skip some commented lines in the beginning of the file and initially we do not read the header data.

```
> pm0 <- read.table("pm25_data/RD_501_88101_1999-0.txt",
+                   comment.char = "#",
+                   header = FALSE,
+                   sep = "|",
+                   na.strings = "")
```

After reading in the 1999 we check the first few rows (there are 117,421) rows in this dataset.

```
> dim(pm0)
[1] 117421     28
> head(pm0[, 1:13])
  V1 V2 V3 V4 V5    V6 V7  V8  V9       V10   V11    V12
1 RD  I  1 27  1 88101  1   7 105 120 19990103 00:00     NA
2 RD  I  1 27  1 88101  1   7 105 120 19990106 00:00     NA
3 RD  I  1 27  1 88101  1   7 105 120 19990109 00:00     NA
4 RD  I  1 27  1 88101  1   7 105 120 19990112 00:00  8.841
5 RD  I  1 27  1 88101  1   7 105 120 19990115 00:00 14.920
6 RD  I  1 27  1 88101  1   7 105 120 19990118 00:00  3.878
```

We then attach the column headers to the dataset and make sure that they are properly formated for R data frames.

```
> cnames <- readLines("pm25_data/RD_501_88101_1999-0.txt", 1)
> cnames <- strsplit(cnames, "|", fixed = TRUE)
> ## Ensure names are properly formatted
> names(pm0) <- make.names(cnames[[1]])
> head(pm0[, 1:13])
  X..RD Action.Code State.Code County.Code Site.ID Parameter POC
1    RD           I          1          27       1     88101   1
2    RD           I          1          27       1     88101   1
3    RD           I          1          27       1     88101   1
4    RD           I          1          27       1     88101   1
5    RD           I          1          27       1     88101   1
6    RD           I          1          27       1     88101   1
  Sample.Duration Unit Method     Date Start.Time Sample.Value
1               7  105    120 19990103      00:00           NA
2               7  105    120 19990106      00:00           NA
3               7  105    120 19990109      00:00           NA
4               7  105    120 19990112      00:00        8.841
5               7  105    120 19990115      00:00       14.920
6               7  105    120 19990118      00:00        3.878
```

The column we are interested in is the `Sample.Value` column which contains the PM2.5 measurements. Here we extract that column and print a brief summary.

```
> x0 <- pm0$Sample.Value
> summary(x0)
   Min. 1st Qu.  Median    Mean 3rd Qu.    Max.    NA's
   0.00    7.20   11.50   13.74   17.90  157.10   13217
```

Missing values are a common problem with environmental data and so we check to se what proportion of the observations are missing (i.e. coded as NA).

```
> ## Are missing values important here?
> mean(is.na(x0))
[1] 0.1125608
```

Because the proportion of missing values is relatively low (0.1125608), we choose to ignore missing values for now.

Reading in the 2012 data

We then read in the 2012 data in the same manner in which we read the 1999 data (the data files are in the same format).

```
> pm1 <- read.table("pm25_data/RD_501_88101_2012-0.txt",
+                   comment.char = "#",
+                   header = FALSE, sep = "|",
+                   na.strings = "",
+                   nrow = 1304290)
```

We also set the column names (they are the same as the 1999 dataset) and extract the `Sample.Value` column from this dataset.

```
> names(pm1) <- make.names(cnames[[1]])
```

Since we will be comparing the two years of data, it makes sense to combine them into a single data frame

```
> library(dplyr)
> pm <- rbind(pm0, pm1)
```

and create a factor variable indicating which year the data comes from. We also rename the `Sample.Value` variable to a more sensible PM.

```
> pm <- mutate(pm, year = factor(rep(c(1999, 2012), c(nrow(pm0), nrow(pm1))))) %>%
+       rename(PM = Sample.Value)
```

17.3 Results

Entire U.S. analysis

In order to show aggregate changes in PM across the entire monitoring network, we can make boxplots of all monitor values in 1999 and 2012. Here, we take the log of the PM values to adjust for the skew in the data.

```
> library(ggplot2)
Loading required package: methods
>
> ## Take a random sample because it's faster
> set.seed(2015)
> idx <- sample(nrow(pm), 1000)
> qplot(year, log2(PM), data = pm[idx, ], geom = "boxplot")
```

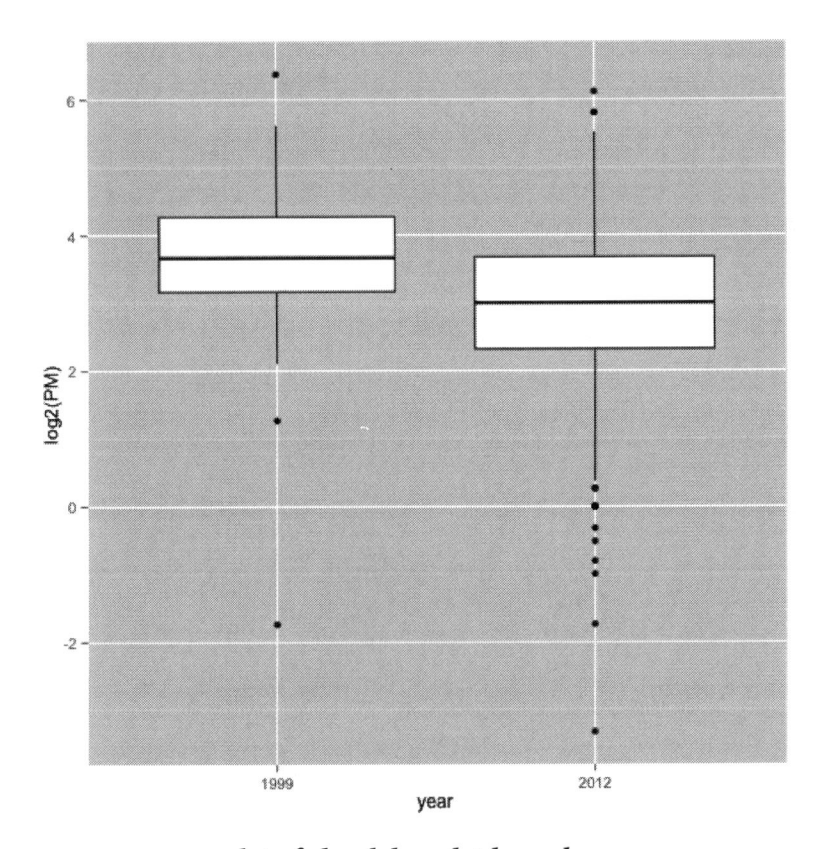

plot of chunk boxplot log values

From the raw boxplot, it seems that on average, the levels of PM in 2012 are lower than they were in 1999. Interestingly, there also appears to be much greater variation in PM in 2012 than there was in 1999.

We can make some summaries of the two year's worth data to get at actual numbers.

```
> with(pm, tapply(PM, year, summary))
$`1999`
   Min. 1st Qu.  Median    Mean 3rd Qu.    Max.    NA's
   0.00    7.20   11.50   13.74   17.90  157.10   13217

$`2012`
   Min. 1st Qu.  Median    Mean 3rd Qu.    Max.    NA's
 -10.00    4.00    7.63    9.14   12.00  909.00   73133
```

Interestingly, from the summary of 2012 it appears there are some negative values of PM, which in general should not occur. We can investigate that somewhat to see if there is anything we should worry about.

```
> filter(pm, year == "2012") %>% summarize(negative = mean(PM < 0, na.rm = TRUE))
    negative
1  0.0215034
```

There is a relatively small proportion of values that are negative, which is perhaps reassuring. In order to investigate this a step further we can extract the date of each measurement from the original data frame. The idea here is that perhaps negative values occur more often in some parts of the year than other parts. However, the original data are formatted as character strings so we convert them to R's Date format for easier manipulation.

```
> dates <- filter(pm, year == "2012")$Date
> dates <- as.Date(as.character(dates), "%Y%m%d")
```

We can then extract the month from each of the dates with negative values and attempt to identify when negative values occur most often.

```
> missing.months <- month.name[as.POSIXlt(dates)$mon + 1]
> tab <- table(factor(missing.months, levels = month.name))
> round(100 * tab / sum(tab))

  January  February     March     April       May      June      July
       15        13        15        13        14        13         8
   August September   October  November  December
        6         3         0         0         0
```

From the table above it appears that bulk of the negative values occur in the first six months of the year (January–June). However, beyond that simple observation, it is not clear why the negative values occur. That said, given the relatively low proportion of negative values, we will ignore them for now.

Changes in PM levels at an individual monitor

So far we have examined the change in PM levels on average across the country. One issue with the previous analysis is that the monitoring network could have changed in the time period between 1999 and 2012. So if for some reason in 2012 there are more monitors concentrated in cleaner parts of the country than there were in 1999, it might appear the PM levels decreased when in fact they didn't. In this section we will focus on a single monitor in New York State to see if PM levels *at that monitor* decreased from 1999 to 2012.

Our first task is to identify a monitor in New York State that has data in 1999 and 2012 (not all monitors operated during both time periods). First we subset the data frames to only include data from New York (`State.Code == 36`) and only include the `County.Code` and the `Site.ID` (i.e. monitor number) variables.

```
> sites <- filter(pm, State.Code == 36) %>% select(County.Code, Site.ID, year) %>% unique
```

Then we create a new variable that combines the county code and the site ID into a single string.

```
> sites <- mutate(sites, site.code = paste(County.Code, Site.ID, sep = "."))
> str(sites)
'data.frame':   51 obs. of  4 variables:
 $ County.Code: int  1 1 5 5 5 5 13 27 29 29 ...
 $ Site.ID    : int  5 12 73 80 83 110 11 1004 2 5 ...
 $ year       : Factor w/ 2 levels "1999","2012": 1 1 1 1 1 1 1 1 1 1 ...
 $ site.code  : chr  "1.5" "1.12" "5.73" "5.80" ...
```

Finally, we want the intersection between the sites present in 1999 and 2012 so that we might choose a monitor that has data in both periods.

```
> site.year <- with(sites, split(site.code, year))
> both <- intersect(site.year[[1]], site.year[[2]])
> print(both)
 [1] "1.5"     "1.12"    "5.80"    "13.11"   "29.5"    "31.3"    "63.2008"
 [8] "67.1015" "85.55"   "101.3"
```

Here (above) we can see that there are 10 monitors that were operating in both time periods. However, rather than choose one at random, it might best to choose one that had a reasonable amount of data in each year.

```
> count <- mutate(pm, site.code = paste(County.Code, Site.ID, sep = ".")) %>%
+         filter(site.code %in% both)
```

Now that we have subsetted the original data frames to only include the data from the monitors that overlap between 1999 and 2012, we can count the number of observations at each monitor to see which ones have the most observations.

```
> group_by(count, site.code) %>% summarize(n = n())
Source: local data frame [10 x 2]

   site.code   n
1       1.12  92
2        1.5 186
3      101.3 527
4      13.11 213
5       29.5  94
6       31.3 198
7       5.80  92
8    63.2008 152
9    67.1015 153
10     85.55  38
```

A number of monitors seem suitable from the output, but we will focus here on County 63 and site ID 2008.

```
> pmsub <- filter(pm, State.Code == 36 & County.Code == 63 & Site.ID == 2008)
```

Now we plot the time series data of PM for the monitor in both years.

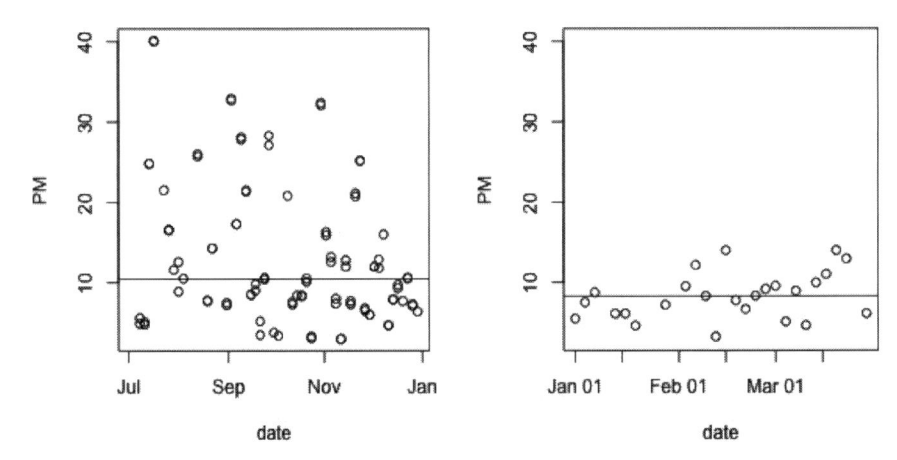

```
> pmsub <- mutate(pmsub, date = as.Date(as.character(Date), "%Y%m%d"))
> rng <- range(pmsub$PM, na.rm = TRUE)
>
> par(mfrow = c(1, 2), mar = c(4, 5, 2, 1))
> with(filter(pmsub, year == "1999"), {
+         plot(date, PM, ylim = rng)
+         abline(h = median(PM, na.rm = TRUE))
+ })
> with(filter(pmsub, year == "2012"), {
+         plot(date, PM, ylim = rng)
+         abline(h = median(PM, na.rm = TRUE))
+ })
```

plot of chunk unnamed-chunk-13

From the plot above, we can that median levels of PM (horizontal solid line) have decreased a little from 10.45 in 1999 to 8.29 in 2012. However, perhaps more interesting is that the variation (spread) in the PM values in 2012 is much smaller than it was in 1999. This suggest that not only are median levels of PM lower in 2012, but that there are fewer large spikes from day to day. One issue with the data here is that the 1999 data are from July through December while the 2012 data are recorded in January through April. It would have been better if we'd had full-year data for both years as there could be some seasonal confounding going on.

Changes in state-wide PM levels

Although ambient air quality standards are set at the federal level in the U.S. and hence affect the entire country, the actual reduction and management of PM is left to the individual states. States that are not "in attainment" have to develop a plan to reduce PM so that that the are in attainment (eventually). Therefore, it might be useful to examine changes in PM at the state level. This analysis falls somewhere in between looking at the entire country all at once and looking at an individual monitor.

What we do here is calculate the mean of PM for each state in 1999 and 2012.

```
> mn <- group_by(pm, year, State.Code) %>% summarize(PM = mean(PM, na.rm = TRUE))
> head(mn)
Source: local data frame [6 x 3]
Groups: year

  year State.Code        PM
1 1999          1 19.956391
2 1999          2  6.665929
3 1999          4 10.795547
4 1999          5 15.676067
5 1999          6 17.655412
6 1999          8  7.533304
> tail(mn)
Source: local data frame [6 x 3]
Groups: year

  year State.Code       PM
1 2012         51 8.708080
2 2012         53 6.364667
3 2012         54 9.821294
4 2012         55 7.914545
5 2012         56 4.005564
6 2012         72 6.048045
```

Now make a plot that shows the 1999 state-wide means in one "column" and the 2012 state-wide means in another columns. We then draw a line connecting the means for each year in the same state to highlight the trend.

```
> qplot(xyear, PM, data = mutate(mn, xyear = as.numeric(as.character(year))),
+       color = factor(State.Code),
+       geom = c("point", "line"))
```

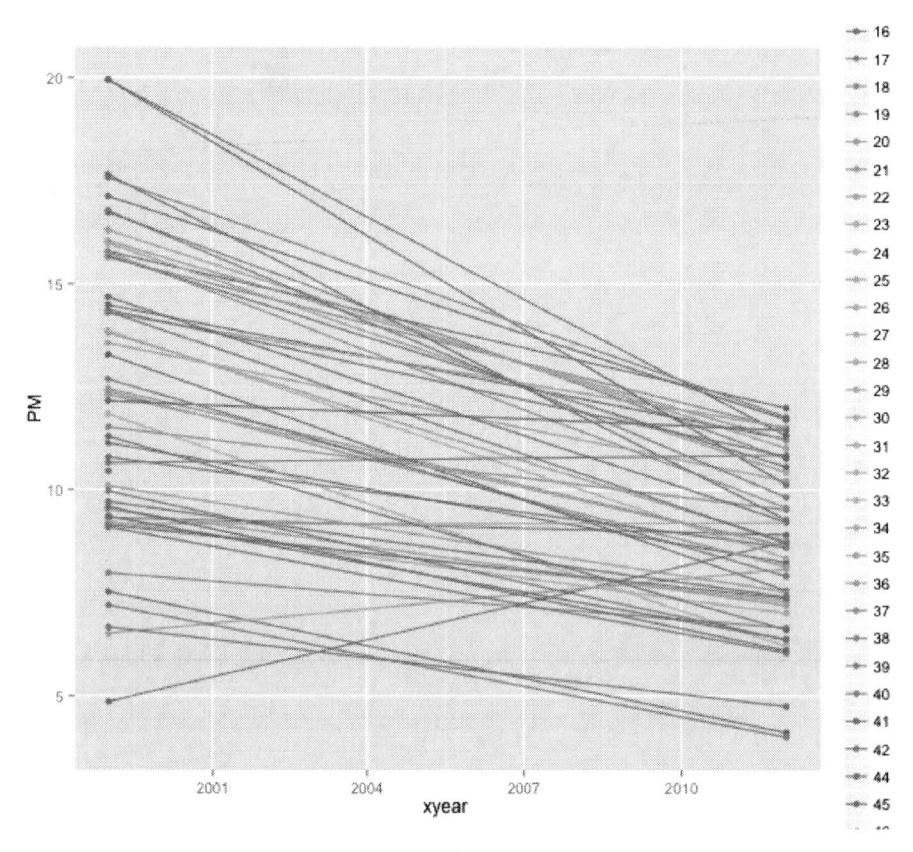

Data Analysis Case Study: Changes in Fine Particle Air Pollution in the U.S.

plot of chunk unnamed-chunk-16

This plot needs a bit of work still. But we can see that many states have decreased the average PM levels from 1999 to 2012 (although a few states actually increased their levels).

18. About the Author

Roger D. Peng is an Associate Professor of Biostatistics at the Johns Hopkins Bloomberg School of Public Health. He is also a Co-Founder of the Johns Hopkins Data Science Specialization[1], which has enrolled over 1.5 million students, the Johns Hopkins Executive Data Science Specialization[2], the Simply Statistics blog[3] where he writes about statistics and data science for the general public, and the Not So Standard Deviations[4] podcast. Roger can be found on Twitter and GitHub under the user name @rdpeng[5].

---

[1] http://www.coursera.org/specialization/jhudatascience/1
[2] https://www.coursera.org/specializations/executive-data-science
[3] http://simplystatistics.org/
[4] https://soundcloud.com/nssd-podcast
[5] https://twitter.com/rdpeng

Made in the USA
Lexington, KY
30 July 2018